Rorschach Responses in Old Age

Also from the Gesell Institute of Child Development

Child Rorschach Responses

Adolescent Rorschach Responses

Rorschach Responses

in Old Age

LOUISE BATES AMES, Ph.D.
Co-Director, Gesell Institute of Child Development;
Past President, Society for Projective Techniques
and Personality Assessment

RUTH W. MÉTRAUX, M.A.
Speech and Rorschach Consultant

JANET LEARNED RODELL, Ph.D.
Formerly Director of Preschool Service

RICHARD N. WALKER, Ph.D.
Director of Research

JASON ARONSON INC.
Northvale, New Jersey
London

THE MASTER WORK SERIES

First softcover edition 1995

Library of Congress Cataloging-in-Publication Data

Rorschach responses in old age / by Louise Bates Ames . . . [et al.].—
   [2nd ed.]
       p.   cm.
   Originally published: New York : Brunner/Mazel, 1973.
   Includes bibliographical references and index.
   ISBN 1-56821-490-1 (alk. paper)
    1. Aged—Psychological testing. 2. Rorschach Test. I. Ames, Louise Bates.
BF724.8R63 1995
   155.2′842—dc20   95-14106

Manufactured in the United States of America. Jason Aronson Inc. offers books and cassettes. For information and catalog write to Jason Aronson Inc., 230 Livingston Street, Northvale, New Jersey 07647.

Contents

List of Tables

Acknowledgments

Our chief acknowledgments, as usual, go to our subjects—in this instance the two hundred men and women between the ages of seventy and one hundred who so cooperatively took the Rorschach test and contributed their life histories.

We wish also especially to thank the Victoria Home for Aged British Gentlewomen at Ossining, New York, and its staff; and the Masonic Home and Hospital in Wallingford, Connecticut, for allowing us to test and interview residents in these institutions. Particular personal thanks are due to Dr. Kurt Pelz of the Masonic Home for the extraordinary cooperation offered by him and his staff. Dr. Virginia Hamilton of Bath, Maine, arranged for a variety of contacts in that city, ranging from public and private institutions to individual subjects living in their own homes.

Dr. Frances L. Ilg, Director Emeritus of the Gesell Institute, not only furnished theoretical help throughout the project but gave the very practical assistance of introducing us to the institutions where most of the research was carried out, and of gathering an appreciable number of the records herself.

Thanks are also due to Mrs. Emily Kirby who as research assistant was of great help in tabulating some of the original material.

Foreword to First Edition

by Arnold Gesell, M.D.

This book is in a sense a sequel. The same four investigators who in 1952 made a systematic report on *Child Rorschach Responses* now offer a comparable survey of the terminal sector of the life span. The sequel, therefore, is also a comparative study. Using the selfsame instrument and similar methods of approach, the present volume brings the first decade into parallel view with the eighth, ninth, and tenth decades. The reader will be intrigued by certain correspondences and resemblances, but he will also be made aware of an interesting variety of unsolved problems and complications which invite further research.

In spite of the complexities, the authors have demonstrated in concrete form a significant gradation of old age responses, ranging from normal adult maturity, to presenile, to senile levels. Once more the Rorschach method has shown its versatility and its efficacy as an implement for behavior analysis. It is a remarkable and welcome fact that the ink blot test elicits almost equal degrees of acceptance and responsiveness from young and old.

This is not altogether surprising because from a developmental standpoint the human action system is built on a unitary plan. There is but one embryology of behavior which begins with conception and terminates with involution and dissolution.

Life expectancy (in America) has increased by almost 20 years since 1900. In 1880 the proportion of men and women over 65 years old was only 3.4 per cent. It is estimated that the proportion of the entire population in 1980 will have risen to 14.4 per cent. Small wonder that the science of gerontology has taken on an increased importance and that geriatric medicine is destined to become a specialty with far-reaching social ramifications.

Gerontology is concerned with the phenomena of aging in all its varied manifestations. The basic life sciences, including biology, physiology, biochemistry, and experimental embryology, are essential for the interpretation of the underlying physical processes. But these processes are so closely linked with the behavioral expressions of personality that the methods of psychology and of cultural anthropology must also be requisitioned. Among the many available techniques, those of the Rorschach type have an essential role because they probe into the patterns and powers of visual perception which undergo growth and decline throughout almost the entire extent of the life cycle.

What is aging? Is it growth? Is it decline, or a changing ratio between growth and decline? The usual connotation suggests a failure of reconstitution on the part of the organism or its tissues. Minot, after years of observation and measurement of guinea pigs, concluded that old age and death are progressive phenomena which begin with life itself. He came to the paradoxical conclusion that the younger we are, the faster we grow old. "Senescence is at its maximum in the very young stages, and the rate of senescence diminishes with age." Precursor signs of potential presbyopia can be identified in the structural growth of the fetal lens! But to what extent are the eventualities of growth dependent upon what happens to the organism within the boundaries of biological time? Abstractly defined, aging refers to those aspects of life cycle change which under given conditions are inherently determined by sheer passage of time.

Although the criterion of such a definition cannot be rigidly applied, the present investigators have made an extensive analysis of attendant conditions, presenting 44 statistical tables and separate chapters on specific variables. By exclusion they arrived at a functional classification of old age Rorschach responses, progressing from normal, to presenile, to senile symptoms. The threefold grouping indicates the double operation of developmental and of individualizing factors. The three summary tables with which the volume concludes can serve judicious clinical and research applications. They should prove particularly suggestive in intensive longitudinal studies of the aging processes both of normal and atypical individuals.

Psychological methods are, of course, necessary for defining mental vitality and longevity. What somatic methods may do in the future to lengthen life span cannot be predicted. It is probable that the human span of life is biologically self-limited, even though the existence span of the fruit fly has been prolonged 900 times by mere temperature regulation. Perhaps the first task of science is to understand rather than to extend old age, and to interpret its potentials.

The characteristics, the peculiarities, the "grandeurs and miseries of old age" have not been neglected in the nontechnical literature of fiction, drama, biography, essays, and memoirs. Cato learned Greek at 80; Cicero in his discourse *De Senectute* gives many instances of high achievement in advanced age. Emerson recorded in his journal that at the age of 62 his memory was failing, but he felt compensated by increased power and means of generalization. He cites Thoreau's remark that man may have two growths like pear trees. G. Stanley Hall in 1922 published a semi-autobiographic volume on *Senescence: The Last Half of Life* as a complement of his pioneering volumes on *Adolescence* (1904). His work on senescence is a unique self-survey, combined with a wide-ranging exposition of the history, the hygiene, and scientific studies of old age. "In a word," he concludes, "the call to us is to construct a new self just as we had to do at adolescence, —a self that both adds to and subtracts much from the old personality of our prime."

One need not look far to find the cultural origins and the social consequences of a science which deals with the aged and aging. Geriatrics confronts problems as vast as those of Pediatrics. Both are concerned with growth problems, normal and abnormal. Both are called upon for preventive and supervisory measures to protect mental health in relation to age. This protection touches many fields of adult education and urgent areas of social welfare.

To direct and to orient this protection in behalf of the aging individual and of society, knowledge as well as humanity is required. The present monograph makes a distinct contribution to the kind of knowledge which may seem remote but which nevertheless serves to clarify the nature and needs of the aging person.

With accumulation of knowledge the problems of aging will be seen in better perspective and in terms of the total life cycle. A personal preventive hygiene of senescence may well begin at the fifth decade with progressive adjustment to the inevitabilities of the years. At any rate, the problems involve profound relationships between the mechanisms of mental growth and of functional aging.

Charles W. Eliot was an exemplar of the fine art of aging. He sums up much in a letter written when he was 60 years old, on the occasion of his twenty-fifth anniversary as president of Harvard University. The letter was addressed (May 20, 1894) to William James, psychologist:

DEAR DR. JAMES—You carry me back farther than anybody else—to 1861. I can see that I then had some of the same qualities and powers that I have now; but I had little range of observation, no breadth of experience, and small capacity for sympathetic imagination. You and I have, I think, the same fundamental reason for being moderately content with the years that are past:—We have a sense of growth and of increased capacity for useful service. We find our lives enriched and amplified from year to year. So long as that enlarging process goes on, we shall be content. If it stops suddenly, we shall be content to that date. . . .

Individuals vary enormously in the depth, the range, and the very patterns of the aging process. The present monograph throws light on this significant aspect of human nature.

Preface to Second Edition

In the twenty years since the original edition of this book was published, the welfare and functioning of the aged has become more and more a national concern. We have seen among professionals an increasing sharing of some of the viewpoints we expressed in that edition: an interest in the behavior of the individual as a reflection of the biological state of his organism and a beginning appreciation of the fact that to give optimum support and help to the aging person one must recognize his developmental state.

The Rorschach test offers a remarkable tool for assessing this developmental status — for seeing which, among a group of old people of similar age, are still mentally robust, which show the beginnings of slowing down, and which are no longer able to function independently. The Rorschach is particularly useful for evaluation in the middle range of this sequence, when the individual has become less capable but when verbalisms may mask the extent of his disability. (It has long been recognized that vocabulary "holds up" well in old age. The person using the impressive vocabulary may not himself be holding up quite so well.)

So we are pleased that this book is to be once again available. We are also pleased to have the chance to confirm some speculations offered in the first edition. Any description of a developmental course using cross-sectional methods is necessarily speculative. In our original edition we proposed what we believed to be typical changes in the Rorschach response as the supposedly typical individual moves on from normal adult functioning through various stages of presenility to senility.

Since for most subjects only one Rorschach response was available when these norms were determined, we were not able to say definitely that as any single individual moved on into old age he actually did follow this hypothetical course.

In the years between the publishing of the original edition and this revision, enough longitudinal data have been gathered that we can say that in perhaps the majority of cases seen by us the aging individual did follow the course which we had originally proposed.

A substantial number of Rorschach tests were given by us to aged subjects at the Masonic Home and Hospital in Wallingford, Connecticut, and were reported in the first edition of this book. The then medical director, Dr. Kurt Pelz, not only cooperated fully in our research, but was quick to see the potential value of an assessment such as the Rorschach could provide as to the level of integration, or disintegration, of the functioning of his elderly patients. He felt that the handling of these patients by hospital personnel could be sensitized and improved if those in charge of the elderly could be helped to appreciate just how far any one individual might have deteriorated in functioning in spite of, often, a superficial air of intactness.

However, in his opinion, the Rorschach, though extremely useful to the initiated, was a highly specialized test not understood by the majority of hospital personnel. At his suggestion we undertook to try out other, simpler, tests to supplement our Rorschach findings. The results of such supplementary testing, as well as preliminary results of ongoing research, are reported here in Chapter 16. Thus in this edition of our book we shall show that the Rorschach can be used in combination with other tests in the practical, effective, assessment of the behavioral status of any aging person.

It is our firm belief that in aging as in childhood, effective work with and planning for the individual requires a reasonable understanding of where he is functioning. It is our hope that the present revision of *Rorschach Responses in Old Age* will stimulate public and professional interest in the potential usefulness of the Rorschach and associated tests in evaluating the behavior level of the elderly individual, who must be understood before he can be helped to function in accordance with his highest potential.

Rorschach Responses in Old Age

CHAPTER ONE

Introduction

"All living organisms undergo progressive changes in structure and function with the passage of time. These changes, which begin at conception and end only at death, constitute the subject matter of gerontology. Thus, in the broadest sense, problems of growth, development, and maturation are as much a part of gerontology as those of atrophy, degeneration, and decline."

This recent definition by Shock (42, p. 353), of the subject matter of gerontology, is strikingly reminiscent of an earlier comment by Gesell, to the effect that development as well as disease falls within the province of clinical pediatrics (18, p. v).

Both of these investigators agree that actually any of the specialties which deal with the behavior of man, whether he be at the beginning of life or the end, are or should be concerned with virtually the same problems: growth, development, and maturation.

It is these very problems which we propose to investigate in the present volume. Though our own field is primarily that of child development, the problems of behavior growth and behavior change are not basically different whether we deal with youth or with old age.

We do not believe that the behavior changes which have concerned us in the first sixteen years of life necessarily stop at the second decade. Our earlier studies have led us to suspect that patterned changes in function take place throughout the lifetime of the human organism. We shall concern ourselves here chiefly with the measurement of changes in intellectual and emotional function in the human subject between the ages of 70 and 100.

Most investigators have agreed that the more widely used intelligence tests are not ideally suited for this purpose. There is general agreement with Shock's statement that "one of the major difficulties in research on intellectual changes with age is that the same test instrument may not be sampling the same mental ability at different ages." Furthermore, "since the so-called 'higher mental functions' such as reasoning, critical thinking, judgment, etc., do not lend themselves to quantitative measurement, most of the beliefs about the effect of age on these functions are based on unquantitated impressions and hunches" (42, p. 359).

When we attempt to assess not only changes in intellectual function, but also changes in personality function with age, we run into further difficulties. Shock notes, "The identification of age changes in this field adds difficulties to the already complicated task of measuring personal qualities. For instance, even if present techniques for the measurement of personality traits are accepted, there is no way of determining what the old man of 60 was like at the age of 40. Thus most of the studies reported deal with age differences rather than age changes. . . . It is obvious that any fundamental contribution to our knowledge about changes in personality with age must await the accumulation of longitudinal data" (42, p. 361).

We agree with Shock that the investigation of problems of growth, development, and maturation is an important aspect of the study of old people. It may be that the most useful tool for making such an investigation is a test which can supply information on both intellectual and individuality factors, and one which can be used throughout the entire age cycle. Ideally such an investigation would be a longitudinal one, following the same subjects throughout their life span.

We have chosen the Rorschach test as our instrument for investigating age changes in the intellectual and emotional functioning of the aging individual because it is the most comprehensive single test we know.

At the first national conference on aging, sponsored by the Federal Security Agency, the complaint was made that, "No intelligence test in existence samples all or even most of the mental abilities known to Psychology. Creative thinking, for example, usually is not measured by our tests, nor is judgment in complex situations" (47, p. 256). The Rorschach test does not fully meet these criteria, but it does so more than any other test which we have used.

Our own earlier investigation (Ames *et al.*, 6) has demonstrated it to be a useful tool for revealing age changes, as well as a test which for most individuals clearly shows the intellectual and emotional status of the organism.

The Rorschach has the advantage that it is well accepted by most subjects of any age (from 2 or 3 years to 100). Furthermore it does not unduly penalize the older person who may be handicapped on other tests by failing memory, slow reaction time, or poor coordination. (True, vision must be fairly adequate to allow a "good" response on this test. But we have obtained excellent protocols from subjects who complained mightily about their failing eyesight.)

In studies of the first sixteen years of life (Gesell and Ilg, 19, 20, 21) we have found that the child's mental age, as measured by such standard psychometric instruments as the Stanford-Binet or Wechsler-Bellevue scales, is only one aspect of development, and may not correspond with his over-all level of maturity. Thus a 10-year-old child may have an I.Q. of 120, but the structure of his general behavior may be like that of an 8-year-old. The Rorschach, perhaps more than any other single clinical measure, has seemed to us to indicate the age level at which the total organism is functioning.

Furthermore if it should be true, as many have suspected, that the old person in some respects at least returns to behavior characteristic of childhood, the Rorschach response is of a kind which could demonstrate this. For example, if human movement responses are in general a more mature response than animal movement, we could determine whether or not the older person returns to a predominance of animal movement responses.

The multidimensionality and objectivity of the Rorschach response also seemed to us to make it a promising test for any exploration of age changes in the aging psyche.

Also it has been our impression in giving the Rorschach to older people that subjects either refused the test entirely (as did occur on occasion), or responded to it wholeheartedly and to the best of their ability —even when the things they saw on the cards were distinctly unpleasant to them. (This was of course only a subjective impression but it was one shared by all four of the present writers.)

The criterion of longitudinality was not met in the present study, except for a bow in that direction. We agree, however, to the desirability of a long-term study which would investigate year by year changes in the response of single individuals.

. . . The present study therefore inquires whether or not patterned age changes in intellectual and emotional functions do take place in the later decades of life as they do in childhood. And if they do, is the Rorschach a useful tool for determining and reporting these changes?

It makes a second major inquiry. Can the Rorschach be used to determine the individual's psychological age? It is now recognized that an individual's physiological age may not necessarily correspond with his chronological age. Similarly it may be that the psychological maturity level may not always correspond with the chronological age. If this supposition is true, and if patterned psychological changes do occur as the individual grows chronologically older, it may be that the Rorschach will prove a useful tool for measuring the psychological age.

CHAPTER TWO

Literature

We shall not in this chapter attempt to summarize the general literature on gerontology, since a number of reviews have been published. A still valuable integration of the earlier studies on old age is Miles' chapter in the *Handbook of Social Psychology* (32). The demographic aspects of old age, stressed throughout the literature, are graphically presented in the Federal Security Agency's *Fact Book on Aging* (45), and are meaningfully organized in Shock's *Trends in Gerontology* (43). Changes in personal and social adjustment in old age are explored by Pollak (38) and by Cavan *et al.* (14). The volume, *Understanding Old Age,* by Gilbert (22) is a comprehensive and readable discussion of these changes.

The present status of knowledge of physiological and psychological aspects of aging is succinctly summarized by Carlson and Steiglitz (13), and by Kaplan (26). An assessment of current knowledge and needed research in gerontology is presented in a report of the Committee on Social Adjustment of the Social Science Research Council (44). The section on personality, intelligence, and mental disorders, by authors who have made distinguished contributions in the field, is outstanding, and the extensive annotated bibliography by Rosenthal is most helpful.

In this chapter we shall confine our comment to mention of studies which specifically report Rorschach findings on elderly subjects. Such studies are few and for the most part somewhat limited as to number of subjects tested.

The first mention of Rorschach responses in old age was made by Rorschach himself (40). He believed that there were three signs "pathognomic" of normal old age: 1) A coarctated *Erlebnistypus,* that is, a diminution of the capacity of old people to make use of their inner resources and a weakening of their reactions to emotional challenges. 2) Vaguely or inaccurately seen forms, indicating a lessening of perceptual

5

acuity and a somewhat lowered level of intellectual efficiency. 3) A highly restricted thought content, demonstrating a narrowing of the range of interests.

These suggestions of Rorschach were confirmed in a study by Walter Klopfer (28), the first investigation that we know of in this country in which the Rorschach test was given to old people. This study, reported in 1946, summarizes responses of 50 persons—30 of them institutional subjects from the Home for Aged and Infirm Hebrews of New York; 20 non-institutionalized subjects. The age ranges for the two groups were 62 to 93, and 63 to 81, respectively, with median ages of 74 and 73.

Klopfer found that:

In the intellectual sphere these aged persons are generally slower, less productive, and less efficient than individuals of an equal capacity in the general population. Though they are still able, for the most part, to deal adequately with the practical problems of everyday life, they have a great deal of difficulty in organizing their experiences for future reference, and are not interested in abstract and theoretical things or the formation of original ideas.

The old people's capacity for making use of their inner resources appears to be diminished. When they do respond to promptings from within, it is to the more instinctive, suggesting a regression to a more infantile level of functioning.

There is no consistent way in which they respond to emotional challenges. Some of the old people are egocentric, labile and highly responsive. Some on the other hand do not respond at all to affective stimuli.

Most of the old people in the group do not have good mechanisms for forming relationships with others. They are critical of other people and find it difficult to make social contacts.

Definite evidence of the presence of strong heterosexual interest is present in 17 cases, as indicated by their reaction to sexual areas of the cards and feeling patterns in respect to the assumption of their respective sexual role in the environment. Six subjects were unable to decide about their preferred sexual role.

Forty-four per cent of subjects give evidence of having a definitely egocentric, uncontrolled and overdependent emotionality. Fifteen subjects are definitely infantile, having regressed to a level of emotional adjustment far below their mental age. Egocentricity is usually of the passive rather than the explosive type.

Only ten subjects showed any strong responsiveness to the finer nuances in the environment; two were oversensitive.

More specifically, Klopfer's findings were as follows:

"Marked constriction aimed primarily at ΣC but with an underemphasis also on M. FM greater than M. Reactions to color more likely to be CF than FC, if present. Color responses found in only 36 per cent of the group. Mean of only 14.1 responses. Long average time per response— mean of 49." A small number of popular responses—54% of the group— had three or less. Emphasis of W at the expense of D. W was overemphasized in 76 per cent of the cases. And lastly, a high A per cent, over 50 per cent in 70 per cent of the cases. Interestingly enough, few significant differences could be found between the institutional and noninstitutional groups. In fact "the trend was definitely toward similarity rather than dissimilarity."

In many respects, as will be seen, subsequent studies bear out the initial findings of Rorschach and Klopfer, and in some instances do not go too far beyond these initial contributions.

The next study appears to be that of Prados and Fried (39) in 1947. These investigators studied 35 subjects between 50 and 80 and found in general a progressive impoverishment of creative intellectual faculties with increasing age.

Subjects of this study were divided into groups according to age. It was found that those between 50 and 70 tended to react with anxiety to an awareness of their own intellectual inadequacy, whereas those over 70 tended to become resigned to this inadequacy. The capacity for emotional responsiveness was found to become relatively shallow with increased age, and there seemed to be little inner conflict. Prados and Fried also found that with increasing age, control over the instinctual demands tends to disappear, and some of the primitive manifestations of childhood tend to recur.

However, since only ten of their subjects were over 70 years of age, their findings will not be reported here in further detail.

In 1949, Chesrow, Wosika, and Reinitz (15) reported a study of 20 subjects from the wards of the Oak Forest Infirmary in Oak Forest, Illinois. Ages of patients ranged from 64 to 83 with an average age of 72. Subjects were given the Wechsler-Bellevue test and the Rorschach.

In general, these investigators report, "a lack of richness both in intellectual and emotional spheres. Intellectual control was found to be within normal limits in all but three of the subjects. All but four showed introversive trends. Neurotic shock was present in most of the records. Other findings of significance were suspiciousness, anxiety and depressive trends. There is a tendency for the subjects to be stereotyped and somewhat conventional in their thinking. Although these records were not typical of organic brain damage, the general findings of delayed responses, reduced number of responses, stereotyped thinking, constriction and impotence might be related to the aging of the mental processes."

Fifteen of the subjects showed, on the Wechsler-Bellevue, deterioration quotients which Wechsler considered pathological. These authors, however, were unable to find any correlation between the intellectual deterioration quotient of the subject and physical findings, or with the results on the Rorschach. Thus "no positive correlation was found between the deterioration score on the Wechsler-Bellevue and the number of organic signs of Piotrowski. This leads us to believe that the organic signs of Piotrowski are not primarily related to the organic process of aging."

Furthermore, "no group scored more poorly because symptoms or signs of serious physical disease were present. The group showing cardiac conditions showed no test peculiarities. This was also true for the group having marked atrophic arthritis, and also for the amputees."

More specifically, the Rorschach findings for this group were as follows:

The number of responses per record ranged from 10 to 40, the average being 18. This is slightly below the average found for normal adults.

The average time per response was 54.

The F+% was above 70% in all but seven cases and in only three of these did it go below 60%.

The A% was above 25% in 18 of the 20 cases. The A% ranged from 0 to 79, the average being 49.

Eleven of the subjects gave no color responses, and five gave only one.

As to movement, four subjects gave no M, five gave only one, six gave two, four gave three, and one gave four. The average M thus was 1.6.

Six subjects made no response to one of the ten cards and one rejected two.

As to Piotrowski's signs, only two subjects had five signs and only one had six signs.

In 1951, Dörken and Kral (16) published findings on a group of 35 committed senile psychotics. Five of these patients did not respond to the Rorschach, but the other 30 were divided, on the basis of Wechsler-Bellevue scores, into a "high" and "low" group. The average ages for these two groups are 76.1 and 76.4 with age ranges of 66 to 86, and 67 to 86.

Considered as a total group these subjects showed an average of 15.1 responses, which is below the lower limits of the normal range. Extent to which the various determinants appeared in these protocols was: 1.1M,

2.8FM, .1m, .7FC, .4CF, .2C. Forty-six percent of cases gave no M, 43 per cent of cases no color.

Area was as follows: 31.3%W, 50.9%D, 17.3Dd. F% was 55.1, F-% was 35.2. Animal percent was 47%.

Thus they found that the responsiveness of the senile patient, as measured by the Rorschach, is limited and of poor quality, and that in general there is a "noticeable lack of variety in the response determinants. The absence of movement and particularly of shading and color in the determination of response is far more extensive than one finds in the normal personality structure.

"This indicates that with deterioration there is not only an intellectual deficit but that the emotional components, the finer nuances that lend individuality to the personality, tend to become lost or obliterated."

Use of shading—generally thought to represent a sensitivity, either of awareness or anxiety—is strikingly meager. "This is consistent with the severely reduced refinement in mental control and lack of free floating anxiety to be found in old people."

Grossman, Warshawsky, and Hertz (23), at the Second International Gerontological Congress, reported a study in progress on the personality characteristics of a group of 50 institutionalized old people selected at random at the Montefiore Home in Cleveland. Subjects were divided into two groups, 60 to 74 years of age, and 75 to 90. The aim of the study was to determine general personality trends, degree of adjustment and balance, and age and sex difference as measured by the Rorschach test.

Data were analyzed qualitatively for the group as a whole, for the younger and older groups, and for the sexes separately, in terms of general group trends, variability, adjustment, neurotic and/or psychotic trends, and changes due to organic involvement.

[Results suggest] that the group functions at a low level of efficiency. Mental productivity is lower and slower than that of the average adult; reasoning ability, imaginative capacity, and motivation are reduced. Thinking tends to be rigid and is often vague and/or irrealistic. Interests are limited. Emotional life is rigid, shallow, and unadapted. Especially evident is the inability to form satisfactory social relationships.

The group as a whole shows varying degrees of adjustment and balance with neurotic and/or psychotic trends frequently in evidence and many indications of personality deterioration due to organic change. Some subjects show, however, healthy well integrated personalities and capacity for high level of performance.

Examinations of the relative performance of the older and younger groups studied shows more of the older group lower in intellectual and emotional flexibility and control, intellectual productivity, sensitivity to and awareness of the environment, and social adaptability. Reliable sex differences are also observed, more women than men being more productive, more intellectually responsive and flexible, more sensitive to the environment, but more unstable emotionally.

However, these authors warn that these results must be considered in terms of the high degree of selectivity of the group studied.

At the same congress a study in progress was reported by Kuhlen and Keil (29) on a larger group—100 men (50 aged 65 to 70 and 50 aged 75 to 80) all of whom were residents in a county home housing mostly old people. The subjects were mainly men of low educational and occupational level; over one-third were single.

Although existing data from other types of studies would lead to the expectation that groups of these two ages (one decade apart in old age) would differ in adjustment, little in the way of statistically significant differences appeared in the case of the Rorschach responses [our italics].

However, statistical contrasts with such "normative" data as are available in the literature showed marked and highly reliable differences. The total number of responses, for the ten cards, for example, averaged 16 compared with an average of 33 for Beck's recently reported normative group. There were also points of similarity with young adult performance. For example, the responses of the old-age group were distributed among W, D, Dd and DW in about the same proportions as are younger adult groups.

In addition to contrasting these two old-age groups one decade apart, and contrasting old age with young adulthood, the paper points up some of the difficulties to be encountered in psychological research on old age using the Rorschach test or utilizing institutional populations.

Wenar (50) in 1952 reported on 20 subjects between the ages 55 and 65, a group below our lower age limit. The purpose of this paper was to compare Rorschach findings on aging subjects with their psychiatric and social ratings and to evaluate the Rorschach findings on these subjects as a measure of the quality of their social adjustment in a group situation, and of their emotional well-being as revealed by the psychiatric examination.

Wenar concluded that the Rorschach can be used as a measure of the general intactness of the personality structure of aging individuals. However, he found it to be of only limited usefulness in predicting the constructiveness of an individual's behavior in actual social situations.

Brief mention should be made of a publication by Piotrowski which, though it does not deal specifically with the responses of old people as such, nevertheless is pertinent here.

One of Piotrowski's many contributions to the literature on the Rorschach is his listing of ten "signs" of central nervous system disorder (37), any five of which are considered diagnostic of a cortical disturbance. These signs are as follows:

1. Total reactions less than 15.
2. Time per reaction exceeds one minute each on an average.
3. One or less movement responses.
4. One or more color naming.
5. F+% less than 75%.
6. Popular % less than 25%
7. Response repetition.
8. Impotence of response. That is, giving a reaction in spite of its recognized inadequacy.
9. Perplexity, distrust of own ability.
10. Automatic or pet phrases.

Chesrow, Wosika, and Reinitz, mentioned above, found no correlation between the deterioration score on the Wechsler-Bellevue, given to subjects, and the number of organic signs of Piotrowski. We, however, found the majority of these signs in many of our presenile and senile records.

This brief summary includes, so far as we know, all the outstanding literature on the Rorschach as used with older subjects. Of the studies listed, Prados and Fried had only 10 subjects within our age range. None of Wenar's subjects were over 65 years of age and all of Dörken and Kral's subjects were senile dements.

Grossman *et al.* observed 50 institutionalized patients 60 to 90 years of age. Kuhlen and Keil had 100 institutionalized male patients, half aged 65 to 70 and half 75 to 80. Thus many of the subjects in both these studies were below our age range. Furthermore at the time of this writing neither of these two studies had appeared in print.

Thus we have actually only the Klopfer and Chesrow studies to compare with our own findings: Klopfer with 50 subjects aged 62 to 93, and Chesrow *et al.* with 20 subjects aged 64 to 83. Table 1, which presents

TABLE 1. COMPARATIVE FINDINGS OF DIFFERENT INVESTIGATORS

	Klopfer	Prados and Fried Normal old age			Dorken and Kral Senile dementia	Chesrow et al.	This study		
		50–60	61–70	71–80			Normal	Presenile	Senile
Age (mean or range)	73.5				76.3	72	70—100		
Number of subjects	50	13	12	10	30	20	41	140	19
R	14.1	20	23	20	15.1	18	25.9	15.7	13.5
M	1.4	2.6	1.9	1.8	1.1	1.6	3.3	1.6	.2
FM	3.2	4.8	5.0	5.1	2.8		2.7	2.0	.3
m	.1				.1		.7	.3	.0
FC	.3	1.8	1.7	.2	.7		1.0	.3	.0
CF	.7	1.5	1.6	.2	.4		1.3	.5	.2
C	—	.2	.2	.3	.2		.2	.1	.1
W%	high	61%	52%	43%	31%		36%	43%	46%
D%	low	37%	46%	55%	50%		47%	47%	45%
Dd%		2%	2%	2%	17%		15%	9%	8%
F%					55%		50%	64%	92%
F+%						70%	93%	81%	50%
A%	high	43%	45%	49%	47%	49%	46%	55%	40%

numerical findings for these two studies, as well as for the others reported here, permits such a comparison.

The findings of these studies are for the most part consistent in reporting general intellectual and emotional impairment in older subjects. Gilbert (22) summarizes the findings as to emotional changes in the personality of some elderly persons as reflected in the Rorschach as follows:

We might say that we find reduced and shallow emotional responsiveness, efficiency and productivity, little inner conflict, reduced control of instinctual demands, constriction, impotence, and a recurrence of the primitive manifestations of childhood.

Several of these investigators have found, as do the present investigators, that there can be marked individual differences among these older subjects—some of the Rorschachs reflecting extremely well integrated and healthy personalities even in quite elderly individuals. They also find, as do we, that *area* is the scoring dimension least affected by increasing age.

CHAPTER THREE

Subjects, Methodology, and Scoring

Subjects and Sampling

During the early stages of this study, records were obtained by interviewing individual old people in their homes. In selecting these cases, we chose subjects over 70 years of age who were known to be, or found to be, reasonably healthy, active, and alert. None of these individuals were bedridden or even, for that matter, temporarily in bed when interviewed. For the most part they were living alone as head of the household, or at least sharing responsibility for the management of their own household. Many handled their own financial affairs, were active socially, traveled.

Practical considerations, however, led to curtailment of this highly time-consuming program of individual interviews, and only a portion of our cases could be gathered in this manner. Consequently, a second group of subjects was introduced. These resembled the first group in that they were reasonably healthy, alert, and active. They appeared to be in good, or at least reasonably good possession of their "faculties" and were able to take part responsively in the test situation. However, the members of this group were housed in institutions for the aged.

From these institutions we asked those in charge to allow us to interview only those individuals whom they considered among the more alert and capable, those who were able to "look out for themselves." The extent to which the Rorschachs of this institutionalized group differed from those of noninstitution subjects is discussed in detail in Chapter Nine.

Thus, our main criteria for selection of subjects were those of age and availability. These criteria being met, we screened out those individuals so grossly incompetent or aberrant in behavior as to suggest senile dementia, and attempted to secure a group of reasonably alert and healthy old people. The composition of the resulting sample may be described as follows.

AGE AND SEX   The joint distribution of our cases by age and sex is presented in Table 2. The number of subjects in each age group drops

TABLE 2.   DISTRIBUTION OF CASES BY AGE AND SEX
(Number of cases in each age and sex group)

Age	Females	Males	Total
70	73	28	101
80	58	28	86
90	9	4	13
TOTALS	140	60	200

with increasing age, and, as would be expected from the differential longevity rate, women outnumber men at all ages.

INSTITUTIONAL STATUS   Sixty-seven cases, one third of our total
sample, at the time of testing were residing outside of institutions—in
homes of their own or of relatives. The remaining two thirds were in
institutions for the aged. The great majority of our institutionalized subjects
were provided by two institutions. The level of institutional life in one of
these is well connoted by its subtitle: *A Home for Aged British Gentlewomen.* The other, maintained by a benevolent organization, similarly
provided accommodations above the typical institutional standard. Finally,
a small number of cases was secured through two other public institutions, about average in their level of accommodations.

SOCIO-ECONOMIC STATUS   A large cluster of different specific items
of information about individuals—their education, occupation, income
level, social class, community status—are commonly grouped under the
general heading of socio-economic status (SES). Since an individual's
status partly derives from his own ability level, and partly determines the
extent and types of many contacts he has with his environment, some
index of this status is generally found to bear a relationship to most
psychological functions that have been measured in the ability and personality fields.

Because of the high degree of interrelationship among the various
items in this cluster, any single item generally serves as a fairly satisfactory
estimate for the total complex. For our old people we have gathered information on the two most accurately classified and commonly used indices
of SES: level of education, and level of occupation in earlier life (husband's
occupation, in the case of married women). These indices tend to stress the
ability aspect of SES, and provide a rough estimate of the range of intelligence of our sample. For purposes of comparison, we include a tabulation of the same data for the total U. S. population in this age range and
geographic area, computed from U. S. Census data (45). Occupation is
classified on the Minnesota Scale of Paternal Occupations (25).

From Tables 3 and 4 it is seen that subjects of all levels of social status

TABLE 3. YEARS OF SCHOOL COMPLETED
Compared with Years of School for White Population
Currently Aged 72-86 Years, Calculated from 1940 Census

| Years of education | Level | Percentage | |
		Total sample	Census
0–7	Grammar school, under 8th grade	8	37
8	Grammar school, graduated	15	37
9–11	High school, 1 to 3 years	16	8
12	High school, graduated	11	9
13+	College, first year and beyond	16	6
	Unclassified	34	3
	TOTAL	100	100

TABLE 4. OCCUPATIONAL LEVELS
Men's Own and Women's Own or Husband's Occupations
On the Minnesota Scale, Compared with the 1920 U. S. Census Data
(When Current Population was Aged 38 to 58 Years)

| Class | Type of Occupation | Percentage | |
		Total sample	Census
I.	Professional	11	3
II.	Semi-professional, managerial	21	5
III.	Clerical, skilled, retail business	21	14
IV.	Farmers	2	19
V.	Semi-skilled, minor business	19	27
VI.	Slightly skilled	8	13
VII.	Day laborers	1	19
	Unclassified	18	——
		100	100

and ability were included in our sample, but that those of higher levels
are overly represented, in comparison with the total U. S. population.
That this is in part a result of our desire to secure healthy, alert subjects
is suggested by studies of Miles and Miles (31) and Owens (33), showing
that individuals with higher ability or educational levels at younger ages,
"hold up" better in psychological performances in old age.

LONGEVITY OF PARENTS   Incidental to our study, but of some interest,
is information on the longevity of the stock from which our elderly subjects

spring. Of our total 200 subjects, 154 reported mother's age and 156 reported father's age at death. Median reported age for the mothers was 76, median for the fathers was 77 years. Both the high average age and the lack of the expected sex differences are surprising.

Appropriate life expectancy figures for comparison are not easy to find. The usual average expectancy is quoted for living infants, and infant mortality considerably reduces the average. The parents of our subjects, however, presumably had had to live to at least age 18 to have had children. The proper figure for comparison, then, would be the life expectancy for individuals aged 20 to 30 years in the years 1860 to 1880. This figure is estimated, from data given by Dublin *et al.* (17) for the English population in 1870 to 1880, to be between 59 and 62 years for men, between 62 and 64 years for women. Thus the median length of life of our subjects' parents is at least a dozen years beyond the average expectation.

The reported age at death of the subjects' fathers, compared with mothers, is especially provocative. In contrast to the relatively much shorter-lived males in the population as a whole, the fathers of our long-lived subjects are themselves particularly long livers. This suggests the very tentative hypothesis that the male's genetic contribution to longevity is of special importance.

How We Gave the Test

The first thirty or so of our subjects were individuals still living in their own homes, and they were tested at home. (With the exception of one man who came to the Gesell Institute, and one who was seen in his office.)

The Examiner, or a secretary, first phoned to request that we be allowed to visit the subject, and to explain briefly the purpose of our visit. We received a few refusals, but most of the subjects approached agreed to take the test.

One, or two, Examiners then visited the subject at home, at the appointed time. Some of our subjects lived alone. If not, they were in nearly all instances examined in a separate room, apart from friends or family.

After greetings and generalized social remarks had been exchanged, the Examiner explained again the purpose of the visit and of the test. We stressed our earlier work in giving this test to children and explained that we were trying to find out what people of different ages saw in the cards. In our explanations to the subjects, the fact that the Rorschach is believed to reveal individuality characteristics was minimized, as was the fact of degeneration or depreciation of patterns in old age. The scientific and research aspect of our efforts was emphasized.

When we first gave the test, it seemed desirable to have two Examiners work together. This was due to the fact that the elderly individual, like the child, seems to require a good deal of personal attention. Attention given to recording and thus taken from the subject seemed to lessen rapport and to reduce responses.

Much encouragement and enthusiasm needed to be directed to the subject. Best results were obtained by looking directly at the subject, praising him, answering all questions, listening to his stories, immediately responding to his remarks.

Though considerable direct encouragement and praise seemed necessary, a few subjects became suspicious and commented, "You say 'good' to everything." Therefore it seemed important to give just the right amount of praise and encouragement, but not too much.

Thus at the beginning of the study one Examiner gave the test and conversed with the subject; a second as unobtrusively as possible recorded subject's responses. Gradually as we became more skilled in working with older people, it became possible for one Examiner to give the test and to record simultaneously, though it was sometimes difficult to get down all the accompanying verbalization. In fact one very productive subject commented to the Examiner, "My observation to you, young lady, is, 'I'm astonished that you haven't learned shorthand.' "

The test procedure followed the usual method with normal adults, except that no additional inquiry was made at the end of the examination. Our usual approach was simply to say, "We have ten cards here which we should like to show you. There are no right or wrong answers. We just want to know what they look like to you or what they remind you of." This, of course, did not preclude questions and answers about the test as it proceeded. But our task and our success were much facilitated by giving this concrete introduction rather than by attempting theoretical discussion or explanation.

As with children, we found that interest lagged after we had been through the cards once. Additional inquiry was difficult to give, and did little to clear up location of responses or reasons for giving them. Subjects tended either to deny, or to be surprised that they had given, the original responses. Or, like children, they would agree to anything the Examiner suggested as to location.

Thus, as in administering the Rorschach to children, we gave as much inquiry as could be given for each card immediately following the subject's spontaneous response.

In the presentation of the blots, modulation of tempo was often as important as we have found it for the young child. Sufficient time had to be allowed for a general slowness of pace even when there was no expansive verbalization. And we had also to gauge very quickly when to cut any inquiry and move on to the next card if restlessness was shown.

One of the outstanding characteristics of this group of subjects was the questioning of Examiner concerning responses, "Is that right?" We always attempted to answer in a noncommittal but encouraging fashion.

At the conclusion of the presentation, the cards were spread out before the subject and he was asked to choose the one he liked best, and then the one he liked least, and to give the reasons for his choice.

After the subject had completed Card X and had selected the cards best and least liked, we conducted a personal interview. The basic topics which we attempted to cover with all subjects were as follows:

1. Subject's name, address, and age.
2. Ancestry and place of birth of parents.
   Own place of birth.
3. Religious affiliation.
4. Educational background of subject and parents.
5. Occupation (past or present) of self and/or spouse.
6. Social history.
7. How socially active is subject at present.
   Degree of independence—does he live at home, etc.
8. Any psychiatric data.
9. Physical health.
10. Health of parents and their age at death.
11. Any special information on siblings or children.
12. Any outstanding events in subject's past history.

However, in most cases the interview covered considerably more ground than this, and not infrequently lasted for at least an hour, and sometimes more. In fact, "getting away" politely was one of the most difficult aspects of the whole procedure.

Many subjects seemed extremely pleased to have a listener who was interested in them and in the details of their lives, and often appeared extremely reluctant to have her depart. Many thanked us for coming. "This is what I consider a first class call," said one of our subjects.

Though most subjects asked, when we arrived, what the test was about and what was its purpose, there was moderately little questioning of the Examiner when the test was completed. A few subjects did request some report as to how "well" they had done and what we had found out about them. In many of these cases a psychogram was drawn up and some interpretations were reported to the subject.

Generally, however, no questions at all were asked, or the subject merely wanted to know if his answers had been satisfactory, if he had given about the same kind of answers as other people, or whether he was or wasn't "crazy." Most subjects were easily reassured that they had done well. Many forgot the test itself in their interest in the interview.

Thus, when the Rorschach was given in the home of the subject we planned to allow about two hours for each visit.

The time per subject was considerably cut down in the testing of institutionalized individuals. Since many of them had been well oriented to the test and to our general purpose by the officials of the institution, very little preliminary explanation was needed from us.

In most institutions, the Examiner was introduced to the subject in his or her room with some such simple phrase as, "Here's the Doctor you were expecting. She's going to show you some pictures and ask you a few questions." (This led to some slight complication in the cases of those subjects who wanted to remove all their clothing at once. But this was easily overcome, and most institutions felt that the more familiar term "Doctor" would obtain better cooperation than a more accurate description.)

If the subject did not want to take the test, mild efforts at persuasion were made but no pressure was brought to bear. Most subjects approached were very willing to cooperate and seemed pleased to do so.

Except for the lessening of the initial explanation, the only outstanding difference in procedure between institution and private home was the shortening of the interviews. We covered all main topics, as to education, health, parentage, marital history, etc., but spent less time in listening to generalized personal reminiscences, on the grounds that we had several of the other people to see. This explanation was readily accepted, and many subjects spontaneously cut short their own reminiscences with the comment, "I mustn't take too much of your time." Several in fact commented adversely about other inmates who, they thought, had taken up too much time.

Scoring

Rorschach scores may be considered under two general categories: absolute scores which are decided upon by the accepted practices of scoring, and relative scores which are determined by criteria that vary according to the particular age or group with which one is concerned. In our general scoring approach we have used the European scoring, a detailed account of which may be found in our book, Ames *et al., Child Rorschach Responses,* Chapter 3. For criteria for the relative scores, D and F+, we have followed Hertz, and the P responses have been determined by a tabulation of the most commonly occurring responses in our group (see Tables 5 and 38). Each response in any record is considered separately and is scored along three primary dimensions: area, determinants, and content. Popular responses are also noted. The categories in each of the primary dimensions are as follows:

Area

W, W	Response to the whole blot without apparent combination and organization=W; and response to the whole figure with one or two small parts omitted=W	D	Response to a normal detail
		Dd	Response to a rarely selected detail
DW	Confabulatory whole	Do	Oligophrenic detail; only a part is seen of a usual whole concept as the heads of the men on III
WS	Response to the whole including the white spaces	S	White space used as area of response

Determinants

F	Response based on form alone.		ant contents, dark, diffuse, gruesome, dismal, threatening. Darkness or blackness is the primary quality
M	Human figures seen in movement or animals (bears, apes) in human activity	FC	Response is determined primarily by the form, with color incorporated in the response
FM	Response determined by animal movement		
m	Response indicating inanimate objects in movement	CF	Response is determined primarily by the color, but some form is present
F(C)	Responses defined or differentiated by shading values		
Clob	(Clob F, F Clob) Response based on a diffuse impression of the blot, stemming from its darkness. Unpleas-	C	Pure color response; response determined by the color alone with no reference to the form

Content

A, Ad   Animal responses. Content of response is an animal form, either the whole animal, A, or part of an animal, Ad

H, Hd   A human form, either whole, H, or part of a human, Hd. Other content categories as in the literature: plant, flowers, object, nature, architecture, geography, painting, paint, food, reflection, map, abstract, science, fire, blood, anatomy

( )   Imaginary forms, either human or animal such as witch or dragon

P   Popular responses, those given by one out of every six individuals. Scored according to the list of populars presented in Table 5

Popular Forms

The forms scored popular (P) in this study are listed in Table 5. These items have been selected on the basis of frequency of occurrence of responses given by our group of old people.* The list generally resembles lists of popular responses derived from normal younger adult samples, such as those of Hertz (24), Beck (10), or Klopfer (27), but differs in omission of some usually found items and inclusion of certain new ones. In this respect, our list is similar to those determined for groups of child subjects (Ames *et al.*, 1), though the overlap of items is greater between young adult and old age lists than between childhood and young adult lists.

TABLE 5.   POPULAR RESPONSES IN OLD AGE

Card	Location	Form
I.	W	Bird, bat, butterfly
	Center	Human figure
II.	W	Two persons
	All black parts	Bears, dogs, animals
III.	W or W	Two persons
	Center red	Bow
IV.	W	Skin, fur rug, pelt
	W	Animal, head at top
	W	Person
V.	W	Bird, bat, butterfly
VI.	W or lower ⅔	Skin, fur rug, pelt
	Top projection	Bird, butterfly
VII.	W or top two tiers	Persons
	Top tier	Person's head
VIII.	Side figures	Animals
X.	Side blues	Crab, spider
	Lower green	Worm, caterpillar, snake
	Top gray	Mice, bugs, animals

* Criteria of minimal frequency for inclusion of a response as *popular*, and a detailed tabulation of frequencies for each of our qualitative groups are presented in Chapter 14.

CHAPTER FOUR

Classification of Cases

Our first approach, in investigating the process of aging as reflected in the Rorschach test, was a straightforward consideration of the records of subjects classified into age groups: the 70-year-olds, 80-year-olds, and 90-year-olds. Examination of this material, presented in Chapter 9, shows that the results of such classification are meager and inconsistent. Age-group means for most Rorschach scoring categories did not increase or decrease steadily from one decade to the next, and over-all age trends tended to differ unpredictably at different socio-economic levels of our sample.

Furthermore, in giving the Rorschach to our elderly subjects, we observed that the records of many subjects differed in no appreciable way from those of any normal adults, and that this normality of response did not appear to be directly related to the age of the subject. Not only did we not find consistent differences between the performances of the 70- and 80- and 90-year-olds as groups, but individually, some 80-year-olds and even some 90-year-olds gave more adequate responses than did some of the 70-year-olds.

These results were at first disappointing, in view of our clinical impression that we had gathered a wealth of material which was highly pertinent to the aging process. We felt strongly that the developmental continuum was there, but our method appeared inadequate to delineate it. We concluded, then, that some division of subjects into groups along other than age lines might be more fruitful than the more conventional age approach.

The most obvious division appeared to be into a "normal" group and a "senile" group. Certainly in a number of our subjects, the extremely high animal or anatomy per cent, the high form per cent, the low correct form per cent, and in some cases complete or virtually complete "static perseveration" (repetition of some concept on several cards regardless of its adequacy as a response) made a diagnosis of senility obvious.

23

TABLE 6. A-List Signs
Omitting Items which were Tried but which did not Occur Conspicuously[a]

*A1.	Thinks own concept is right or wrong
*A2.	F% over 50%
A3.	A% over 50%
*A4.	Static perseveration
A5.	Dynamic perseveration[b]
A6.	"Perfect" this or that
*A7.	Low F+% (80% or under)
*A8.	Tells own experiences
*A9.	Gives qualifying remarks
*A11.	M+FM=0
*A12.	FM=or>M
A14.	Interest in other people's responses
*A16.	Qualifying verbs as "could be," "might be"
*A17.	Initial exclamations
*A20.	Low R (15 or fewer)
*A21.	Narrow content (4 or less)
*A22.	Refusals
*A25.	Looks on back of card
A29.	Would know what it was if it were a picture of something else
A31.	Suggests changes in the blot to make it fit his concept
*A32.	Says "too hard" or that he doesn't know, and then responds adequately
*A33.	Bird or animal response to human figures on III

[a] Of the original 35 A items, area items and several others which when checked occurred too seldom to be tested by χ^2, were omitted in the final list. The original numerical designations—A1, A2, etc.— were retained, to show how many of the original items tried turned out to be usable.
* Starred items in Tables 6 and 7 are included in χ^2 table, pages 28–29.
[b] Dynamic perseveration = the same response given repetitively but in a form which changes slightly but adaptively from card to card.

However, the majority of our 200 cases seemed, in our judgment, to occupy a position somewhere between these two groups. By no means yet senile, these subjects still differed conspicuously, in their responses, from the normal individual. These subjects we designated as presenile.* We thus used the term as the term preadolescent is customarily used: not to designate *any* age or behavior period preceding adolescence (or senility), but rather to indicate the age or behavior period *just* preceding—in this case—senility.

It became evident immediately that in many of these presenile protocols, scoring differed conspicuously from normal scoring. Especially was this true of the A% and F%, both of which appeared to be excessively high in many of the records. F+% and number of responses, on the other hand, were both low, as was variety of content.

More striking were the qualitative ways in which the responses of many of these older people differed from those of the individual under 70.

* The term apparently corresponds to "senescent" as used by some investigators, who thereby imply a definite, but relatively benign, state of decline.

TABLE 7. B-List Signs

Omitting Items which were Tried but which did not Occur Conspicuously[a]

*B1.	One or more anatomy responses
*B2.	Concept of "oughtness"[b]
*B3.	Abstraction or idealistic concept
*B4.	Quarreling responses
*B5.	H% of 15% or more
*B6.	New shading response, inside upper side portions of IV (Hertz's Area #38 [17]).
*B7.	Complains that brains aren't good, is stupid or dumb, etc.
B8.	Describes people as "having a high old time"
B9.	0ΣC
B10.	Thinks there is a trick to getting the right answer
B11.	Tone of voice[c]
B12.	Quotes a nursery rhyme
*B13.	Mention of midline
*B14.	Mention of symmetry
*B15.	Laughter
B16.	Questions card, addressing it directly
B17.	Compliments card
*B18.	"Eah (Ayah)," confirming comment to own response
*B19.	Discusses own response with self, pro and con
*B20.	Questions Ex. as to what "answer" is
*B23.	F—on populars
*B24.	Physical excuses for poor performance (headache, pain in arm, etc.)
*B26.	Implies without naming. That is, tells what subject is doing without identifying subject
*B29.	Split up middle
*B30.	Indefinite use of "something," or "somebody"
B31.	Dogs on VIII watching other part of blot, or other new connections between parts of blot
*B32.	Thinks Ex. knows the answer
B33.	Legs off human figure on III
*B36.	Perseveration of remarks
*B37.	"Of course"
B40.	Subject says he is "stuck"
B42.	Stories about bats
B43.	One blot connected with another in confabulatory response
*B44.	General expressions of insecurity or inadequacy
*B45.	Prefaces response with "Well!"

[a] Of the original 51 items, several when checked did not occur frequently enough to be tested by χ^2, and thus have been omitted in the final listing.
[b] Subject thinks that he "ought" to be doing better. Or that people or animals on card "ought" to be behaving differently. Or that other subjects "ought" to give certain responses.
[c] Subject uses gentle, wondering, surprised, pleased tone of voice as one might use in addressing a young child.

All aspects of the individual's Rorschach performance which seemed to us to be likely "signs" of aging were noted, and were listed in two separate lists. Group A contained those kinds of responses which we had earlier observed in children's records, but not in the records on adults. Group B contained those responses which to our knowledge did not characteristically appear in normal adult records or in children's records.

As we gathered our cases, more and more of these tentative qualitative signs suggested themselves to us, i.e. responses which were not typical of normal adult records, but which we had found earlier in children, or, responses which we had never found conspicuously in any earlier age group. Eventually the frequency of appearance of each sign was tabulated for all of our cases. Tables 6 and 7 list A- and B-list signs. Table 8 indicates the percentage of normal, presenile, and senile subjects who showed each of these signs.

Classification of all cases into three major groups—normal, presenile, and senile—was then effected on the following basis:

Subjects were classified as *Normal* when the total patterning of their records was about as rich and varied as one would expect to find in any normal adult sample, and when they showed none of the qualitative signs of presenility, or when just one or two such signs appeared in an otherwise full and normal record. Ideally, there should be no such signs in a normal record, but often an extremely normal-seeming record was classified as normal in spite of a few such signs.

Classification in the *Presenile* group was determined by our clinical judgment of the over-all adequacy of the record and by the presence of several of the specific qualitative signs listed in our A and B lists in any one record. A few records were classified as presenile even without many of these signs on the basis of the patterning of scores mentioned earlier, especially high animal per cent and high form per cent.

A small number of cases in our estimation belonged in neither the normal nor presenile groups. They were classified as *Senile* when: the animal per cent or the anatomy per cent or a combination of the two was close to 100% and when at the same time there was a very high F% and a very low F+%. Complete or virtually complete static perseveration was also a basis for classification in the senile group.

We made the assumption that our senile cases were not senile dements, since in institutions we specifically requested exclusion of cases diagnosed as such, and since we excluded the records of any individuals who did not make a reasonably good adjustment to the test situation and give at least some kind of attention to each of the ten cards.

In all but 10 per cent of our cases, classification was made directly on the basis of the Rorschach test response. However, when there was some doubt, and when the investigators disagreed as to classification, the examiner's judgment of the subject's general behavior was taken into account. Thus if the question were between senile and presenile, and the individual's general behavior appeared to be excessively senile, that fact would influence the decision.

After all cases had been gathered and classified along these lines as normal, presenile, or senile, we tabulated the occurrence of each of these A and B list qualitative items for each group of records. This appears to be a circular method of approach to the problem—first to differentiate the groups according to a list of signs, and then to check to see if the groups showed different frequencies of these signs.

Actually, our tabulation and tests of the frequency of occurrence of these signs in the different groups served several purposes. For one thing, it showed the actual frequency of a number of specific aspects of performance in the Rorschach situation for a group of old people. More important, it allowed us to discard a number of items which we had thought allowed discrimination between our three qualitative groups, but which actually did not. This sharpened our criteria and our precision in separating the groups.

Most important, though, is not the differentiation of the three groups on these items alone, but the extent to which these groups hang together *as* groups in other aspects of performance. That is, it is not primarily important that one group uses a half-dozen specific phrases which are not commonly used by another, but that these two groups, differentiated by the specific items, show real intragroup homogeneity in the total patterning of response. We believe that we have actually "lifted ourselves by our own bootstraps" in this process of first crudely, then more precisely, separating these empirical groups.

The χ^2 test of significance was used to evaluate the significance of the differences in frequency of items among the groups. It is here only a very approximate test, because of the decided nonrandomness of the samples, but it is clearly better than no test at all, pointing up as it does the items which show greatest differences among the groups. In all, we tabulated 86 different items. The theoretical number of comparisons thus possible was 258. The number of comparisons which could actually be made by χ^2 (in some instances the behavior did not occur often enough to be testable) was 133.

The number of differences expected to test significant at the 5 per cent level or better by chance alone was 7. The number which did so test was 55. The number expected to test significant at the 1 per cent level by chance alone was 1. The number which did so test was 38.

Of the original 86 items, 38 allowed at least partial testing by χ^2, and

TABLE 8. QUALITATIVE DIFFERENCES BETWEEN GROUPS
Percentage of each Group Showing each "Sign"

	Frequency of occurrence			Significance of differences		
	Normal	Presenile	Senile	N–PS	N–S	PS–S
I. *Increasing Items*						
A. Normals and preseniles similar; seniles higher						
A11 M+FM=0	0%	5%	74%	0	**	**
B1 Anatomy responses	31	35	63	0	*	*
B37 "Of course"	7	15	26	0	–	–
B. Normals lower; preseniles and seniles similar						
A1 Thinks right or wrong ans.	26	68	47	**	**	0
A4 Static perseveration	7	41	47	**	–	0
A8 Relates own experiences	22	52	42	**	0	0
A22 Refusals	17	36	42	**	–	0
B7 "My brains are no good"	15	44	31	**	–	0
B15 Laughter	9	25	15	*	–	0
B18 "Eah" or "Yeah"	2	19	20	*	–	–
B20 Questions examiner	15	52	63	**	**	0
B36 Perseveration of remarks	19	61	52	**	–	0
B44 Insecurity	9	62	58	*	**	0
B45 "Well"	34	59	53	**	0	0
C. Normals below preseniles; preseniles below seniles						
A2 F% over 50%	53	79	100	**	**	–
A7 F+% below 80%	5	32	79	**	**	**
A12 FM=or>M	44	64	89	**	**	*
A20 Low R (15 or fewer)	17	55	78	**	**	*
A21 Narrow content (4 items or less)	19	55	100	**	**	**
A25 Looks on back of card	5	12	36	–	–	*
B9 ΣC=0	15	47	78	**	**	*
B13 Midline emphasis	19	30	44	0	*	0
B23 F– on populars	2	20	52	**	–	**
II. *Special presenile items. Normals and seniles similar; preseniles higher*						
A9 Qualifying remarks	26	56	5	**	–	**
A32 "Too hard," then answers	5	60	36	**	–	*
A33 Bird or animal for man on III	10	25	10	*	–	–
B2 Sense of oughtness	2	16	5	*	–	–
B6 Special shading on IV	2	20	5	*	–	–
B19 Discusses ideas with self	19	59	10	**	–	**
B24 Physical excuse for inadequacy	4	16	0	*	–	–
B26 Implies without naming	0	16	0	**	–	–
B29 "Split up middle"	12	24	5	*	–	–
B30 "Something" as response	24	61	5	**	–	**
B32 Thinks Ex. knows answer	9	24	10	*	–	–

TABLE 8. QUALITATIVE DIFFERENCES BETWEEN GROUPS—*Continued*
Percentage of each Group Showing each "Sign"—*Continued*

	Frequency of occurrence			Significance of differences		
	Normal	Presenile	Senile	N–PS	N–S	PS–S
III. *Decreasing items. Normals and preseniles similar; seniles lower*						
A16 Qualifying verbs	39	50	21	0	0	*
A17 Initial exclamations	51	60	26	0	0	**
B3 Abstract responses, idealism	19	10	5	0	–	–
B4 Quarreling	27	19	5	0	–	*
B5 15% or more humans	41	50	10	0	0	*
B14 Symmetry	22	15	5	0	–	–
B26 Asks what test is for	15	21	0	0	–	–

Key to significance symbols:
  $-$ = Not testable by χ^2 (too few cases in cell)
  o = Tested by χ^2 and not found significant
  * = Tested by χ^2 and found significant at 5 per cent level
  ** = Tested by χ^2 and found significant at 1 per cent level

Total number of items tabulated for all three groups: 86
Theoretical number of comparisons between groups: 258
Number of comparisons actually made by χ^2 (tests not possible in some cases because of theoretical frequency in a cell being too small for valid use of the test):   133

Number of differences expected to test significant at the 5 per cent level or better by chance alone: 7
Number actually obtained: 55

Number of differences expected to test significant at the 1 per cent level by chance alone: 1
Number actually obtained: 38

results of the testing are presented in Table 8. As will be seen, a three-way comparison was made: between Normal and Presenile groups; between Normal and Senile; and between Presenile and Senile.

Items are tabulated under the following headings:

I. Increasing items:
   A. Normals and preseniles similar, seniles higher
   B. Normals lower, preseniles and seniles similar
   C. Normals below preseniles; preseniles below seniles
II. Special presenile items: normals and seniles similar, preseniles higher
III. Decreasing items: normals and preseniles similar, seniles lower.

Those items which test significant under each of the above categories have been graphed in Figure 1. The curves for individual items are not labeled because of the great overlap within each category, but the general similarity of configuration of items within each grouping is striking. The steepness of many of the curves attests to the success with which we have separated our three clinical groups.

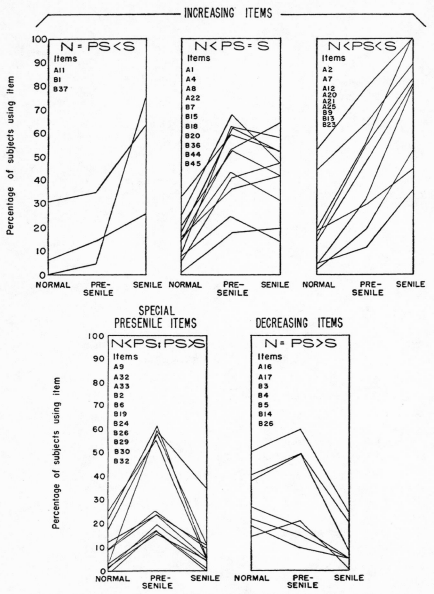

Fig. 1. Percentage occurrence of the significant qualitative items in each clinical group

In addition, we list below A and B items which did not occur frequently enough, or with enough difference between the groups, to be tested by χ^2, but which nevertheless seem to us at least noteworthy when they do occur.

A-list items not testable by χ^2

A5. Dynamic perseveration (9%, 2%, 0%).

A6. Comment that concept is a " 'perfect'————" (14%, 18%, 15%).

A14. Interest in other people's responses (18%, 16%, 0%).

A29. Says he would recognize blot if it were a picture of something else (0%, 3%, 5%).

A31. Suggests changes in blot to make it fit his concept (0%, 7%, 0%).

B-list items not testable by χ^2

B10. Thinks there is a trick (0%, 3%, 0%).

B11. Special tone of voice (12%, 25%, 10%).

B12. Quotes nursery rhymes (9%, 8%, 0%).

B16. Addresses card directly (0%, 5%, 0%).

B17. Compliments card (0%, 10%, 10%).

B31. Dogs on VIII watching something else, or other new connections between parts of blots (12%, 9%, 0%).

B33. Legs off at III (9%, 9%, 0%).

B40. Subject says he is "stuck" (15%, 17%, 36%).

B42. Tells stories about bats (2%, 7%, 0%).

B43. One blot connected with another (0%, 4%, 5%).

CHAPTER FIVE

Statistical Analysis of Rorschach Scores

Several different statistics have been used to describe the distribution of the major Rorschach variables for each of our qualitative groups. These statistics supplement each other in giving a picture of the central tendencies and variabilities of each group. The principal values given for each Rorschach score are the *mean*, together with its standard deviation, and the *median*, together with the mid-quartile range and the over-all range. In addition, we also list for each scoring category the percentage of subjects obtaining a score greater than zero.

Distribution of Scores: Means and Standard Deviations

The means and standard deviations for each scoring category for the sexes separately and combined for each qualitative group are presented in a master table, Table 9. Included are the results of testing the significance of the differences between the sexes within each group, and of the differences between groups.

A note is in order with regard to the interpretation of the tests of significance. We have used Student's *t* test, which is an exact test only when certain underlying assumptions are fulfilled: those of randomness of sampling, of normality and common variance of the population distributions, and of independence between tests.

The first condition, that of randomness, is not fulfilled. Our subjects were collected miscellaneously, rather than selected randomly. Further, they were divided into groups partially on the basis of several scores which are here being tested for significance of difference. The second and third conditions—normality and common variance—are approximated in the case of some variables, but not in the case of others. Finally, each group mean has been tested twice—against each of the other group means—leading to slight inflation of the probability values.

32

As is usually done in such cases, we have gone ahead and used the *t* test anyway, terming it an "approximate" test. It is the best rule-of-thumb we have for judging the importance of observed differences. Particularly in the case of the very large *t* values, there seems to be little question of the reality of the differences between scores.

It seems reasonable to say that, using our method of separating the three qualitative groups, some real differences in scores do obtain among the groups. Most important, as we have emphasized before, is the fact that though we have separated the groups on the basis of certain scores, the groups hang together qualitatively *as* groups, with significant differences between other, non-criterion, scores.

Distribution of Scores: Percentiles

In Table 10 is presented the over-all range, mid-quartile range, and median for each qualitative group for every score that occurs with appreciable frequency. This table should be of particular clinical value, since it can show directly the standing of any given individual's scores in relation to the distribution found in each of our groups of old people.

These same data are depicted in Figure 2. This graph presents, quite vividly we believe, an immediate impression not only of the differences between group averages but of the differences in variability and in the amount of overlap between groups. The low degree of overlap for many scores lends considerable corroboration to our clinical impression of essential differences between the three groups.

Distribution of Scores: Percentage Using Each Category

Also in Table 10 is listed the percentage of cases in each group who use each particular scoring category one or more times. This statistic throws light on the "universality" of a scoring variable, rather than on its magnitude. It supplements measures of central tendency by showing how the different individuals in the group have contributed to the average. It can indicate, for example, whether a "moderate" average score for a determinant results from a large percentage of subjects obtaining moderate scores, or from a very few individuals achieving very high scores, even though most subjects neglect that determinant.

TABLE 9. MASTER TABLE
Means, Standard Deviations, and Significance of Differences between Mean Scores

Score		Normal			Presenile			Senile			Significance of sex differences			Significance of group differences		
		Female	Male	Total	Female	Male	Total	Female	Male	Total	Normal	Presenile	Senile	Normals vs. preseniles	Normals vs. seniles	Preseniles vs. seniles
R	Mean	27.3	22.6	25.9	16.7	13.2	15.7	17.8	8.8	13.5	0	**	**	****	***	0
	SD	13.7	13.4	14.6	7.7	4.6	7.0	7.6	3.8	7.6						
ΣW	Mean	7.7	7.3	7.6	6.2	6.2	6.2	5.5	4.4	5.0	0	0	0	***	***	*
	SD	2.4	2.7	2.5	2.1	2.5	2.2	3.6	2.9	3.4						
W%	Mean	34.4	41.1	36.1	41.7	47.9	43.5	40.2	52.8	46.2	0	0	0	*	**	0
	SD	21.9	26.5	22.9	18.6	21.3	21.0	31.0	19.6	26.8						
D	Mean	13.6	10.4	12.8	8.6	6.5	8.0	9.7	3.6	6.8	0	*	*	***	**	0
	SD	7.6	8.2	7.9	5.0	3.9	4.8	6.9	2.9	6.2						
D%	Mean	49.5	41.0	47.2	48.5	44.5	47.4	49.5	39.3	44.7	*	0	0	0	0	0
	SD	9.1	19.1	13.2	14.0	19.2	15.8	26.1	21.4	24.5						
ΣDd	Mean	6.0	4.9	5.7	2.1	1.1	1.8	2.6	.8	1.8	0	0	0	***	*	0
	SD	8.0	9.3	8.4	3.3	2.1	3.1	4.4	1.2	3.4						
Dd%	Mean	14.9	16.8	15.4	10.1	7.0	9.2	10.3	7.7	8.0	0	0	0	**	*	0
	SD	16.6	15.7	16.4	11.0	10.2	10.7	12.7	10.8	8.6						
F	Mean	15.3	11.8	14.4	10.7	9.2	10.2	16.4	8.1	12.5	0	0	**	**	0	0
	SD	11.9	11.0	11.7	6.0	3.8	5.5	6.8	4.1	7.0						
F%	Mean	51.2	46.6	50.0	62.7	66.7	63.9	92.3	90.7	91.5	0	0	0	***	***	***
	SD	16.7	18.2	17.2	16.5	6.6	14.6	5.8	16.0	11.8						
F+%	Mean	93.0	93.9	93.2	80.0	82.6	80.7	33.1	69.8	50.5	0	0	**	***	***	***
	SD	6.7	6.1	6.5	22.3	23.9	22.8	22.8	21.3	28.7						
M	Mean	3.4	2.9	3.3	1.7	1.2	1.6	.3	.1	.2	0	0	0	***	***	***
	SD	2.1	1.3	1.9	1.5	1.4	1.5	.2	.3	.5						

		1	2	3	4	5	6	7	8	9	Sig 1	Sig 2	Sig 3	Sig 4	Sig 5
FM	Mean	2.7	2.8	2.7	2.2	1.4	2.0	.2	.3	.3	***	***	*	0	*
	SD	2.0	2.4	2.1	1.6	1.6	1.6	.4	.7	.8					
m	Mean	.7	.9	.7	.2	.3	.3	0	0	0	0	***	***	0	0
	SD	.8	1.0	.9	.5	.6	.6	0	0	0					
F(C)	Mean	2.3	1.4	2.1	.9	.7	.9	.6	.1	.4	*	***	***	0	0
	SD	2.4	1.0	1.9	1.4	.7	1.3	1.0	.3	.8					
FC	Mean	.7	1.2	.9	.4	.1	.3	0	0	0	*	***	***	0	*
	SD	.8	1.6	1.1	.6	.4	.6	0	0	0					
CF	Mean	1.4	1.1	1.3	.5	.3	.4	.3	0	.2	0	***	***	0	0
	SD	1.4	.8	1.1	.7	.7	.7	.5	0	.4					
C	Mean	.3	0	.2	.1	.1	.1	.1	0	0	0	0	0	0	0
	SD	.6	0	.5	.3	.4	.3	.3	0	.2					
ΣC	Mean	2.3	1.7	2.1	.8	.6	.7	.4	0	.2	*	***	***	0	0
	SD	1.9	.9	1.8	1.0	.9	1.0	.8	0	.6					
A+Ad	Mean	12.5	9.2	11.4	9.0	7.6	8.6	4.0	4.1	4.2	***	***	0	0	0
	SD	7.6	4.3	7.0	4.6	3.7	4.4	4.1	2.8	3.6					
A%	Mean	46.8	42.4	45.6	55.9	52.6	55.0	30.0	50.1	39.5	***	0	**	0	0
	SD	12.1	16.1	13.4	18.7	20.9	19.4	35.7	25.3	33.3					
H+Hd	Mean	6.4	5.0	6.0	3.1	2.8	3.0	.7	.3	.5	***	***	***	0	0
	SD	6.1	2.0	5.4	2.2	1.7	2.1	.9	.5	.9					
H%	Mean	22.7	26.6	23.7	16.9	18.2	17.3	4.3	5.4	4.8	***	***	***	0	0
	SD	13.8	8.4	13.6	8.4	12.9	9.9	5.2	6.3	7.0					
Anat	Mean	.9	.4	.6	1.4	1.4	1.4	12.7	3.6	8.4	***	***	0	*	0
	SD	1.0	.5	.9	3.6	2.1	3.0	9.8	4.5	9.0					
Anat%	Mean	2.8	1.4	2.4	6.1	8.2	6.9	63.2	29.2	47.1	***	***	0	*	0
	SD	3.3	1.9	3.0	12.9	14.1	13.3	34.5	33.3	37.9					
P	Mean	7.0	7.2	7.1	5.5	5.2	5.4	1.9	2.2	2.0	***	***	***	0	0
	SD	3.1	2.3	3.0	2.1	2.0	2.1	1.2	1.2	1.7					
P%	Mean	31.5	37.4	33.3	35.8	39.2	36.8	12.2	37.3	20.4	**	*	0	*	0
	SD	11.6	12.3	17.1	14.6	13.5	14.4	13.3	30.2	24.7					

Key: 0=Non-significant difference by *t* test.
   *=Difference significant at 5 per cent level
   **=Difference significant at 1 per cent level
   ***=Difference significant at 0.1 per cent level

TABLE 10. DISTRIBUTION OF MAJOR RORSCHACH SCORES
Median, Range, and Quartiles; and Percentage Obtaining a Score of
One or More in Each Qualitative Group: Normal (N),
Presenile (PS), and Senile (S)

Score	Group	Percentage giving 1+	Percentiles				
			1	25	50	75	99
R	N:	100%	9	17.5	21.5	32.0	61
	PS:	100	4	11.9	14.7	19.0	42
	S:	100	3	10.0	13.0	14.0	34
W	N:	100%	2	5.9	7.9	10.1	14
	PS:	99	0	4.7	6.1	7.6	12
	S:	95	0	2.1	4.8	8.0	10
D	N:	98%	0	8.5	11.3	16.5	33
	PS:	98	0	5.2	8.3	9.3	26
	S:	89	0	2.5	5.5	8.3	20
Dd+S	N:	71%	0	.9	2.1	7.0	31
	PS:	50	0	0	.6	2.6	18
	S:	63	0	0	.9	1.5	14
FM	N:	80%	0	.9	2.8	3.8	8
	PS:	78	0	.6	1.5	3.2	7
	S:	21	0	0	0	0	2
F(C)	N:	78%	0	.7	1.7	3.0	8
	PS:	52	0	0	.6	1.4	9
	S:	21	0	0	0	0	3
FC	N:	59%	0	.1	.8	1.5	5
	PS:	26	0	0	0	.5	3
	S:	0	0	0	0	0	0
CF	N:	68%	0	.4	1.1	1.9	6
	PS:	34	0	0	.3	.9	3
	S:	16	0	0	0	0	1

W%	N:	100%	4%	25%	33%	45%	100%
	PS:	100	0	28	39	57	100
	S:	100	0	24	46	68	100
D%	N:		0%	41%	50%	56%	69%
	PS:		0	36	47	58	85
	S:		0	31	54	59	85
Dd%	N:		0%	1%	10%	26%	52%
	PS:		0	1	6	16	45
	S:		0	0	6	14	32
F%	N:		22%	39%	51%	63%	78%
	PS:		18	54	65	75	100
	S:		50	85	95	100	100
F+%	N:		74%	90%	94%	99%	100%
	PS:		31	73	85	93	100
	S:		0	32	50	73	100
M	N:	98%	0	1.8	3.6	4.3	9
	PS:	84	0	.6	1.4	2.4	7
	S:	16	0	0	0	0	1

ΣC	N:	85%	0	.4	1.9	2.9	8.5
	PS:	54	0	0	.3	1.3	4
	S:	16	0	0	0	0	2.5
A%	N:	100%	1%	36%	45%	55%	77%
	PS:	100	10	42	55	68	100
	S:	89	0	10	45	70	100
H%	N:	98%	0%	15%	23%	30%	55%
	PS:	89	0	8	17	23	65
	S:	42	0	0	0	8	25
Anat%	N:	44%	0%	0%	0%	6%	11%
	PS:	40	0	0	2	9	74
	S:	63	0	0	55	86	100
P	N:	100%	3	5.8	7.0	9.0	10
	PS:	100	0	4.0	5.7	7.2	10
	S:	89	0	1.0	1.5	3.0	6
P%	N:		5%	17%	31%	46%	72%
	PS:		0	28	34	48	71
	S:		0	7	10	33	100

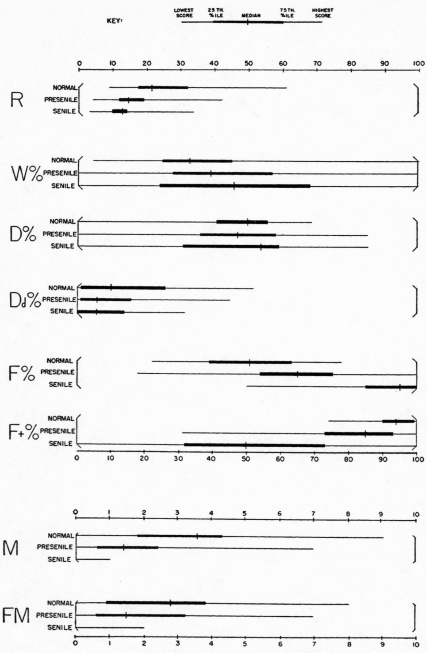

FIG. 2. Median, quartiles, and range for each major Rorschach score

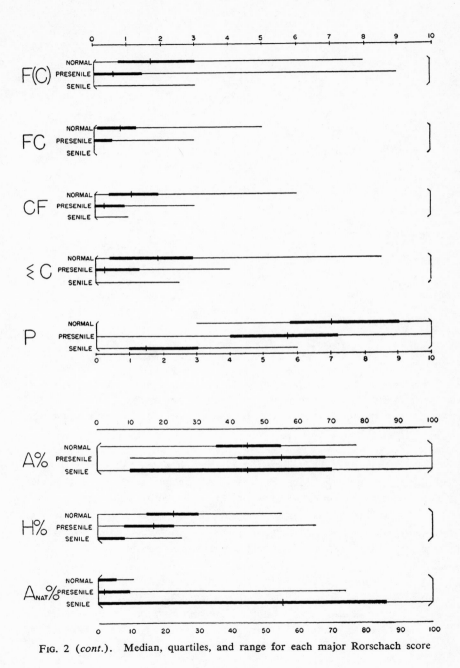

Fig. 2 (*cont.*).   Median, quartiles, and range for each major Rorschach score

CHAPTER SIX

Normal Responses

R = 25.9	50%F	11.4A or 46%A
	93%+	6.0H or 24%H
36%W		3.3 objects
47%D	3.3M, 2.7FM, .7m,	1.8 plant or flower
15%Dd	1FC, 1.3CF, .2C, 2.1F(C)	.7 nature
	.1FClob	.5 anatomy
		.4 geol. or geog.
	3.3M : 2.1ΣC	.3 scene
		.3 food

Description of Rorschach Response

The actual quality and content of responses of our group of "normal" old people was not, in the opinion of the investigators, as remarkable as the fact that such a large proportion of our subjects between 70 and 100 years of age could be classed as normal on the basis of their Rorschach response.

This classification of normality was made on two counts: 1) close correspondence of the actual Rorschach scores with those of normal adults of younger ages, and 2) absence of the qualitative signs which we have identified as indicative of presenility and senility.

Of our 200 subjects aged 70 to 98, 41 fell into the normal category. These 41 subjects ranged in age from 70 to 92. Many of them were considerably older in years than other subjects classed as presenile or even as senile.

The responses of this group of apparently normal older people closely approximate and do not differ in any systematic way from those found in any group of presumably "normal" members of any adult population.

As to actual scores: the average number of responses in our normal subjects was 25.9, which falls well within the normal range.

As to area of the blot responded to: distribution of responses approaches that of the normal adult but is already diverging slightly toward the distribution typical of presenile and senile subjects. On the average, 36% of responses are global, 47% are details, and 15% small details. Thus we have slightly more W and Dd and slightly less D than is expected in a normal adult record.

With respect to area perhaps more than any other determinant, our group of normal old people differs from the younger normal population. Furthermore it is in this respect that our own three groups (normal, presenile and senile) are least clearly distinguishable one from the other.

The average F% (number of responses determined by form alone) is 50%. This number falls just at the top limit of any presumably normal distribution. Thus most of our normal old people are only slightly more restricted in this respect than is usual in a normal adult population. The F% increases sharply in presenility and even more sharply in senility, as Table 9 indicates.

Not only the mean F% but also the mean F + % is within normal limits; in the case of F + %, well within normal limits. The mean F + % of our group of normal old people is 93%. Accurate form holds up rather well even in our presenile subjects, being 81% in that group. But in the seniles it falls sharply to an all-time low of 50%.

The mean experience balance in our normal group is 3.3M to 2.1ΣC. Within the introversive sphere, the movement response scores are virtually identical to those expected in the normal adult: 3.3M, 2.7FM and .7m, human movement slightly exceeding animal. This gives us a W:M ratio of 7.6W : 3.3M, which is very close to the ideal normal 2:1 ratio for these determinants.

On the color side, there is a slight but not excessive divergence from the expected normal adult scores. Mean color scores for our normal old people are 1FC, 1.3CF and .2C. Thus CF slightly exceeds FC rather than amounting to only half FC as prescribed. Pure C is virtually nonexistent.

It is interesting to note what changes presenility and senility bring about in both movement and color scores. In presenility, both human and animal movement scores fall off, and also a change in proportion takes place, with animal movement coming to exceed human. Inanimate movement drops to .2. In the senile subject each of these scores again drops sharply, in fact nearly reaches the vanishing point. The proportion remains as in presenility.

As to color, the proportion of FC, CF, and C responses remains the same in presenile subjects as in normals—CF responses lead, then FC, and lastly C. In the preseniles the scores are .3FC, .5CF, and .1C; in seniles, 0FC, .2CF, and .1C.

In the normal old age group, shading is a further determinant which falls within normal limits, there being on the average 2.1 shading responses. This number drops sharply in the preseniles and seniles. Clob responses are not found (mean .1) in this group nor in those which follow.

Animal per cent in this normal group is on the average 46%, which falls within the normal adult expectation of 35–50%. This number increases in the preseniles to 55% and then drops back in senile subjects to 40%.

Human responses, interestingly enough, reach a mean of 24% in our normal subjects—being considerably higher than the normal expectation. This figure drops to 17% in preseniles and 5% in the seniles.

Content is fairly varied in this group, leading content categories in addition to animal and human, being object, plant, nature, anatomy, geology and geography, scenes, and food.

Sharp contrasts between our three groups are found when we consider the percentage of cases using any given determinant. For example, human movement responses are given by 98 per cent of our normal cases and 84 per cent of our preseniles, but by only 16 per cent of the seniles. Similarly, animal movement responses are given by 80 per cent of the normal group, 78 per cent of the preseniles, and only 21 per cent of the seniles. Inanimate movement appears in 49 per cent of the normal records but in only 19 per cent of the preseniles and none of the seniles.

As to color responses: 59 per cent of the normal subjects use the adaptive FC; but only 26 per cent of the preseniles and none of the seniles. Sixty-eight per cent of the normals give CF responses, 34 per cent of the preseniles, and 16 per cent of the seniles. C responses occur in 20 per cent of the normals, 11 per cent of the preseniles, and only 5 per cent of the seniles.

Seventy-eight per cent of the normal group give shading responses, 52 per cent of the preseniles, and only 21 per cent of the seniles. FClob or ClobF responses occur in only 9 per cent of the normals, 2 per cent of the preseniles and in no senile cases.

Thus in every respect the normal record appears as richer than the presenile, which is in turn less restricted than the senile.

QUALITATIVE SIGNS   One of the outstanding findings of the present study is the identification of two groups of qualitative signs, the occurrence of which in any number appears to indicate presenility. One of these two groups (Group A) includes ways of responding which are customarily present in child subjects but which usually drop out in adulthood. In these respects the presenile subject thus once again responds as does a child. The second group (Group B) includes kinds of response never seen before to any extent in the entire life span, either in childhood or in normal adulthood, but appearing with presenility.

So far as we know, no investigator has ever checked a group of normal adult records for the presence of such signs. Nor have we. But we believe that though a few may occasionally occur, most of them are not present conspicuously or consistently in normal adult records.

A few of these signs do occur in our normal old people. These are listed in tabular form below:

A-list signs

Those which occur in one quarter or more of our normal subjects but which occur most extensively in preseniles:

26 per cent of normal subjects think there is a right or wrong "answer" to the blots

26 per cent make qualifying remarks

39 per cent use qualifying verbs "could be," "might be"

51 per cent give an initial exclamation

44 per cent have an A% of over 50%

Those which occur in normals but most extensively in seniles:

53 per cent have an F% of over 50%

24 per cent have a W% of over 50%

48 per cent have a Dd% of 9% or less

B-list signs

24 per cent fail to formulate responses explicitly but use vague terms "something," or "somebody"

44 per cent give one or more anatomy responses

34 per cent preface remarks with a delaying "Well"

Psyche of the Normal Old Person

The picture of the "normal" 70 to 100 year old individual which we obtain from the Rorschach is not unlike that of the theoretical "average" normal adult.

In terms of actual Rorschach scores we have the picture of an individual who prefers to generalize though he can also be quite concrete and practical. (It is perhaps in the area category that we see the more common bond in all our older persons, whatever the classification.)

He is able to refine his judgment to a perfectly normal degree, with perhaps even an excessive tendency in this direction in some cases. Where the Dd% is especially high and the F response is over 50%, we might expect a fussy, fretting, worrying individual, somewhat demanding and compulsive. It is in this way that the culture often thinks of the older person, but we find that this type of response occurs no more in this group than in the normal population.

The CF and C combined are greater than the FC, implying a lessening of adaptability, and an increase of egocentricity in old age. It may be here, as in the area category, that we will begin to see the signs of aging more readily than elsewhere.

The amount of shading combined with the predominance of introversivity indicates a sensitivity to others, a normal empathetic response, and the presence of caution and restraint in emotional and intellectual adaptation.

The average A%, which is at the high normal limit, indicates adequate stereotypy and ability to conform easily. The spread of the content categories implies a breadth of intellect and interest as great as that of the normal adult. The high H% indicates a strong interest in others and in making and maintaining adequate interpersonal relations which is especially characteristic of this particular age group. This high H% combined with the frequency of the anatomy responses also indicates strong interest in self. This characteristic plus the egocentricity indicated by the ratio of the color responses might again be a configuration one would expect in the protocol of an older person.

As to the meaning of the qualitative signs which appear in this group of older persons whom we have termed normal, some of them are fairly patent indications of insecurity, such as the feeling that answers are or are not correct, and the use of qualifying verbs "might be," or "could be," and the prefacing remark, "Well." The fact that they think that there is a right or wrong "answer" implies also a rather naive approach to a situation and a dependence on others (in this case the Examiner) and the assumption that there is a simple resolution to any problem. It may also imply a diminution of intellectual potential. The vague expressions used such as "something" or "somebody" also imply a reduction of clear-cut intellectualization, or an evasive type of response which indicates inability to specify or a need to respond with as little "engagement" as possible. We are inclined to believe that it supports the other signs of diminution of intellectual dynamism and potential.

However, the stereotypy of behavior observed so conspicuously in senile subjects and to at least some extent in members of our presenile group, does not appear among normal subjects. Thus, records of this group are no more alike one another than are records of any group of normal subjects.

For our senile cases we have found that individual psychograms do not reveal too much more than does an average psychogram for the whole group. This is not true of the normal subject. Of our three groups of cases there is the greatest variation from individual to individual among the normal subjects on nearly all scoring variables. Normals show the widest intragroup variation on: number of responses, Dd%, F%, and on *all* the determinants—M, FM, m, F(C), FC, CF, and C.

On the other hand, for a few variables, there is even less variation from individual to individual in the normal than in the other groups. This is the case for F+% and A%. Apparently there is great latitude in the extent to which normal individuals are responsive to the blots, and in the ways in which they utilize different aspects of the blots for responding. But there is very little leeway, among individuals considered normal, in the degree of clarity or accuracy of perceptions and judgment, or in the adequacy of stereotyping and conforming functions.

Behavior of Normal Subjects as Observed in the Rorschach Situation

The general behavior of our normal older subjects during the test situation does not differ consistently or conspicuously from that of any group of normal adults. Furthermore there is about as much variation from one person to another as would be found in any group of normal individuals.

Most noteworthy is this fact that behavior so much resembles that of alert younger people. This not only in the actual Rorschach scores but in the general social manner and response to the social aspects of the situation.

We shall thus make no effort to categorize this behavior, but shall instead quote sample comments of examiners, made directly at the close of the Rorschach examination:

Mr. F., aged 78: "Very alert, clear, pleasant, and quite interesting. Does not ramble. Answers questions about his life in an interesting, clear manner. Comments that his life has been rather a failure materially, but feels that it was not necessarily a failure spiritually because he has gone through a lot and learned a lot."

Miss K, aged 70: "Much interested, and very sociable during the test. Makes good general conversation. Seems like a woman in her early sixties, completely alert, energetic and interested in what is going on."

Miss A. S., aged 76: "Seems healthy both physically and mentally. Excellent sense of humor."

Miss G. S., aged 76: "A very vivacious, interesting woman. Extremely entertaining and a lively sense of humor."

Mr. H., aged 81: "Subject with keen, quick speech, who moves easily and with great dignity, has a lively sense of humor, appears to be widely informed and to have an easy, unembarrassed, factual approach to almost any subject."

Classification of Cases

AGE RANGE   Twenty-seven of our 41 normal subjects were in their seventies; 11 in their eighties; and 3 in their nineties.

SEX   Of this group, 30 were females, only 11 males. This comprises 18 per cent of all the male subjects, 21 per cent of the females.

EDUCATION   Eighteen of these subjects had less than a high school education or its equivalent; but the larger number—23—had a high school education or in some cases considerably more.

INSTITUTION VS. PRIVATE HOME   Subjects were evenly divided on this score. Twenty-one lived in institutions; and 20 still lived in their own homes.

Examples

Two examples only have been selected from among our normal cases—that of Miss A. S. aged 76 and that of Mr. H. aged 81.

These two records are not presented to give a composite picture of the normal aging psyche, because the variation in response from subject to subject is too great to make such an attempt feasible. Rather the two samples are given to illustrate the resemblance to the normal young adult record of records found in an appreciable percentage of an older population.

Sample Record of Miss A. S., Age 76 Yrs.: Normal Group

D	FM	A		I. In center point looks as though it might be two apes. Both imitating each other. (*Inquiry:* Top center from middle up, with rounded center humps as heads and two other small center top projections as hands.)
W	F+	A	P	Taken as a whole might be a butterfly or wasp. (*Inquiry:* Shape.)

D	M	H		A very interesting thing. Good lady running to catch the train. A fly-away coat and puffed sleeves, scooting for all she's worth. Fur hat. Nothing but a fur hat could be formed like that. (*Inquiry:* Left side detail.)
	Repetition			Apes in center.
	Elaboration			Too substantial for a butterfly. Moth is the thick one and butterfly transparent.
	Repetition and elaboration			This has some relation to this. The right is more masculine than the left, first on account of cap, and then again the face. Very substantial head and face there on the right. I can't see his legs, but his overcoat goes down to his knee. The man is also in pursuit of the train. (*Inquiry:* Right side detail, same as above, except that it is now a man.)
Dd	F(C)	Ad		Bear with a smile. (*Inquiry:* Shading in center of right half. Sees head only.)
Dd	F+	Hd		Leg might be the well upholstered leg of a woman, tip of toe and heel and fur around it. (*Inquiry:* Lower right side projection. *Reminded you?* The way it's shaped.)
Dd	F+	obj.		Music. (*Inquiry:* Tiny dots off left side of main blot are music notes.)
Dd	m	obj.		Little stones. Movement of people's feet made them fly. (*Inquiry:* Same dots off main blot, now on both right and left.)
W	M	(H) reflection	P	II. Christmas. Santa Claus looking at himself in the glass. Has some animals in his arms, carrying them. (*Inquiry:* Usual figure, right and left, is Santa Claus, with usual hands and projections, outside top of each black, appearing to her as animal he is carrying.)

	Elaboration			His suit. (*Inquiry:* Bottom red.)
D	↗m C	blood		I don't like the red down below there. Looks too bloody the way it's splashed for me. (*Inquiry:* Bottom red.)
	Elaboration			Knees. (Points to usual rounded part in center as knees of Santa Claus.) I can't understand why he's holding his hand here in greeting.
W	M	H	P	III. My goodness! What are they contending over? Of course! Over a bow. Each wants that bow for their neck. (*Inquiry:* Usual figures with center red as bow.) ·
D	m	obj.		This is the night before Christmas. This is his stocking night-cap like the French wear. He's smoking a cigar. St. Nick. This extension might be that he's a toy Nick and is hanging up on the wall. Cap only goes as far as there. (*Inquiry:* Side red.)
	Elaboration			These are the coat tails of these two dandies who are contending for the bow. (Elaboration of first response.) Something like—I can't think what. (Indicates center gray.)
W	↗F(C) F+	A		IV. Oh, this is an animal upside down. My heavens! It looks as though you had turned him inside out and upside down. Eyes. The figure looks as though it must be dead since it's opened, but the eyes must be alive. I won't attempt to explain this little thingamabob. Hair on nostrils, ears proper. These are the legs that used to be, opened out. I can't account for the thinness of the arms. And here's the vertebrae. (*Inquiry:* Whole. Sees head at bottom center, with vertebrae up the rest of the center.)

| W | M | A | P | Looking at it as whole, it looks like an ape striding out. All out of proportion. (Here she tells a long story about Puerto Rican boy painting Superman.)
(*Inquiry:* Head at top with usual arms and legs.) |
|---|---|---|---|---|
| D | F(C) | mask | | Now look, a good theatrical mask there. That's the thing I wouldn't like to see in my sleep.
(*Inquiry:* Upper central area, eyes in shading.)
My observation to you, young lady, is, "I'm astonished that you haven't learned shorthand." |
| W | F(C) | A | P | V. (She tells about reading *Quo Vadis* in German, her first German book, and getting the nose bleed!)
Oh, a bat, a bat! Vampire—its face here turned out here (right side of upper center detail). Its little legs are slightly extended more than in real life. Must I have it up that way? ∨ No, it is grotesque that way. ∧
That's the more perfect picture to me. Furry part continuing on legs.
(*Inquiry:* Whole. *Reminded you?* The furry look and the way the fur comes down on its legs.)
By the way, were you born here in this country? |
| W | F(C) | obj. | P | VI. ∨ You know, these things remind me most of all—unless I pick them to pieces— of skins of animals. What in the world is this creature? Have you anything to do with the fur trade? (Laughs.) A nice piece of fur well marked. It's given you some very good shadings. Is it water color? If I had more to do with animals I could tell you more. Seems very symmetric. It's clear to me that it's been doubled over. I suppose it would occur to others. It's too perfect.
(*Inquiry:* Whole seen as piece of fur. Shows Ex. doll clothes that she is making, to illustrate doubling.) |

W	FM	abstr. ↗ A	VII. This picture suggests jollification. They're having a high old time. Little dogs —Scotties. This is a field.

(Inquiry: Scotties are top two tiers and field is at bottom. The dogs have one paw up and out as seen in projection on second tier.)

D	F(C)	arch.	Down here is a light stone building, and here is the casement window. These little parts that go up here are parts of the castle. I could suggest this pathway or lighting to the sky. It's too high—not placed right for a pathway, and yet it looks like that. I meant the lights and shadows, you know, when I said the lighting.

(Inquiry: Third tier with casement window at center bottom. Midline of third tier is "pathway or lighting to the sky.")

I would rather dream of this than the other (Card IV) because it suggests jollification.

D	FM	A	P	VIII.>This suggests two animals treading across with its first foot onto that spiky thing. It's footing there and there. < The other one is exactly the same. It's in duplicate, isn't it? It's an animal without a tail.

(Inquiry: Usual animal.)

W	↗F(C) CF	flower	V This thing suggests more of a flower, because of the shading, I think. If you see flowers from the distance it would suggest that and these would be the leaves. This would be the heart of the flower in here. I couldn't account for that at all, except that it is a connecting link between leaves or stalk and plant. A plant with which the wind has taken liberties, because it's not perfect in shape. Flowers always are. And too fresh looking to be withered. Color is good and harmonious.

(Inquiry: Pink and orange is flower with blue and gray as leaves. Heart of flower is center of pink and orange and center midline between pink and blue is "connecting link between leaves and plant." *Reminded you?* The color gave me the idea.)

W	↗CF F±	obj.	IX. Griffins—two griffins. The British coat-of-arms. No, unicorns—the one-horned unicorn. (*Inquiry:* Orange as unicorns. *Reminded you?* The horn gave me the idea, and the unicorn is at the top of the British coat-of-arms.)
D	m ↗ FM	A	These here suggest that they are held in tow or caught—not exactly the word I want to use—they are held fast by these creatures. Held up by the neck. Might suggest a dog, little shaggy haired creature. (*Inquiry:* Green, with smaller animal at top of green holding up dog which is main part of green.)
S	F+	(Hd)	And you know, looking out of center, something like an ogre. It would appeal to a child. (*Inquiry:* Face in center space detail with slits as eyes.)
D	FC	food	The pink, I'm sorry to say, doesn't suggest anything. These two end ones might suggest a cherry—with stem. Don't know what connection it has to dog. (*Inquiry:* Side pink. *Reminded you?* Shape, but color too.)
W	CF	flowers	X. ∨ This is exceedingly pretty, but—flowers, that's all I can make out of that. It's airy-fairy. (*Inquiry:* Whole. *Reminded you?* Color and shapes.)
D	CF	plant	A leaf. (*Inquiry:* Side yellow and orange. *Reminded you?* Both color and shape.)
D	CF	plant	Piece of last dead leaf turned back from stalk. (*Inquiry:* Side brown. *Reminded you?* The color.)

D	FM	A	Except for color, reminds you of a peacock's tail. Here's the peacock, very imperfect shape. Here's its legs. It should be filled out here. Coloring in this very well shaded. (*Inquiry:* Lower green with center as peacock and usual worms as tail. Card is still inverse. *Reminded you?* A peacock with his tail spread.)
D	F±	nat.	Part of coast line in miniature. In this case the white would be water—closing this out of your mind altogether. (*Inquiry:* Pink is coast line. She omits everything between the pinks. *Idea?* Shape.)
D	CF	flower	Sea flower. (*Inquiry:* Center blue. *Idea?* Color and shape.)
D	FC	obj.	That's very clearly brought out. It suggests a little pendant to jewelry. (*Inquiry:* Center orange. *Idea?* The shape and the color.)
D	CF	flower	It might be the stalk of a flower broken off here with two little yellow buds. It's the most perfect shape on the paper as far as I can see. (*Inquiry:* Same detail. *Idea?* The color.)
D	F+	A	There's quite a lot in that. It's pleasing because of shades and colors. This figure up here amuses me. It could be a lamb, but you'd have to cut off these things. (*Inquiry:* Side green. *Idea?* The shape.)

Best: X. The most peaceful of them. IX next.

Least: IV. A nightmare!

R=33	8F=24%F	10A, 1Ad=33%A
	6F, 2F±=85%F+	
11W=33%W	5F(C)	2H, 1(H), 1Hd, 1(Hd)=15%H
17D=52%D	2FC, 6 CF, 1C	6 obj.

$\dfrac{4\text{Dd}}{1\text{S}}=15\%\,\text{Dd}$ 4M, 5FM, 2m

11W : 4M   1→CF, 2→F(C), 2→m

Succession:

Loose-orderly Reactivity: 4M : 8½ΣC

Shock: None   7P

1 blood
1 mask
1 arch.
4 flower
2 plant
1 nat.
1 food

COMMENT The most outstanding thing here is the configuration of total scores, which in itself indicates the vigor of the intellectual and emotional activity in this subject. From the scoring alone, one would not be able to identify this individual with any particular adult age group, even though qualitatively a few of the signs of aging do begin to appear.

It is not our purpose here to write a detailed individual psychogram, but from the scoring and the quality of the response, it is apparent that such a protocol would lend itself quite easily to a study of the individuality of this subject. This becomes more and more difficult as our subjects range into the presenile and senile groups.

This, then, might be a representative protocol of any "normal" adult and the fact that this subject is 76 years old does not necessarily mean that she belongs to a particular age classification. Within perhaps certain physical limits, she would appear to be as active and productive as any individual in the normal population.

Sample Record of Mr. C.R.H., Age 81 Yrs.: Normal Group

WS   F+   anat.   I. Well, it looks to me very much like the hip bones, somewhat mauled, but the pelvic arch.
(*Inquiry:* Whole. *Idea?* It looks like it. Here the pelvic bones, fossae, condial where back bone comes down. Space details are where "back bone comes down.")

W   F+   A   *Else?* No, there are a good many things that might—but that's the most important. Though incidentally it might also pass for one of the giant rays, the big Manta. (This reminds him of a story of a movie in which the giant ray appeared.)
(*Inquiry:* Whole. *Idea?* Giant rays have a grasper like these here. Upper center details have given him idea of Manta.)

W	FM	A	P	II. Two bears dancing in front of a candle or a pair of candles. (*Inquiry:* Bears are black, top red are candles. Bears are looking up at candles, paws together.)
W	M	(H)	P	III. They look to me like two characters from one of the comic strips, but just why they should have sort of
D	FC	obj.		a pink brassiere between them, I don't know. (*Inquiry:* Usual men, with center red as brassiere. "Here are their legs, bending here, facing each other, hands down." The brassiere is not related to the men. *Idea?* "Two shields, but the fact that it was pink added a little more touch to the likelihood.")
W	F+	obj.	P	IV. Well, except for color it looks not unlike a polar bear skin which the brother of a friend of mine scared the daylights out of his brother by getting in it. (*Inquiry:* Whole. Does not see it as on a person, but only as a skin. *Idea?* Shape, head, roughly the shape of a bear skin, a mat.)
D	F(C)	Hd		And as I turn it up, I get the face of a Chinese mandarin glaring at me. (*Inquiry:* Top center shading detail. *Idea?* Appearance. He now tells the story about the skin again. Also says he has been having a diet of Chinese engineering references in which the author is constantly throwing rocks at the Chinese. "Perhaps that made me think of it.")
W	↗FClob F+	A	P	V. Well, the thing that I think about there is a bat. It doesn't look very much like a bat. Ears up, legs back, awfully ragged. About all I can think of
W	ClobF	nat.		except a thundercloud and not too much like that

	Humorous remark			or a whale.

(*Inquiry:* Bat is whole. *Remind you?* Ears and hind legs and black wings. Thundercloud is whole. *Idea?* Black and rough. *Whale?* "Is it Hamlet where he or one of his friends is wresting about something and he says, 'is it a black cloud, or a whale, or . . .' just a bit of levity.")

W	M	(H) tend. abstr.	O

VI. If I was an impressionist, I'd say it was a human being just bursting its shell of sin and getting its first glimpse of heaven.
(*Inquiry:* "Here's a weird creature just spreading his wings and spurting out of something [top D] and that [lower D] looks as much like sin and woe as a blob of anything like that could, I think.")

W	F+	obj.	P

The thing that constantly occurs to me with these weird smears is skins—animal skins. This one is upside down. ∨ No, that might be his tail [top D]—there are fluffy tails. I've played a little bit with natural history and for that reason perhaps have a sense of hides that shows.
(*Inquiry:* Whole as skin. *Idea?* Neck, front paws, hind paws, and tail.)

D	M	(Hd)	P

VII. Again the comic strip and there are two children making faces at each other—either children or queer animals.
(*Inquiry:* Top two tiers. Points out mouth and nose and head dress. "Arms stretched out, no feet, windshield wiper type." This last remark refers to a joke which the subject had told the Examiner at the beginning of the examination.)

W	FM	A	P

VIII. Oh now, now we've got something. We've got a pair of chameleons climbing out of an orchid.

D	CF	flower	

(*Inquiry:* Usual animals with pink and orange as orchid. *Idea?* Shape of animals while with the orchid it is the color and shape).

W	FM	A		IX. Well, I don't know so much about what is below there, but those two fellows look like two marine beasts—I think they call them copepods—with sea lettuce beneath. They're coming out of that form of sea weed. Not too unlike our sand fleas.
D	FC	plant		(*Inquiry:* Copepods are the orange. *Idea?* Looks of the beasts. Green is sea lettuce. *Idea?* Shape and color.)
D	F+	A	P	X. Well, we have two blue spider crabs there beautifully. (*Inquiry:* Side blue. *Idea?* Not the color, the shape. They're gray.)
D	FM	A	P	And we've got two little black beasts facing each other. I don't know what they'd be. (*Inquiry:* Top gray. *Idea?* Looks like two animals of some kind, miniature buffaloes perhaps standing on their hind legs.)
W	FC	plant		But looks very much like a hunk of seaweed with some of the sea creatures on it. (*Inquiry:* Pink with all the attached parts. *Idea?* A pink seaweed, one of the edible ones—the dolce that the Scotch eat.) There are a number of queer things of that sort from the Sargasso Sea with all kinds of queer appendages.

Best: My first statement would be none, but I think the one is the two little figures facing each other—comes nearer to something that is something. III.

Least: When you fall into a rose bush it's hard to say which thorn pricks the most. I don't know as there is any comparison. III is the least disliked. Would not like to choose another.

R=19

$\dfrac{11W}{1WS}$ = 63% W

6F=31% F

6F+ =100% F+

7A=37% A

2(H), 1Hd=16% H

1 anat.

7D=27% D

1F(C), 1 ClobF

3 obj.

12W : 3M

3FC, 1CF

1 nat.

2 plant

Succession: Orderly

3M, 4FM

2 flower

Shock: ? Clob

1→FClob

9P

Reactivity: 3M : 2½ΣC

1O

COMMENT Here again we see a very acceptable configuration of scores which one might find in any "normal" record. The total response is low, but with the high W and the 100% F+, the implication is that of a very synthesizing and abstract mind rather than a deteriorating one. The individuality is more apparent than any of the signs of age.

As we noted earlier, one of the most outstanding characteristics which we observe as subjects show increasing signs of age as judged by the Rorschach, is the disappearance of those responses which might be termed "personal." (Any particular personal response is most likely to have been given only by one particular subject, because of the personal identification shown by the uniqueness of its composition.)

Both this and the foregoing protocol contain many personal responses and thus show individual rather than any particular age characteristics, and we feel that both can be classified with the normal adult population. Characteristics of aging, as we have been able to define them in this study, appear to have no simple direct correspondence with chronological age. Many aging individuals show integrity of emotional and intellectual reactions, no matter what their chronological age.

CHAPTER SEVEN

Presenile Responses

R=15.7	64%F	8.6A or 55%A
	81%F+	3.0H or 17%H
43%W		1.4 anat.
47%D	1.6M, 2.0FM, .2m,	1.8 object
9%Dd	.3FC, .5CF, .1C, .9 F(C)	.6 plant, flower
		.3 nature
	1.6M:.7ΣC	

Description of Rorschach Responses

The actual Rorschach scores for our presenile group are distinctive, distinguishing these subjects from normal and senile individuals with respect to most determinants. However, even more distinctive than the actual scores themselves are the qualitative items which characterize this group. As our sample presenile records demonstrate, the presenile Rorschach response stands quite unique, unlike the response of child, mature adult, normal old person, or even senile old person. It is in most instances quite easily identified.

Considering the actual Rorschach scores, we obtain the following picture of the performance of the presenile individual.

The presenile subject gives on the average sixteen responses. This is markedly less than found in the normal adult and only slightly more than given by senile subjects. Thus quantity of output is not great in presenile individuals. Though more than found in the first five years of life, it is about equal to that of the average 6- to 10-year-olds whom we studied (Ames *et al.*, 1).

As to area of response, the presenile performance is very close to that of the senile. Compared with the response of the normal old person, there are more global responses, fewer small details, and about an equal number of large details. Distribution is: 43%W, 47%D, and 9%Dd.

When we consider the number of responses determined by form alone, as well as the matter of accurate form, we find that the change from normal to presenile is far less than that from presenile to senile. That is, in this respect presenile subjects appear to be holding up very well and giving a good performance. The proportion of responses determined by form alone in the presenile group is on the average only 64%, a rise of only 14% from that found in the normal subjects. This figure then increases sharply in the seniles to 92%. Conversely F+% falls only from 93% in normals to 81% in preseniles, but then drops very sharply to a mean of 50%F+ in senile subjects. Thus with respect to both F% and F+%, the presenile subjects make quite a creditable showing. Both approximate the figures found in 5½- to 10-year-old children.

Comparing movement responses of preseniles to those given by normals we find that animal movement holds up best, dropping only from a mean of 2.7 in normals to 2.0 in preseniles. This figure decreases to .3 in senile subjects. Human movement, averaging 3.3 in normals, falls by half to 1.6 in preseniles and then almost disappears in seniles (mean of .2). Inanimate movement, .7 in normals, falls to .2 in preseniles and then drops out completely. The distribution of movement responses in presenile subjects approaches that of the 7- to 10-year-old child.

As to relative distribution of FC, CF, and C responses, the ratio is close to that found in our normal, and also in our senile subjects. As to quantity, however, ΣC is only .7 in preseniles as against 2.1 in normals and .2 in seniles. Thus it has fallen off by more than half, and we have mean color scores for the preseniles of .3FC, .5CF, and .1C. This is very close to the distribution of color responses found in the 3-year-old child.

The number of shading responses is halved from normals to preseniles and again from preseniles to seniles. Mean figures are 2.1F(C) in normal old people, .9 in preseniles, and .4 in seniles. Shading occurs in our presenile subjects to about the same extent as in 8- to 9-year-old child subjects. Clob responses have virtually disappeared in presenility.

Animal per cent reaches its high point in this group, rising from an average of 46% in normals to 55% in preseniles. This figure drops again in senile subjects because of the large number of anatomy responses. This high A% is not seen after 4 years in normal children.

H% on the other hand, drops from a mean of 24% in our normal group to 17% in preseniles, and falls further to 5% in seniles. This H% of 17% is close to that obtained in the 8- to 10-year-old child.

Different number of content categories falls off from normals to preseniles—anatomy, object, plant, or flower being the only conspicuous content categories besides animals and humans. Except for the anatomy responses this is approximately the same content that is found from 2 through 6 years of age.

From these figures it is clear that responses in our presenile subjects are quantitatively distinctive when compared with those of normal old subjects. The presenile group is, however, most clearly distinguished by the presence of so-called "qualitative" signs.

As suggested earlier, some of the qualitative signs which characterize presenility were already found in children's records, but for the most part disappeared in normal adult records. These are the A-list signs. Other signs (the B-list signs), so far as we know, are not typically seen in youth or middle age. For a comparison of the extent to which these qualitative signs occur in normal, presenile, and senile records, see Table 8.

The most conspicuous of these signs, and the ones whose presence leads us most surely to a classification of presenility, are as follows:

A-list signs, present also in childhood:

1. Items which especially distinguish the presenile subjects and occur very little in normal or senile old people:
   68 per cent of presenile subjects seem certain that the inkblots are real pictures, representing definite objects, and that there is thus a right and wrong "answer" to the blots.
   52 per cent of presenile subjects interject long stories of their own experiences into their responses.
   56 per cent heavily qualify responses and 50 per cent use qualifying verbs— "could be," "might be."
   Animal movement equals or exceeds human movement in 64 per cent of presenile records.
   25 per cent of subjects see a bird or animal on Card III instead of the usual human figures.
   60 per cent make delaying initial exclamations.
   60 per cent respond by saying, "I don't know" or "I can't tell," and then giving a good response.
   Dynamic perseveration, the same response given repetitively in a form which changes only slightly from card to card, is present in 2 per cent of preseniles and in no other subjects.
   16 per cent express an interest in what other people have said and in how "well" others have done.
   18 per cent comment that blot is a "perfect" whatever it is.
   30 per cent comment that cards are "hard" or "easy." Or that they "get worse and worse."

2. Items which characterize presenile records though they do not reach their peak in presenility but in senility.

Restriction of response is reflected in the fact that 79 per cent of presenile subjects have an F% of over 50%. Conversely F+% decreases—32 per cent having an F+% of 80% or under.

41 per cent of subjects perseverate on one or more concepts.

55 per cent of subjects have a narrow content of four or fewer content categories.

36 per cent of subjects refuse at least one card.

12 per cent look on back of card.

3 per cent comment that if picture were something else they could tell.

B-list signs, which characterize presenility and senility but which are not present to any extent in the records of children or normal adults:

1. Items which especially distinguish the presenile group and which occur less in normal older subjects and in senile subjects:

61 per cent of presenile subjects express themselves vaguely: they see something but are not quite clear as to what it is—"Somebody doing something to something," for example.

59 per cent carry on discussions with themselves, as, "A butterfly. No I don't think it would be a butterfly. Butterflies don't have legs like that. But I guess it probably is."

21 per cent ask suspiciously what the test is for. 24 per cent think Examiner knows the correct "answer."

61 per cent perseverate in their remarks, as "They all have this line up the middle," or "You've got me there, sister," on several cards.

16 per cent express a sense of "oughtness" in one form or another. They think they ought to give better answers or may feel that people or animals seen on the cards "ought" to be behaving differently.

25 per cent laugh a good deal as they answer; 14 per cent describe people seen in the cards as having a "high old time."

20 per cent see animal figures within the shaded area of the upper portions of Card IV.

44 per cent complain that brains are not good or they would do better; and 15 per cent give physical excuses for not doing better: "I could have done better if my shoulder hadn't been hurting me."

16 per cent give a concept by implication only. Thus: "Why, they're arguing with each other about something," without identifying "them."

50 per cent have an H% of 15% or more.

25 per cent describe objects or animals as "split up the middle."

25 per cent have a special, gentle, wondering, reasonable, pleased kind of voice which they use when they question or elaborate their own concepts.

2. Qualitative items which occur least, or scarcely at all, in normal old subjects, conspicuously in preseniles, but even more in seniles.

10 per cent of presenile subjects compliment the cards or the "artist."

19 per cent confirm their own response, after giving it, with an extremely confident "Eah!," or "Yeah, that's what it is all right." 15 per cent follow their response with the comment, "Of course."

62 per cent express varying degrees of insecurity as to their ability to give an adequate response. 59 per cent delay with the prefacing comment, "Well." 4 per cent say "Wait a minute, wait a minute." 17 per cent say "I'm stuck," or "I'm stumped."

20 per cent give F− responses to portions of the blot usually responded to with popular responses.

47 per cent have a ΣC of 0.

30 per cent give midline responses.

Anatomy responses increase, the mean being 1.4 per subject (40%).

7 per cent tell stories about bats; 6 per cent compliment their own performance; 5 per cent address questions directly to the cards: "Now what are you doing?" 3 per cent think there is a "trick" about the whole thing, which they have, or have not mastered.

Psyche of the Presenile

The emotional and intellectual life of the subject whom we have termed presenile can be very clearly determined from the Rorschach response.

Even more than the actual Rorschach scores, the so-called A- and B-list qualitative items reveal the individuality of the presenile subjects as a group.

Above all, there is in presenility an element of uncertainty of self and suspiciousness of others. A large majority of presenile subjects express the fear that they are giving a "wrong answer" to the cards. There is a good deal of apology, both on the basis of ill-health and of general stupidity. Subjects comment that "My brains aren't very good," "You'll find out how dumb I am," or "I can't do these very well because it's so long since I went to school." Or, qualifying verbs are used—Might be, Could be. Or, subjects say that they don't know, or can't possibly tell, and then do proceed to give perfectly adequate responses.

Further expression of feelings of inadequacy in the face of what seems a difficult task are the frequent complaints that the cards are hard or that "they get worse and worse."

Refusal of blots, which occurs in 36 per cent of the presenile subjects, and admissions that they are "stuck" or "stumped," express similar feelings of inadequacy.

Uncertainty as well as a certain vagueness in both perception and expression are shown in the fact that presenile subjects often give a response and then argue and discuss with themselves as to its accuracy. Or they characteristically use such vague terms as "Something," "Somebody."

This same vagueness and inaccuracy of perception is also indicated by the lessening F + % (only 81% F+) and by the large number of F— responses which are given in place of the usual correct form popular responses.

Suspiciousness of others is found in the questioning and requestioning of Examiner as to the purpose of the test, and also in the belief expressed by many that there is a "trick" to the test to which they do or do not catch on. Or in the belief, which several have, that the cards become more and more difficult as the test proceeds and that this is done on purpose.

Presenile subjects, when presented with a situation such as one of the inkblots, which they do not feel fully qualified to meet, have several characteristic methods of dealing with such a situation. They may refuse it entirely. They may complain about its difficulty. They may protect themselves by saying, "I don't know," or "I can't tell," and then going on to answer adequately. They may delay with the admonition to the Examiner, "Wait a minute! Wait a minute!" Or they may simply give an initial delaying exclamation of "Well . . . ," or "Oh my!" and then proceed to answer.

There are several paradoxes in the behavior of presenile old people. Though suspicious and egocentric, they are nevertheless, as shown by the high H% and their questions about what other people said or how well other people have done, considerably interested in other people.

Furthermore, though vague and uncertain much of the time, many presenile subjects are extremely certain, definite, and rigid at other times. They give a response and not only think it is "right" or "perfect," but they feel that other people "ought" to give the same response and "ought to know better" than to give a different one. For example on Card VIII one subject remarks: "Bears. Plainest thing I've ever seen. Do most people think they're bears?" Examiner says that many do, but that some think they are rats or something. Subject says, "They ought to know better than that. Rats can't climb trees."

Or they confirm their own responses with "Of course," or "Eah! That's what it is all right."

This degree of belief in the correctness of one's own perceptions helps explain the "setness" and inflexibility of many old people and the difficulty that those living with them often experience in getting them to "see reason" or to change their minds.

Presenile individuals are not only rigid but definitely restricted as suggested by an F% of 64%, a basic equation of only 1.6M : .7ΣC, and an A% of 55%. Restriction is further suggested by the lessening of R (now only 15.7 on the average); and by the narrowing of content (there being now only *five* major content categories—anatomy, object, plant, animal, and human).

Though interested in other people, and though given to considerable laughter and to ready tears, individuals in this group are not the victims of or even the possessors of strong emotions. As indicated, ΣC is only on the average .7, with .3FC, .5CF, and .1C. Subjects are definitely, though not strongly, introversive. Lack of emotional vulnerability is also reflected in the absence of Clob responses.

Some childishness and egocentricity is suggested by the fact that FM responses outnumber M (1.6M, 2.0FM) and CF responses slightly outnumber FC.

The aging individual is commonly considered to be both garrulous and repetitive. Both of these characteristics are well illustrated in the Rorschach response—the first in the long personal anecdotes with which 52 per cent of subjects interrupt their response, as "Singlehanded I've killed five bears in my life with a club"; the second in the perseveration or magic repetition which occurs in 41 per cent of cases. Not only is there perseveration of specific concepts but subjects also perseverate with certain general remarks and comments.

Many presenile subjects express very high standards for themselves, and sometimes for others. In spite of probably waning abilities, they nevertheless give an average F+% of 81%. In spite of, or perhaps along with, feelings of inadequacy, they strongly express the feeling that they "ought" to do better. They may excuse themselves with the explanation that if the card were only a picture of something else, they could tell what it was.

Though presenile subjects in their own anecdotes may be extremely (though sometimes inaccurately) detailed, in responding to external stimuli there is often a conspicuous lack of attention to detail. W% has in this group increased to 43% at the expense of Dd which has dropped to 9%. D remains at 47% as in our normal group. Lack of attention to small detail and also to the finer nuances of life is also suggested by the sharp decrease in shading responses which in this group average only .9.

Presenile individuals are commonly found to have some difficulty in communication with others. This is partly because they cannot always follow what is being said to them, partly because their own remarks are not always entirely clear. In the Rorschach we see this lack of clarity when subjects plunge into a description of what "they" are doing without first identifying "them."

The increasing anatomy response (mean of 1.4 or 7% of all content) reflects an increasing interest in self. Other signs of egocentricity have been mentioned. But the interest in self of the presenile individual is more or less like that of any egocentric person. It in no way approaches the extreme and absorbing interest of the senile subject in his own anatomy, sex parts and excretory functions. It is still well within normal limits.

A rather unusual and attractive characteristic of a small group of our presenile subjects—mostly women—is the giving of abstract and extremely idealistic responses. Such responses as "Evolution," or "New life," or "Everyone striving for something better," seem to reflect a positive and constructive idealism which suggests a certain wisdom and spiritual outlook on life.

Description of Accompanying Behavior

The group of subjects which we have identified as presenile is not an entirely homogeneous group. Though we can identify here no clear-cut gradient such as we have suggested within the senile group, there do appear to be several gradations within presenility.

First, there is a group of subjects who in many ways strongly resemble the normal individual except that Rorschach scoring is shifting slightly from normal to presenile and, more important, a few characteristic presenile "signs" appear in their protocols.

A second group, comprising the majority of what we have designated as presenile subjects, show clearly many of the qualitative signs of presenility.

A third group of presenile subjects include the few individuals whose functioning is still intact enough for them to show qualitative presenile signs but who because of stereotypy or restriction of response or very high animal or anatomy response and very high F%, give evidence of their rapidly approaching senility.

In this section, we shall discuss the behavior of the second, largest, and most typically presenile group.

In many respects the behavior of individuals in this group is like that of any normal adult. There is some suspiciousness, some hesitancy, and some worry that they may not do well or may show themselves up as stupid; some embarrassed laughter and joking. But otherwise, subjects respond much as does any normal adult when faced with the Rorschach for the first time.

The majority establish a good friendly and responsive relationship with the Examiner. They understand the instructions, give good serious attention to the cards, and seem interested in the cards and in what they can make of them.

Emotional attitude toward the cards varies, as with any adults, with the individual. Some think they are beautiful, some think they are amusing, some think they are horrible.

In what way then, is the general behavior of the presenile individual during the test situation different from that of any normal adult? Chiefly in the fact that the presenile subject tends to *take over* the situation. For all his cooperativeness, his apparent wish to do well on the test and to do what the Examiner wants him to do, he—much more than the normal adult—directs the course and the tempo of the situation. (This tendency increases as the subject advances in presenility.)

This directive behavior on the part of the presenile subject varies from a slight tendency toward strong-mindedness, to such a marked degree of this same behavior that the Examiner sometimes feels that she has encountered a steam roller.

The subject, though apparently fully cooperative, is often so talkative that it may take some time to direct his attention even to the first card, which he holds in his hand as he talks.

And even once started, he readily and frequently diverges from the task at hand. Many times during the entire test, and often several times during one card, his attention strays from the task at hand to stories of his own life experiences—often to things that have happened in the far past. These stories he tells with great enthusiasm and interest. It is often extremely difficult, without seeming rude or importunate, to get him back to responding to the individual blot.

The whole procedure is rendered more difficult by the fact that the presenile individual, unlike the senile, is in such good contact with the social environment and so socially alert that he requires full responsiveness from the Examiner at all times. A perfunctory, "That's very interesting, but now let's get back and see what you can see here," is by no means adequate. Most presenile subjects like to have the Examiner look them directly in the eye and show full and enthusiastic interest in what they are saying. This large amount of responsiveness required often makes recording extremely difficult.

Not only is there a good deal of preliminary conversation, but once the formal test is finished, then most presenile subjects settle down for a real good long chat—or, actually, monologue. Encouraged by the questions in the life history interview, they launch out. An hour goes by quickly, and much more than an hour, Examiner permitting. The Examiner often gets the impression of being bound to the situation with strong ropes of words. If there are two Examiners, one Examiner backs up the other with farewell comments of "That was fine. We thank you very much. And now I'm afraid we'll have to be going." To no avail.

Subjects happily recount every illness they have ever had, with doctors' names and details of medication. Sometimes they even go into complete detail of their mothers' or fathers' last illnesses. They give complete occupational histories.

All of this is done with such enthusiasm and goodwill that it seems heartless as well as rude to interrupt.

There is also a good deal of philosophizing—extremely interesting summaries of what they make of life—how they feel about the total experience of living. Some of this, inevitably, is pessimistic. But in others it is gratifyingly optimistic and positive.

Others comment on their probable approaching death in a realistic and calm manner: " 'Bout through here," "My time is nearly up, I think."

A great many make reference to the Deity, his plans for them, his goodness to them, how miraculously he has saved them from danger and disaster even though at times things may have looked rather black.

There is inevitably, much reference to parents, spouses, siblings, and children who are no longer living. This varies from extremely tearful recital, if the bereavement has been recent, to a calm, peaceful, and often apparently pleasurable reviewing of past happy relations: "I buried three lovely wives!" Several single women recount that their home life, as children, was virtually a paradise and that they have never cared to marry because nothing could ever equal their lives at home.

Though there is considerable tearfulness, it does not seem to indicate vast or deep grief in most cases, and is usually fairly easily diverted.

There is not too intense interest in the Examiner's evaluation of what the test showed about the subject. A few pursue this intently (and if they do so, are given a subsequent report). Most, however, easily accept the explanation that this is research in a somewhat new field and that till it is completed, we cannot tell too much. Thus, in spite of often considerable worried comment during the test situation as to how well they are doing, most subjects do not follow this up with any marked degree of curiosity.

Other characteristics of the behavior of presenile individuals during the Rorschach situation have already been indicated by the Rorschach response itself. Thus presenile subjects, in the Rorschach and in behavior, characteristically show themselves to be somewhat insecure, uncertain, suspicious, worried that they will not make a good impression, vague and unprecise, yet rigid and immovable. They are egocentric, but also much interested in human relations and especially hopeful that things will be harmonious between people.

Classification of Cases

AGE RANGE   Of our presenile subjects 68 were in their seventies; 62 in their eighties; 10 in their nineties.

SEX   Of the presenile subjects, 41 were men; 99 were women.

EDUCATION   Fifty-eight of these subjects had a high school education or more. The larger number—82—did not graduate from high school.

INSTITUTION VS. PRIVATE HOME   The majority of this group, 96 subjects, came from institutions; 44 were still living in their own homes.

Examples

Seven sample presenile protocols are given. The first two, of Mr. J. S. and Mrs. W., show subjects who may be considered just barely presenile but whose records strongly resemble in many ways those of the normal older subject.

The next two cases, Mrs. A. and Mrs. R., may be considered as mid-range preseniles.

The next three cases, Miss H. B., Mrs. C. B., and Mr. W. L., are examples of quite markedly constricted responses which approach the senile type of record.

Sample Record of Mr. J. S., Age 75 Yrs.: Beginning Presenility

W	FM	A	P	I. Isn't that a bat? *(Inquiry:* Whole. *Idea?* Way a bat will rest in this manner—they fly at night and they rest in this manner, with extended wings.)
W	F±	map		Looks like a map of something. *(Inquiry:* Whole. *Idea?* Some geography somewhere, presents a country with peninsulas.)
W	F+	A	P	II. Well, two bears. *(Inquiry:* Sees black as whole bear. *Idea:* Bears look something on this order.)

∨ Course I don't know what this part would mean (center hands) or this here (top red.) < If you had it this way—maybe there is something, but I wouldn't—

Dd   F+   Ad

III. First place you gotta be a student of many things to know these things. I've never seen these things before. > What could that be? ∧ These heads. It's probably some animal I'm not familiar with.
(*Inquiry:* Sees neck of usual men as an animal neck, but will not interpret the heads. "There is a neck but no head.")

D   F+   Hd

∨ Well, then you turn it around this way, there's faces of a colored race.
(*Inquiry:* Usual lower center heads. *Idea?* Heads, skull of colored people—no American Negro, some other country.)

W   F(C)   A

IV. ∨ < ∨ (Long regard.) That's rather strange to me. I never saw in animal life— unless there is some sea animal—a good many you don't see—they're in the bottom —they might be sea animals. These things here (usual boots) don't have any connection with it except it might be growing at the bottom of the sea—this might be something we're not familiar with.
(*Inquiry:* Lower center head is sea animal. *Idea?* It looks like it might be deep down in the sea. He now includes the rest of the blot as a sea plant which might also be in the sea.)

W   F+   (A)   P

V. ∨ ∧ Well, I had one (he is referring to Card I)—this looks more like a bat than anything else, but it's spread out—it's something disguised. This looks more like a bat than the others—it's got legs and a face.
(*Inquiry:* Whole. *Idea?* It doesn't look like a bat, it just reminds me of a bat.)

D   F±   (A)   P   VI. V Λ Had I known these were your
questions, I would have gone to the library.
You caught me unawares. This reminds me
of a kind of humming bird—this head would
be similar, but it would be disguised—or
an insect built like this on the side.
(*Inquiry:* Top D only reminds him of a bird
or insect. *Idea?* The antenna.)

D   F+   Hd   P   VII. V Λ (Long regard.) Something—a
face with eyes and all this here built up, but
I don't know anything living that has a head
of this sort—it would be a primitive female
with those heads.
(*Inquiry:* Top tier. *Idea?* Some primitive
female because of the top knot. I don't know
any animals like that.)

D   F(C)   arch.   V This looks like a building somewhere—
in the distance, on the other side in the
clouds.
(*Inquiry:* Third tier as clouds with building
the small light detail at the bottom center.)

D   F±   map   Or the Panama Canal connecting two oceans.
(*Inquiry:* Midline of third tier is canal, sides
of tier are two oceans. *Idea?* The connection
there, very small.)

D   F+   A   P   VIII. Well, there are two animals—let's see
what sort of animals would they be. They
might be beavers. And let's see what they
would be doing. The faces look like beavers.
Beavers are usually around the water, but
there isn't any water here.
(*Inquiry:* Usual animals.)

S   FC'   flower   This may be some sort of flower, with a long
stem blossoming.
(*Inquiry:* Center space detail is flower with
stem in midline through pink and orange.
Idea? I've seen flowers with white blossoms
like that, and this is the stem.)

       Repetition — This looks like beavers. Now what this bottom would be. This looks like beavers, but they don't belong in any spot like that—they belong on the brink of a pond. I don't know just what they're doing though—maybe they're not beavers.

W   CF   nat. — IX. > (Long regard.) Some kind—going in an airplane above the clouds you see all scenery in the colored clouds—might be clouds—you see all colors, dark, bright colors. (He repeats his words constantly.) You go up in an airplane, etc.—various forms though no particular shape to it. (*Inquiry:* Whole. *Idea?* Color of the clouds.)

D   F+   A — X. ∨ ∧ These look like lobsters, just on the side.
(*Inquiry:* Side blue. *Idea?* All of these are not perfect, just indicative of something, but it has head and legs like a lobster.)

W   F±   A — All kinds of insects.
(*Inquiry:* Whole. *Idea?* All these shapes look like insects.)

       Repetition — These look like lobsters on the side. (Repetition of first response.)

D   F+   A — Here's something—well, crabs, lobsters.
(*Inquiry:* Top gray animals. *Idea?* Crabs are shaped like that.)

D   F(C)   nat. — This might be the brink of the ocean where the waves beat, but I can't understand the connecting blue pieces.
(*Inquiry:* Pink. *Idea?* Where the water creates this appearance, lighter at the edge and darker as it approaches the beach, but the blue I don't understand.)

D   F+   Ad — This is the head of a rabbit.
(*Inquiry:* Usual lower green.)

D	FM	A	P	But those things are caterpillars on the side. I guess I don't know what that has to do with the head of the rabbit.

(*Inquiry:* Usual lower green. *Idea?* Caterpillars will climb and twist like that.)

Best: It's like buying antique furniture—it's all broken—like modernistic painting. These are not bad, VIII, IX, X.

Least: III. I don't understand this.

R=20   Time: 13 minutes

7W =35% W

11D=55% D

1Dd
   =10% Dd
1S

7W : 0M

Succession: Loose

13F=65% F

9F+, 4F±=84% F+

3F(C)

1FC, 1CF

2FM

Reactivity: 0M : 1½ΣC

8A, 2Ad, 2(A)=60% A

                  2Hd=10% H

2 map

1 arch.

2 nat.

1 flower

7P

Shock: ? Red, ? Clob

COMMENT In this record, which shows a relatively intact psyche, we nevertheless see some of the beginning signs of aging—more in the qualitative signs concomitant with the interpretations than in the actual scores themselves. The area perception, the F+%, the shading, the color, the FM, the H%, and the number of categories all indicate the adequacy of the intellectual and emotional productivity of this subject. The increased F%, the high A%, the absence of M do point to areas where aging begins to appear.

But it is in qualitative signs that we feel that this subject begins to show most clearly the signs of age. His questioning of the Examiner, his apology for the inadequacy he feels, the many evidences of insecurity as he debates his response, and his repetitiousness, are among the most obvious of these characteristics.

This subject is undoubtedly functioning very adequately even though there is a diminution in his reactivity. In such a study as this we recognize the need of longitudinal research in order that we may compare a subject's performance to his own earlier performance, to determine when differences begin to appear in each individual.

Sample Record of Mrs. W., Age 77 Yrs.: Beginning Presenility

Dd	F+	obj.	I. Oh gosh, I wouldn't know what that was. Top across there is like a monument.

(*Inquiry:* Small top center projections. *Why?* Looks like it.)

D	F+	H		Two men. (*Inquiry:* Center detail. Sees two figures together.)
W	FM	A	P	II. Two dogs. I don't know what they're looking at. Holding onto something. Little feet. One was blowing bubbles. (*Inquiry:* Black are dogs, top red are bubbles.)
W	F+	A		III. Well, that I think is apes. Long, long neck. Very peculiar feet. (*Inquiry:* Usual men.)
D	F±	A		Little things look like squirrels. Maybe I'm wrong. (She laughs continuously.) (*Inquiry:* Side red. *Reminded you?* They look like squirrels.)
D	F(C)	A		IV. Some more dogs, face and eyes and tail. (*Inquiry:* Shading detail at each side of top center.)
W	F+	A	P	I don't know what—big animal. (*Inquiry:* Whole. *Reminded you?* She points to feet, arms, and head.)
W	F±	A		V. Almost looks like two deer, meeting in the middle. Maybe not right, but what I see. (*Inquiry:* Whole. She sees them facing each other, heads at top center.)
D	F−	A		VI. What is this all for? Mine always seem to be a lot of animals. That looks like two animals. Don't know what kind. Almost like sheep. I don't know what the top is. I want to be careful about not taking up too much time. One woman at lunch said she took one hour and a half of the doctor's time. That is awful. We're Scotch and don't want to waste time. (*Inquiry:* Lower D. She sees the projections as feet, but is unable to specify the rest of the animal precisely.)

W	F(C)	nat.		VII. That would look to me almost like clouds in the sky. (*Inquiry:* Whole. *Reminded you?* Looks like clouds you see in the sky sometimes.)
W	↗FC FM	A	P	VIII. Ho-ho-ho-ho! This looks like squirrels, two of them, trying to climb up a tree. Very beautiful tree. Can't tell you what they're standing on, but that's what it looks like to me. (*Inquiry:* Usual animals, center is tree.)
W	F(C)	nat.		IX. More? Could be clouds again. (*Inquiry:* Whole. It is the shading and not the color which reminds her of clouds.)
S	F+	Ad		But it could be a big animal too. (*Inquiry:* She does not see the animal, she only sees the slits in the center as the eyes of an animal.)
D	F+	obj.		Statue in the middle. (*Inquiry:* Blue center of large white detail. *Idea?* Just an outline of something.)
D	FM	A		Could be butterflies fighting each other. (*Inquiry:* Orange.)
W	CF	flowers		X. Hard ones till last. Beautiful flowers! Beautiful flowers! All of it could be beautiful flowers. (*Inquiry:* Whole. *Idea?* The colors and the way it looks.)
D	F+	obj.	(P)	Flower glass with ornaments—two squirrels holding it up. (*Inquiry:* Top gray. The squirrels are part of the ornament.)
D	F+	obj.	(P)	Little vase upside down. Held with two hands. Those are little snakes holding it. (*Inquiry:* Lower green. She sees it upside down without turning the card. Again the snakes are part of the ornament.)

D	FM	A	Little animals jumping.

(*Inquiry:* Side brown. She does not specify the animal.)

Best: X.

Least: VI.

R=19

8W=42%W	11F=58%F	10A, 1Ad=58%A
9D=47%D	8F+, 2F±, 1F−=81%F+	1H=5%H
	3F(C)	
$\frac{1Dd}{1S}$=11%Dd	1CF	4 obj.
		2 nat.
8W : 0M	4FM	1 flower
Succession: Loose	1→FC	3P + 2→P
	Reactivity: 0M : 1ΣC	

COMMENT In this protocol, as in that which just precedes, the scores themselves indicate only a few areas where signs of age appear. High F%, FM, and no M response, high A% and low H% are the most evident points of change. However, the subject sees the card upside down without turning it, a characteristic usually found in children of 3½−4 years of age. She uses qualifying words such as "Could be," "Might be," or "Looks to me like." There are initial exclamations as "Oh gosh." She says, "I wouldn't know what that was," and then gives an adequate interpretation. She gives an animal response for the usual popular response at III, and she feels that there is a "right" answer to the cards. There is questioning about the test, a good deal of laughter, and a tendency to repetition of expressions. Thus, even though much of the scoring is not grossly deviant, the questionable scoring signs we have indicated, plus the qualitative characteristics, which we have described, would give clear indication of aging in this subject—even though deterioration is by no means marked.

Sample Record of Mrs. A., Age 82 Yrs.: Midrange Presenility

D	FM	A	I. (Long talk in advance before she could get into the cards.) Well, I could give you a dozen things. One, two, four birds. I don't know—birds or bats. I'll say birds. Very uncomfortable position, but they're going to try and make it and fly away. I talk too much?

				(*Inquiry:* Birds are top corners outside and the two center hands. Hands are "smaller birds—they can't fly so well. They may wait awhile till they're a little older.")
W	F+	design		Else? You can see many things, but—it might be used for a < ∧ decoration on the wall of a—let me see—we wouldn't want it—well, suppose you put it on a wall of a doctor's office. (She tells about her daughter being a doctor.) They're always in a hurry you know, those doctors, and they can hardly stop to eat. (*Inquiry:* Whole. *Idea?* Like a design.) I don't think I see anything else really.
W	M	(H)	P,O	II. (Smiles.) Oh, this is a Mother Goose story, I think. No—well, let's see. Couldn't be Jack and Jill. Well, really isn't any hill for them, no! Line but I can't quote it. (Whistles and shakes her head. Hands card back to Ex.) (*Inquiry:* She agrees reluctantly to Jack and Jill as the two figures.)
W	M	H	P	III. Well, this is really worse! Oh yes! They're scrapping for the red tie. I should have studied Mother Goose, I think. They're
D	FC	obj.	P	broken. No, not broken hearts! Broken limbs here. ∨ Mmm! (*Inquiry:* Usual figures. She is conscious of the separation of the legs from the body.)
W	F(C)	A	P	IV. Well! This is a great big fellow in the Zoo. He nearly got out one day. His feet are much too large. His head is about the right size but pedal extremities too big. Heavy fur! They use that fur to make—well, it wouldn't be a mink coat, but some fur coat. And I think he's really too warm for this weather. Doesn't look like a Mother Moses' painting. (Arm's length.) ∨ No. (*Inquiry:* Whole.)

W	FM	A	P	V. ∨ ᵥ Well, I don't know. (Arm's length.) It's the head of an animal, but he only has two legs. Well, its legs, forelegs have grown into wings and he's flying to the sky. < ∨ Here is a big—no, that's just the same. ∧ This is about the least of a picture to me. (*Inquiry:* Whole. Two legs are bottom center, then forelegs become wings and whole animal becomes a bird.)

W   ↗F(C)
     FM   A   O

VI. Mmmm! Something is broken open here. (Whistles.) I think it's—what did we call those green bugs—(thinks for a long time) praying mantis, being hatched. I think he's coming out but he's too thick. Anyway, some insect is being hatched out here— maybe Japanese beetle. (Tells about how they attack her roses.)
(*Inquiry:* Sees top D as insect emerging from an egg or chrysalis which is lower D.)

∨ What is this woolly thing? They look so warm. Let me see, he's got a head here and whiskers. No! Oh, I haven't the faintest idea. (She rejects this response before it is specific.)

D   FM   A   O

VII. Oh! Mmm! Some more Mother Goose. Let me see! I think these are flamingos, two, necks are long.
(*Inquiry:* Top tier with hair as neck and bill the tiny point at top. Birds are facing out from center. *Idea?* They have such long necks.)

D   F(C)   Ad

Eyes or face.
(*Inquiry:* Sees face looking out from center and down on tier 2. *Kind?* Animal face.)

D   ↗FM
     F(C)   A

Same hatching we had before, but bugs are already out.
(*Inquiry:* Tier 3 with midline as chrysalis and bugs on each side.)

	Elaboration			Birds when they take a drink, raise their heads and are thankful. Give thanks to Heaven for water. (This is evidently a comment about first response.)
W	↗F(C) M	H		V Ballet dancer with clouds above them— arms swung out here. (*Inquiry:* Whole with tier 3 as clouds.)
W	FM	A	P	VIII. You're going to be tired out! Here's some animals, four legged. Bear. But a bear shouldn't be that color and he shouldn't be crawling on leaves. But two bears very distinctly. Really a puzzler, but two distinct bears here. Branch of tree, but bears don't climb around like that, but whatever animal can it be? I hope you're not writing all I say. No, you couldn't. Fell to earth I know not where! Pretty, but I don't get anything
D	CF	plant		out of it. Leaves are not leaves. The bears are crawling nowhere. I suppose some people get this right off! Too much for me. I think all of them are. On the back it tells you what it is. (She says this as she looks on the back of the card.) (Now tells story about her eyes and Bates method of training them.) Take your time. (*Inquiry:* Usual animals. *Tree?* Because it is green and this looks like leaves.)
D	F±	A		IX. Well, if I look at this—some pigs— no—too pretty to joke about! (*Inquiry:* Pigs are top orange. *Idea?* Well, it looks something like pigs, but not too much. She does not reject this response, but she is not satisfied with it.)
D	C	food		That looks like watermelon, but no, it couldn't be—well, just the inside, just the color. (*Inquiry:* Pink.)

W	↗FM CF	A	O	What did anybody say that is? Well! ∨ Let's try it this side. Better this side. Let's see. Well, this is birds singing in shade of tree—well, not tree, shrubs. Over them the boys have put up some balloons. They reflect their color on the birds. The birds are really white, but reflected color. Couldn't say, "under the spreading chestnut tree"—no village smith there. That's really pretty and the green and pink, but I really couldn't make any sense out of it. Same pictures to each person? (*Inquiry:* Birds are orange, balloons are green and pink.)
D	F+	A	P	X. ∨ (Shrugs.) So many things. Two mice, what are they doing? (*Inquiry:* Top gray. *Idea?* They look a little like mice.)
D	F±	A		I think these are lobsters but not the right color. (*Inquiry:* Side blue. *Idea?* Shape.) This (pink) I don't know. (Shakes head.) Well, I think I could make a better picture than that myself. And I'm no artist. Looks more as if it—(doesn't finish sentence.)
D	F±	anat.		Throat. (*Inquiry:* Top gray center. *Idea?* "Like the throat here" as she points to her own throat.)
D	F±	anat.		Intestines. (*Inquiry:* Lower green. *Idea?* The shape and the way they curve around.)
D	CF	blood		Bloody lines. They didn't take care of that so well. No, I couldn't say. Frame it. Put it on the wall. (Joking.) (*Inquiry:* Pink. *Idea?* The color like a smear of blood.) *Best:* In what way? Color? For color VII. Would frame it. For fun, II. *Least:* None make sense. Where was that silly thing? V.

R=22

9W = 41% W

13D = 59% D

9W : 3M

Succession: Loose

6F = 27% F

2F+, 4F± = 66% F+

3F(C)

1FC, 3CF, 1C

3M, 5FM

2→F(C), 2→FM

Reactivity: 3M : 5ΣC

11A, 1Ad = 54% A

2H, 1(H) = 13% H

2 anat.

1 blood

1 food

1 design

1 obj.

1 plant

7P

4O

COMMENT   This lady has retained a good sense of humor and an awareness of present-day happenings as well as a good deal of originality. There
is also marked emotional reaction and sensitivity to both internal and external
stimuli, though her intellectual perceptions are perhaps a bit dulled as indicated
by the 66% F+. A% is high and the appearance of 2 anatomic and 1 blood
response would indicate the areas of approaching senescence.

Among the outstanding qualitative signs indicative of presenility are the
fact that she thinks the answers are on the back of the card, inquires what other
people have said, makes initial exclamations or prefaces her response with
"Well." She discusses with herself about the response; perseverates on "Mother
Goose," and "Bugs hatching" responses. The quality of the response at V and
VIII which shows the hesitancy and indecision of this subject, is also characteristic of presenility. The concept of things "broken" is also strong with the
older or aging persons, as it is with the children.

Thus, although emotional vigor is active, the intellectual perceptions of
this subject are diminished, and signs of presenility are marked.

Sample Record of Mrs. R., Age 80 Yrs.: Midrange Presenility

W   FM   A

I. A couple of animals that's climbing up
over here. Head, arms, feet. I don't know
what kind of animal. Climbing up over the
thing in the middle, and kinda watching to
see what goes on outside. A very lovely
picture and full of suggestions.
(*Inquiry:* Whole. Animals are either side and
are beginning to crawl toward middle.)

| W | FM | A | P | II. You know the worst of it is they all remind me of animals. Nose of the animals, their eyes, their ears, but the mouth is peculiar, very peculiar. You wouldn't think that they were kinda trying to get something away from each other would you? (*Inquiry:* Black as animals.) |

| W | M | H | P | III. (Intent regard.) Well now, these two fellows are going away on a journey and they're each picking up their bags. They seem to be a little antagonistic to each other, don't they? (Ex. agrees.) I thought so! Maybe that fellow has picked up that fellow's bag. Otherwise they're coming apart, they're parting. (*Inquiry:* Usual figures. She is conscious of break between leg and body.) |

| Dd | F(C) | Hd | | IV. Well, this has a different outlook, though I can see, yes, if I study real long there's a mouth there, a mouth and eyes. I should get something better. Mouth has kind of a—like a man all hunched up, doesn't it? Yet for all that he's only got two feet and a side to each side, but—cranium, eyes—his mouth |
| W | ↗FClob
M | H | P | couldn't be quite as big as that, could it? All I can find in it. Man all hunched up like that. (She demonstrates the position and looks quite threatening as she does so.) (*Inquiry:* Face is shading detail at top center left, and is a separate response, but this leads to the whole response of "man all hunched up.") |

| W | FM | A | P | V. ∨ You gotta take it this way. Oh, that's a bird on the wing. Yes! Yes, all I can find. (*Inquiry:* Whole.) |

| | | Refusal | | VI. ∨ Oh! ∧ ∨ (Returns to Ex., looking quite sober as she does so. Her expression does not brook further encouragement.) |

D	M	Hd	P	VII. Ha! That might be two naughty boys kinda having a scrap, don't you think so? Yes. Yes. Two naughty boys having a scrap. (Seems rather amused and satisfied.) I can't hear it! Nose, mouth and eyes. I don't know what else it could be. (*Inquiry:* Top tier only.)
W	FM	A	P	VIII. Very beautiful! Very beautiful. Now this—two cats here and climbing up a couple of pillars. Yes. I think they're going to take a nap. Cause here's a couple dogs ready to jump on these two, huh? Very plain, huh? (*Inquiry:* Usual animals are cats. Dogs are center pink looking up toward cats.)
		Cn		IX. Oh! V (Intent regard.) Somebody had a very beautiful idea of coloring. That pink is a very beautiful shade and this greenish yellow is beautiful and so is that—what do you call that—that orange. A beautiful conglomeration of colors. (She gives no further response and cannot be encouraged to do so.)
D	↗FC' FM	A	P	X. I gotta find something in this one. Right away I find two little kittens going through this hole, maybe running away. (*Inquiry:* Top gray animals are kittens.)
D	F+	A	P	Do those look like crabs to you? (Ex. agrees.) Yes, they are. (*Inquiry:* Side blue. *Idea?* Just like crabs.)
D	F±	arch.	O	And this is their home. Look like that to you? The coloring is very beautiful. Regular shade of a mouse. (She is referring to her first response which was "kittens," but which she now calls "mouse.") (*Inquiry:* Home of crabs is pink, both sides, including the white space between.)

Best: These three (colored ones) are about on a par. Very beautiful painting. And very suggestive which make it difficult to give it a name.

Least: VII. I don't like those two imps. They're just ready to spit at each other, aren't they?

R=11

Time: 14 minutes

6W=54%

2F=18% F

6A=54% A

4D=36%

1F+, 1F±=75% F+

2H, 2Hd=36% H

1Dd=9%

1 F(C), 1→FClob, 1→FC'

1 arch.

6W : 3M

3M, 5FM

8P

Succession: None

Reactivity: 3M : 0ΣC

2O

Shock: ? Clob

COMMENT Here again we have a midrange presenile protocol. Both age and individuality factors show themselves clearly in this response. Subject expresses considerable aggressivity and shows herself to be (as she actually is) possessed of extreme vigor of personality, suggested by the high M and the very low F%.

However, signs of presenility are more conspicuous here than are individuality indicators. Characteristic of the presenile response are: the narrow content, the lowered F+%, the questioning of the Examiner, the strong belief in the reality of things seen in the cards, color naming, refusal, the men at Card III "coming apart," and the expressed feeling that she "should get something better."

Sample Record of Miss H. B., Age 85 Yrs.: Advanced Presenility

W   F+   A   P   I. Hold it this way or that? Some animal cut in two and spread out. Don't know that I could label the animal. An insect I think. More like a grub. Might be a butterfly or beetle.
(*Inquiry:* Whole. *Idea?* Is still undecided about insect, but thinks it has wings.)

W   F±   A   Lobster at first. I've seen them divided in that way.
(*Inquiry:* Whole. *Idea?* Lobster is split down the middle.)

W	M	(H)	P	II. A couple of clowns playing bean porridge hot, bean porridge cold. (*Inquiry:* Whole, usual figures.)

W	M	H	P	III. How are you? (She addresses the figures in the card. Long delay.) Well, I'll say two boys facing each other around a bowl of something. (*Inquiry:* Usual figures.)

D	FM	A	And these red things flying around here, I don't know what they are. I think they're bugs. (*Inquiry:* Side red.)

D	↗m F(C)	fire	This red may be smoke from the fire, something warm anyway. I don't know why it should be red. They're jolly little fellows. (*Inquiry:* Center red is emerging from center black and gray which she sees as "fire," though she denies any color influence.)

W	F(C)	A	IV. This is a furry friend. Doesn't look like my cat. Too black and doesn't look like her anyway. I think it may be a dog. I don't think so though, not the right kind of tail. Guess he's a squirrel, head, feet, tail, and hind feet. (*Inquiry:* Whole. Head is lower center, feet are usual boots and arms, tail is at top.)

W	F(C)	A	V. I didn't know I was going to be examined like this. Thought you might ask about my teaching experience, etc. (Smiles.) Now who are you? (Again addresses card.) Looks like another furry friend, I know that much. Long ears—they stand up good and straight. Maybe feathers. Could be a chicken. Tail and headgear, legs, chicken legs and feathers. (*Inquiry:* Whole. She responds to the shading, but the identification of parts makes the concept very imprecise.)

D	F+	A	

VI. (Sits back from card, delays.) I suppose this is some animal that's had a chance to see, isn't it? (Ex. doesn't understand, but agrees that it is.) Well, all right! He hasn't much of a tail, has he? (Breathes heavily throughout. Long pause and regard.) Well, when I'm stumped you'd have to put that down, wouldn't you? I'm not stumped yet. Well, I'll not say a pigeon because I know it isn't a pigeon. (Ex. says it could be.) No, it couldn't be. An insect. No, it isn't. Some kind of a bat. No, most like an insect.
(*Inquiry:* Top D. *Idea?* The wings.)

W	F−	A

VII. Ah ah! Now you would think of somebody! I should think he was an insect. I don't think that's so much—four legs. He's a crawler, head and legs. Don't think it's a mosquito though.
(*Inquiry:* Whole. Head is tier 3, legs are projections on tiers 1 and 2. *Idea?* Just looks like four legs.)

D	F+	A	P

VIII. Mmmm! A fancy one! I wish they wouldn't make it red cause it makes me think of a lobster and I don't suppose it is. (Laughs.) These fancy things look like animals, so that you wonder if they were folded together how they would look. I don't know his name.
(*Inquiry:* Usual animals.)

WS	F−	A

IX. This looks like a dragonfly. Head, his wings.
(*Inquiry:* Whole. Center space detail is head, wings are each side. *Idea?* This looks like his head.)

D	F+	A	P

X. They're trying to make me think it's a lobster or crab. That is trying to mislead me, I'm sure. But I'm obliged to say a crab. Rest doesn't look especially like it. (*Rest look like something else?*) Now let's see. (Regards for some time and then just inconclusively hands card back to Ex.)

(*Inquiry:* Side blue as crabs. *Idea?* All these legs.)

Best: II. Looks like something I did know something about.

Least: X. Doesn't look like anything I ever saw except the crablike things.

R=13

$\frac{7W}{1WS}$=62%W

5D=38%D

8W : 2M

7F=53%F

4F+, 1F±, 2F−=64%F+

3 F(C)

2M, 1FM, 1→m

10A=77%A

2H=15%H

1 fire

5P

Succession: None   Reactivity: 2M : 0ΣC

COMMENT Here we begin to see the constriction that becomes more marked as the individual progresses toward senility. It is most noticeable in the increased A% and the narrowing of content. The F% is increasing and the F+% is markedly reduced. The qualitative signs are also strong: increased consciousness of the midline, animals cut in two and spread out, the manner of addressing the card directly, allusion to her own cat, long discussion with herself about a response, the imprecision of her concepts, the belief that there is a trick to the cards or "that is trying to mislead me." These are all signs of presenility veering toward senility and the evidence here begins to appear more clear-cut than in the preceding protocols where fewer signs appear and where the emotional and intellectual reactions are more vigorous and active.

Sample Record of Mrs. C. B., Age 82 Yrs.: Advanced Presenility

———

I. I couldn't tell you. It looks like some image, but I couldn't tell you.

II. All I ask from anyone is confidence and love and I try to do good to them, cause I know I can't stay much longer.

D   F±   obj.

I don't know. The red looks like candle sticks. Is that right? (Ex. commends her.) So I can see good.
(*Inquiry:* Top red. *Idea?* They just look like candlesticks to me.)

D   F±   obj.

III. That's a pipe.
(*Inquiry:* Side red. *Idea?* Here's the stem.)

D	F+	A		Butterfly.

(*Inquiry:* Center red. *Idea?* Like a butterfly.)

I'm much better than when I came. I've been here only six weeks.

W	F+	A	P	IV. That's some kind of an ape.

(*Inquiry:* Whole. *Idea?* Big like an ape.)

W	F±	A		V. I don't know. Some kind of an animal, but I couldn't tell. I admit the doctors help me.

(*Inquiry:* Whole. *Animal?* Still cannot specify.)

W	F+	A		VI. That's a butterfly. I got that right, didn't I? But I've gained since I've been here.

(*Inquiry:* Whole. *Idea?* Just a butterfly.)

D	F+	Ad		VII. You've got beautiful teeth. I've got all the time in the world. That looks like faces. I think they're monkeys.

(*Inquiry:* Top tier. *Idea?* Just the face of a monkey.)

D	F+	A		VIII. Oh, that's pretty, isn't it, but I don't know what it is. Isn't that funny? That looks like butterflies down here, but I'm no good at bright colors.

(*Inquiry:* Pink and orange. *Idea?* Because it had wings up here and small right here.)

D	FM	A	P	I respect everybody and everybody's religion, and I try to do what's right. Is that some animal climbing up there? No, I don't know.

(*Inquiry:* Usual animals.)

	———			IX. I don't know what that is. It looks like an animal of some kind, but I can't distinguish it.

(*Inquiry:* Cannot specify area or animal.)

W	F±	obj.	

X. I don't know what that is, but it's pretty. I don't know. It isn't an animal. That's an ornament. Is that what it is? Does the doctor examine all those? I'm happy to tell you I answered all but one, and I got all but one right.

(*Inquiry:* Whole as ornament. *Idea?* Just all those parts of an ornament.)

Best: II. It's colorful, agreeable and shaking hands. I love the colored ones, but I can't see them. It's been a pleasure to talk to you.

Least: VI. That one, because I couldn't see it.

R=10 (2 not scored)

4W=40%W	9F=90%F	6A, 1Ad=70%A
6D=60%D	5F+, 4F±=78%F+	3 obj.
4W:0M	1FM	2P
Succession: None	Reactivity: 0M : 0ΣC	

Shock: None
      ? Initial

COMMENT Here we have a sharp drop toward senility, as also in the protocol which follows. The scores of this subject begin to resemble those in the senile gradient. As we read the entire protocol, we see the marked difference between this and a so-called normal response, and begin to get the feeling of the change which takes place as an individual approaches senility.

We can even see the difference between this protocol and the first samples in the presenile group which more closely approach the normal. We have noted elsewhere our awareness of the gradations in the presenile group, though only further study will allow us to classify them adequately.

Noteworthy here are the low number of responses (10), the high A% (70%), the high F%, the equation of 0M : 0ΣC, the restricted content. Conspicuous also are the several presenile qualitative signs present even in this rather limited protocol. These include initial refusal of a blot followed by an adequate response; asking Examiner, "Is that right?"; perseverative remarks about own health; inability to specify exact area or to tell what gave her the idea for her response; giving response in the form of a question and then arguing with herself about it.

In spite of all these factors, however, this subject appears to be in reasonably good contact with her environment. Her F+% is 78%, and many of her extraneous remarks are at least reasonable: "I try to do good . . . cause I know I can't stay much longer."

Sample Record of Mr. W. L., Age 85 Yrs.: Advanced Presenility

W	F±	anat. position		I. These two top parts, shoulders and arms outspread; hips and spine. (*Inquiry:* Shoulders and arms are top and wing projections, hips are rounded sides right and left, and spine is center. *Idea?* He just names the parts again. He seems to be listing anatomical parts rather than describing a person. They seem to be given as one response, however.)
W	M	H	P	II. Ho ho! Fella and I go this way tellin' a joke—pease porridge hot. (He demonstrates with hands.) (*Inquiry:* Usual figures.)
W	M	H	P	III. Oh! That's two comedians. (*Inquiry:* Usual figures.)
D	F±	Ad		Don't know what this might be—mule's ear? (*Inquiry:* Side red. *Idea?* Can't say.)
D	F+	plant		Down here limbs. (*Inquiry:* Men's legs. *Idea?* Like the limbs of a tree.)
W	F(C)	obj.		IV. Oh gee! Looks like my old raccoon coat. Two arms there. (*Inquiry:* Whole. *Idea?* Like my fur coat.)
W	F+	A	P	V. Bat! (*Inquiry:* Whole. *Idea?* Just a bat.)
W	F±	anat.		VI. These all for men? Women get the same ones? (He evidently doesn't think that is too appropriate.) Well, that looks like the spine and back and hips and short arms. (*Inquiry:* Spine and back are midline, hips are bottom right and left, arms are side projections. This is again as on Card I where he seems to be listing anatomical parts without necessarily describing a person although it is given as one response.)

VII. (Laughs.) Those butterflies?
(*Inquiry:* This, he says was not a response, but appears to be a joke with him.)

D	F−	anat.	

Lower part of body.
(*Inquiry:* Tier 3. *Idea?* Just here, as he points to abdomen.)

D	F−	anat.	

Upper part shoulders and arms.
(*Inquiry:* Top two tiers. *Idea?* He points to projection on tier 2.)

Got a ? here? I could tell you about a ?.
(Ex. cannot understand even after questioning what it is he is talking about.)

D	F+	A	P

VIII. Mice.
(*Inquiry:* Usual animals.)

W	F−	anat. position

They get that body in there all the time. Hips, lungs, head, hair. Like me—born with no hair.
(*Inquiry:* Hips are pink and orange, lungs are center blue, head is top gray. *Idea?* He names them again.)

D	F+	anat.

IX. Whew! Oh gee, you leave the hard ones till last. This one would suit a man more than a woman, wouldn't it? Man's spine and testicles opened out. I guess that's about all.
(*Inquiry:* Pink. *Idea?* This pink here. Further questioning seems to indicate that no color is involved in interpretation.)

D	F−	anat.

X. Rear view is it? (Long regard.) Buttocks?
(*Inquiry:* Pink. *Idea?* Can't specify.)

D	F±	anat.

Little things that make all the trouble.
(*Inquiry:* Side brown. *What?* He cannot name the part. *Idea?* Just the way they look.)

Best: Mostly all relating to surgery. III good but IX best physical one.

Least: II.

R=15   Time: 7 minutes

7W=47%W   12F=80%F   2A, 1Ad=20%A
                        4F+, 4F±, 4F−=50%F+   2H=16%H
                                                          8 anat.

                                                          1 plant

8D=53%D   1F(C)   1 obj.

7W : 2M   2M   4P

Succession: Loose   Reactivity: 2M : 0ΣC

COMMENT   Here, though we classify the subject as presenile, we again see scores which approach those of senile subjects.

In individuals at the bottom of the presenile, and in the senile classifications, either animal or anatomy responses tend to predominate. This subject gives 53% anatomy responses. These, with the 80% F, indicate an extremely restricted approach. F+% is low—only 50%.

These factors as well as the quality of the entire protocol suggest the intellectual and emotional impoverishment which occurs as presenility verges toward senility.

However, the two movement responses, the shading response, and the H% of 16%, all suggest that this record belongs in the presenile rather than in the senile category. Especially noteworthy is this subject's certainty that the anatomical (sex) responses are what he sees them to be—definitely pictures of male parts, not suitable for women subjects.

CHAPTER EIGHT

Senile Responses

R = 13	92%F	4A or 40%A
46%W	50%F+	.5H or 5%H
45%D	.2M, .3FM, 0m	8.4 anat or 47% anat
8%Dd	0FC, .2CF, .1C, .4F(C)	.4 object
	.2M : .2ΣC	

Description of Rorschach Response

The response of the senile individual is, above all, characterized by the predominance of animal responses, anatomy responses, or both. The statistical averages of 40% animal and 47% anatomy which we have found in senile subjects do not present a true picture of the individual response. Though a few give a fairly equal number of these two types of content, in the majority either animal or anatomy predominates and sometimes reaches 100%.

We have, therefore, divided our senile subjects into two main groups: those in which animal responses markedly predominate (mean of 69%A), and those in which anatomy markedly predominates (mean of 83% anat.). Table 11 indicates how extremely different these two groups of subjects are in every respect.

The subjects who give predominantly animal responses give only a few (mean of 8.7) responses, nearly 50% of which are whole responses. Accuracy of form is considerably higher in this group than in the other, even though far below normal limits (71%F+). A large proportion of their responses are simple populars: P% = 41%.

Subjects who give chiefly anatomy responses give many more responses (mean 17.8), have a slightly lower percentage of whole responses, and a much lower F+% (32%F+). Very few of their responses are populars: P% = 9%.

TABLE 11. SENILE GROUP: DIFFERENCES BETWEEN CASES
EMPHASIZING ANIMAL RESPONSES AND THOSE EMPHASIZING
ANATOMY RESPONSES

Mean scores for cases where A% > Anat% and for those where Anat% > A%

Score	Animal A% > Anat% 3 female, 6 male	Anatomy Anat% > A% 7 female, 3 male
R	8.7	17.8
W%	49%	43%
D%	42%	47%
Dd%	8%	10%
F%	90%	93%
F+%	71%	32%
M	.1	.3
FM	.3	.3
F(C)	.1	.6
ΣC	.3	.2
A%	69%	13%
H%	7%	3%
Anat%	7%	83%
P%	41%	9%

This predominance of animal or anatomy responses is probably much more of an individuality than an age factor. The marked discrepancy in all determinants in these two groups suggests how much any group average hides when we are dealing with such a test as the Rorschach.

However, the figures given at the beginning of this chapter, and elsewhere throughout this book, in referring to senile subjects refer to the group as a whole—not making this distinction between the "animal" and "anatomy" groups.

Considering the group as a whole, we have tentatively identified a rather clear-cut gradient of performance, from what appear to us to be the most intact to the most deteriorated individuals.

In the best-preserved subjects, animal responses predominate and there are few if any anatomy responses.

Slightly less intact individuals give a combination of animal and anatomy.

The most deteriorated, however, give exclusively or almost exclusively, anatomy responses. And even here there are gradations. The most intact within this group give a good variety of parts of the body, and the form is fairly good. Subjects who are holding up less well do not have a good variety of anatomy responses and tend to perseverate on just one or two body parts, as "skeleton," "spine," or "heart."

Even more deteriorated subjects give almost exclusively sex parts. It is rather astonishing sometimes to hear a benign-looking white-haired old lady giving such responses as: "Women's parts," "Man's back passage," or "The vagina. A wonderful organ for the female body."

Next come those who see the blots as pictures of themselves: "My thighs," or "My ——."

Last and most deteriorated, within this group of presumably non-psychotic seniles, are those who name either the organs of excretion or excretory products.

The senile group can be distinguished from other subjects also by the extremely poor form of its responses (only 50%F+). In no other group is the form equally poor, though the 2- and 2½-year-old approaches this low point, with an F+% of 54%. Our normal old people give an F+% of 93%, and even the presenile group holds up to an F+% of 81%.

The high number of responses determined by form alone is also one of the indications of senility. In our senile subjects, an average of 92% of responses are so determined. This contrasts sharply with the mean F% of 50% in our normal group of old people, and of 64% in the preseniles. Only the 2-year-old child gives so restricted a response.

With so high an F%, the *Erlebnistype* is necessarily extremely restricted, the average being .2M:.2ΣC. This means actually that a good many senile subjects have a basic equation of 0M:0ΣC.

Movement responses other than human are, on the average: .3FM, 0m. The distribution of the few color responses given is on the average as follows: 0FC, .2CF, .1C. (Only 16 per cent of subjects give human movement, only 21 per cent, animal movement. No senile subjects give FC responses, only 16 per cent CF, and only 5 per cent give C.)

Thus actually neither movement nor color response predominates in this group which is ambi-equal as well as coarctated. The distribution of color responses suggests that the senile individual has very limited powers of adaptability, and though the amount of emotionality which he expresses is slight, such as it is it is primarily egocentric.

There are no Clob responses, and shading responses average only .4, only 21 per cent of subjects giving such responses.

The mean number of responses is only 13, a definite drop from the mean of 26 in the normals and 16 in the preseniles. This low output is equalled only at 3 years and under, in children.

Other than animal and anatomy responses, the only type of content which occurs conspicuously in the senile group is human responses which occur to the extent of 5%. Animal, anatomy, and human responses together reach a mean of 92%, and few other content categories appear. Eighty-nine per cent of subjects give at least one animal response, 63 per cent give anatomy, and 42 per cent, human.

The only respect in which the senile group cannot be quite clearly distinguished from our other two classifications for old people is with respect to the area of the blot chosen. As in the first ten years of life, there are once again more global than detail responses, but only to the extent of 46%W, 45%D. The D response is just about the same as that found in the normal and presenile subjects, whereas the W has increased at the expense of Dd, which was 15% in the normals, 9% in the preseniles, and is 8% in the seniles. Twenty-six per cent of the seniles give the oligophrenic Do response —the most of any group.

Thus the picture of the emotional and intellectual capacities of the senile subject appears to be distinctively different from that of either normal or presenile older people, and more restricted in most respects than even that of the 2-year-old child which it in some ways resembles.

So much for the actual Rorschach scores. More is revealed by the so-called "qualitative" items described in our A- and B-lists which appear in Tables 6, 7, and 8. Though these items have proved most useful in identifying presenile subjects, several of them as listed below also characterize the senile individual.

A-list signs, present also in childhood

1. Items which occur most in senility:
   47 per cent of senile subjects perseverate on one or more concept.
   36 per cent look on the back of the card.
   42 per cent refuse at least one blot.
   5 per cent comment that they could identify the blot if it were only a picture of something else: "I'd like one of a cow with a good bag on it or something like that. Then I could tell."
2. Items which characterize senility though they occur most in presenility:
   47 per cent of senile subjects believe that there is a right and wrong "answer" and that their own response is right or wrong.
   42 per cent interrupt their response to give long stories of their own life experiences.

36 per cent reply at once that they don't know or can't tell, and then proceed to give an adequate answer.

B-list signs which characterize presenility and senility but which are not present to any extent in the records of children or normal adults

1. Items which occur most in senile subjects:
   63 per cent give anatomy responses; 78 per cent have a ΣC of 0.
   63 per cent emphasize the midline. 52 per cent give F− responses on the customary popular responses.
   36 per cent comment that they are "stuck" or "stumped."
   58 per cent give general expressions of insecurity or uncertainty.
   53 per cent protect themselves with the initial delaying comment, "Well."
   10 per cent give lavish compliments to the blots or to the person who made them.
2. Items which occur most in presenility but which are conspicuous in the seniles:
   31 per cent worry that their brains aren't good. 15 per cent laugh excessively.
   52 per cent make perseverative comments, as commenting on all cards that "They all have this funny line up the middle." Or may just repeat words and phrases as, "Bees, bees, bees," or "Very beautiful, very beautiful."
   20 per cent worriedly comment that this test is "hard" or that it "gets worse and worse."
3. Characteristic presenile behaviors which largely drop out:
   Little interest in interpersonal relations—few subjects project either quarreling or "having a high old time."
   Few physical excuses for poor performance.
   Few abstract and idealistic responses.
   Little comment that they "can't think of the words." Little groping for concepts. Senile subjects appear to be more definite within the narrow range in which they operate.

Psyche of the Senile

The picture of the senile psyche which is thus revealed is one of marked restriction and intellectual underproductivity and impoverishment.

The R of only 13 is lower than at any other age after 3 years in the entire life span. Combined with the high F% of 92% and the high number of refusals it indicates an extremely restricted outlook. And the concepts that are produced are inaccurate as often as not, as shown by the F+% of only 50 and the large number of F− responses given even to those parts of the blot so obvious as commonly to attract so-called popular responses.

There is virtually no inner creativity (.2M). The fact that FM predominates over M as in childhood suggests feelings of dependency, and also suggests that the individual may be prone to project his own demands and difficulties onto the environment.

In spite of the many comments which express uncertainty and self-doubt, however, absence of real feelings of frustration or of suppressed aggressivity is suggested by the absence of m responses.

Responsiveness in the extratensive sphere is as limited as that in the introversive. A ΣC of .2 indicates virtually no responsiveness to environmental stimuli. Such few color responses as do appear suggest little adaptability and relatively strong egocentricity, as in the young child. In fact the response of the very old person is in many respects strikingly reminiscent of that of the very young child. High egocentricity is also expressed in the fact that some subjects actually ask if the blots are supposed to be pictures of themselves. "Why I don't know if it's a picture they took of me?" or "That's where I have the trouble." Or, one woman, when asked which card she liked best replied: "You mean which card would suit me the best being as I'm not very well? Well, I have a bad shoulder and a bad throat. Let me see where's the shoulder and the throat. (Shows Card VIII.) I think that this is best. Here's the shoulder where I hurt and here's my throat. That has everything I got."

Restriction of intellectual outlook is clearly indicated not only by the high F% but by the extremely limited content. Many senile subjects limit all responses to one or two content categories—mostly animal and anatomy. Subjects who confine themselves largely to animal responses reveal themselves as extremely stereotyped and conforming. Those who give chiefly anatomy responses indicate not only stereotypy but an overconcern with themselves and their own bodily functions.

Overconcern with self is combined with a marked lack of interest in other people. H% is only 5% and there is a marked decrease in responses portraying interaction between people. No senile subjects show interest in the responses of other individuals or ask what others have said, as do subjects in other groups. An average shading response of only .4 suggests only a remnant of sensitivity to others.

In the perceptual area, the high global response suggests that senile subjects do not differentiate details, and especially ignore tiny details. There is a lack of practicality, a lack of refinement of judgment, and a lack of analytical approach.

There are several indications that senile subjects lack the ability to modulate, to see things in perspective, or to question their own behavior.

The number who give qualified responses has dropped from an average of 56 per cent in the presenile group to 5 per cent in the seniles. This finding is supported by the fact that 15 per cent of the seniles confirm their responses with "Definitely a ————," or "A perfect ————," and 26 per cent assure the Examiner, "Of course that is a ————," or comment, "Yes, I thought so," on being assured that they have given a good response.

Senile subjects appear to operate within a narrower sphere than do subjects in other groups, but to be more definite within this sphere.

However, the inconsistency of senile subjects is shown by the fact that along with a marked confidence in their own responses and lack of self-criticism, we find extreme expressions of insecurity and self-doubt. Fifty-eight per cent of subjects express some degree of self-doubt, insecurity, or worry about their intellectual ability and the correctness or adequacy of their answers.

Childishness, repetitiousness and a paucity of intellectual productivity is suggested by the large amount of perseveration, both of concepts and of remarks.

The traditional garrulity of the old person is expressed in the fact that though actual responses to the blots are usually brief, 42 per cent of the senile subjects interrupt their test response to tell long stories about themselves and their experiences.

And finally, in the most deteriorated members of our senile group, we come to those whose interests are centered not only on themselves and their own bodies—as shown by a predominance of anatomical responses—but have narrowed down to a concern with sex parts and excretion.

Thus we seem to see in the response to the Rorschach a picture of the senile subject as extremely restricted, unproductive, stereotyped, intellectually and emotionally impoverished, uncritical but insecure. Little interested in those about him, his interest gradually narrows down to complete concern with self and bodily parts and functions, particularly a concern with the eliminative functions. The divinely human spark reflected in the response of even quite young children is indeed burning low.

Behavior of Senile Subjects as Observed during the Rorschach Situation

Senile subjects were for the most part friendly and cooperative, though not always too coherent in what they themselves said or in their understanding of what the Examiner said. Many showed great good will and willingness to cooperate, and even gratitude for the Examiner's "visit," but were uneven in their clarity. There was in fact variation from subject to subject, and in one subject from one part of the examination to another. Institution authorities commented that some of the subjects we classed as senile were sociable, friendly, and jolly but not too clear or reliable intellectually. Several were more lucid in spontaneous conversation than in answering questions.

In general, the cooperation of senile subjects was better than that of the preseniles, due at least in part to the fact that senile subjects were less suspicious of the Examiner and her purposes and intentions, and accepted the situation more readily and more passively.

Several showed an almost "fixed idea" as to Examiner's occupation and intent, or as to the purpose of the test. It was difficult to break into or change this idea. Thus one subject commented, on being shown the first blot, "No thank you, dear, I've bought all my Christmas cards. And I don't think these are very pretty anyway." And this notion could not be overcome enough for us to proceed with the test.

Others were extremely garrulous and repetitive in their spontaneous conversation. They told long stories about their youth, or discussed their health in great detail. It was often most difficult to break into their verbalization to get the test started, and later to proceed with the test, which they interrupted frequently.

There was a great tendency in their flow of speech to enumerate small details rather than to make any generalized statement. Many thus enumerated all the doctors they had ever had; every position they had ever held (with dates); or gave the details of old romances, or of illnesses their mothers or fathers had suffered. Such stories or recitals were extremely detailed but often a little confused as to detail. Dates appeared to be inaccurate, or brothers and husbands were confused. (This detailed verbalization about the past occurred even more, and in greater detail, in the presenile subjects than in the senile.)

Not only was it difficult to break into spontaneous stories of the senile subjects, but it also seemed more effective not to cross or contradict them.

There was much concern with and discussion of the subjects' physical health and also general discussion of disease. Respect was expressed for how wonderfully the human body is made.

Senile subjects appeared to be much more introversive than extratensive; much more influenced by their own inner promptings than by what was being said to them.

There was great readiness to tears, especially as subjects remembered past friends and relatives. But this emotional lability, as in children, did not seem to represent deep emotion, and was readily overcome. A few seemed to be a little silly, but most were not. In fact several senile subjects appeared in general conversation much more alert and in touch with the world than the Rorschach record would indicate. However, there was much less self-criticism than in the presenile group.

As with children, subjects expressed considerable need for rapport with the Examiner. Often it was difficult to maintain rapport with the subject and at the same time to record his responses. Also as with children, it seemed most effective to go through the cards fairly rapidly, and not to delay for too much inquiry. (Otherwise they got off the track of responding to the Rorschach and back onto the track of telling about their own experiences.) A further way in which the senile subject resembled the child was that inquiry did not as a rule clear up anything. Subjects either forgot, and denied that they had made the response, made new, entirely different responses, or agreed to anything that the Examiner suggested as to location.

Classification of Senile Cases

AGE RANGE   Of our 19 senile cases, 7 were in their seventies, 12 in their eighties, none in their nineties. The average age of these subjects is 80.

SEX   Our cases are evenly divided as to sex, there being 9 men and 10 women.

EDUCATION   The majority of these subjects (14) have less than high school education. Only 5 have a high school education or more.

INSTITUTION VS. PRIVATE HOME   The majority of the group not only belong to the lower educational level but also were among the institution population. Only 3 of the senile group were in their own homes. The remaining 16 were institution cases.

Examples

Rather than quoting extensively from the subjects' records, we have chosen to present six of the nineteen records obtained from our senile subjects, in full. The reader can thus see for himself the exact nature of these responses.

The six records given illustrate, in order, the descending steps of our hypothesized senile gradient, proceeding from what appear to be the "best" of the senile records to the most deteriorated.

Thus the first record, that of Mrs. I. P., aged 85, is an example of the predominantly animal response. Next comes Mr. P., aged 85, who gives a combination of animal and anatomy concepts.

Then come the almost purely anatomy responses as follows: Mrs. K., aged 76, good variety of anatomy responses. Then Mr. R., aged 76, perseveration on one anatomy concept. Mrs. McN., aged 88, who confines herself to "spine," "womb" and "rectum." And lastly Mrs. S. B., aged 82, who combines anatomy with excretion responses.

Sample Record of Mrs. I. P., Age 85 Yrs.: Senile Group
(1) Animals

W	F+	A	P	I. (Looks on back.) Looks like an eagle, don't it? Eagle belongs to the U.S. (*Inquiry:* Whole. *Reminded you?* Wings.)
W	F+	A		II. Those are elephants. They're very friendly, too. (*Inquiry:* Black. She does not indicate any movement, finds it difficult to point out any part except the "trunk.")
W	F−	A		III. What are they? Are they donkeys? (*Inquiry:* Usual men as donkeys. Is unable to specify any part except head.)
W	F+	A	P	IV. A monkey. I'm not up on these things. (*Inquiry:* Whole. *Reminded you?* Points out arms and legs and indicates head at top.)
W	F+	A	P	V. ∨ That's a bat, isn't it? New for me. New lessons. (*Inquiry:* Whole. *Reminded you?* The wings.)
W	F±	A		VI. ∨ You've got me there. What is it? I should think a bat. (*Inquiry:* Whole. *Reminded you?* I don't know.)
D	F±	Ad		VII. Looks like pigs, pig head, don't it? (*Inquiry:* Top tier only without top knot. *Reminded you?* Is unable to specify.)
D	F+	A	P	VIII. That's a mouse. (*Inquiry:* Usual animal, L side only. *Reminded you?* Shape.)
D	F+	A		IX. Looks more like lobsters? Do I love them! (*Inquiry:* Orange only. *Reminded you?* These spikes.)

D	F−	A		X. I don't know those animals.

(*Inquiry:* Center blue. Cannot specify animal or define parts.)

D	F+	A	P	Mice.

(*Inquiry:* Top gray animals. *Reminded you?* The shape.)

D	F+	A	P	Crabs.

(*Inquiry:* Usual side blue. *Reminded you?* The shape.)

D	F+	A	P	Eels.

(*Inquiry:* Lower green. *Reminded you?* The shape.)

Best: Can't tell.

Least: Can't tell.

R=13   Time: 9 minutes

6W=46%W   13F=100%F   12A, 1Ad=100%A

7D=54%D   9F+, 1F±, 2F−=77%F+

Reactivity: 0M : 0ΣC   7P

COMMENT   Senility, as judged by the Rorschach protocol, is not to be recognized by one attribute alone, but is, as we have been able to show by at least six rather well defined protocols, a complex of individuality and age patterns. These combine to make personality differences even in senility recognizable.

This first protocol appears to us to fall into a senile classification mainly because of the 100%F and the 100%A response. Even the youngest children whom we have studied usually have at least one or two categories outside the animal, and this subject does not. There is also a lack of ability to define answers once they are given. This is again like the very young child. Attempts to specify only seem to make the form less precise. With the child this is the beginning of an intellectual process; with the senile old person, it is a diminution of this same process.

There is also a lack of color and movement response which is indicative of the paucity of potential for inner creative experience and emotional reaction to external stimuli.

But this subject is undoubtedly quite lucid, and is as responsive to the demands of the group as her age and reduced potentials allow her to be, for even though there is a reduction of intellectual and emotional capacity, she gives seven popular responses. This would imply that she is able to identify with and participate in cultural thinking, and she probably has very stereotyped but adequate response in everyday routines and social situations. It is for this reason that we feel that this type of protocol indicates the more intact senile individual even though it falls within the senile group.

Sample Case of Mr. P., Age 85 Yrs.: Senile Group
(2) Combination of Animals and Anatomy

W	F—	A	I. Ha! Well, I know but I can't tell you. Some kind of an animal. (Looks on back as if for clues.) (*Inquiry:* Whole. Cannot specify animal or point out any part.)
W	F—	Ad	II. I ain't boastin' on animals. Might be part of an animal. Might be his front paws. (Laughs.) (*Inquiry:* Whole. Is very vague about paws, but indicates two sides as what he has seen.)
D	F±	Ad	III. I'm lost there! (Laughs.) ∨ Those couldn't be the hoofs, could it? (*Inquiry:* Indicates head of usual men. *Reminded you?* Shape.)
Do	F+	Ad	IV. He-he! You're puttin' me right on the fence, I tell you. I couldn't tell that. Those couldn't be the feet could they? (*Inquiry:* Usual feet. *Whose?* Feet of animal, but does not see rest of animal.)
D	F± midline position	anat.	This might be the backbone. (Looks on the back of card.) (*Inquiry:* Center of blot. *Reminded you?* This middle.) I bet you have some funny experiences.
Dd	F+	Ad	V. I can't answer that one I don't believe. (Touches card.) These couldn't be the heads, could they? (Looks on back.) (*Inquiry:* Part of top center only. *Kind of heads?* Animal heads.)
D	F— midline position	anat.	VI. This is a nice one. (His hand trembles.) This couldn't be where they fitted two together for a backbone? (*Inquiry:* Center of whole blot. *Reminded you?* This line here.)

D	F±	Ad	
	? position		

This be connected with head in some way? (*Inquiry:* Top D. *Reminded you?* He is unable to say. *Kind of head?* Animal head.)

Refusal

VII. Oh this is a hard one! (He regards card for some time and then hands it back to Ex.)

D	F±	anat.	
	? position		

VIII. It's just one animal, isn't it? That to me is a hard one. Couldn't be on the side and the bone that goes through the back? (*Inquiry:* Includes usual center ribs and whole center of blot as backbone. *Reminded you?* He just indicates center ribs and center line again.)

D	F+	A	P

These couldn't be animals could they? They'll say "he must have been crazy to say such things." (*Inquiry:* Usual animals. *Reminded you?* The way they look.) I like to come here pretty good. I come for a couple of weeks every year.

Dd	F+	Ad

IX. Ha ha! They're too much alike. Could those be the horns on an animal? (*Inquiry:* One of the spikes on top orange.)

V Can they be more than one part of an animal? Could they be two animals? (Now points out "horns" on each side. This is only an elaboration of the first response.) I don't know. I'm afraid I fall down on this one. (Turns card repeatedly.) I'd like one of a cow with a good bag on it or something like that. Then I could tell. My that's some job for you. (He is commenting on the Examiner's recording.)

D	F+	A	
	? contamination		

X. These are animals that play in the grass. (*Inquiry:* Lower green. *Reminded you?* That's the way they look.)

D	F+	anat.

This maybe is backbone to an animal. I don't know. (*Inquiry:* Top gray. *Reminded you?* Just looks like it.)

R=13 (+1 refusal)   Time: 12 minutes

2W=15%W   13F=100%F   4A, 5Ad=69%A

8D=61%D   6F+, 4F±, 3F−=61%F+   4 anat.

$\frac{2Dd}{1Do}$=24%Dd   Reactivity: 0M : 0ΣC   1P

COMMENT This protocol, with both animal and anatomy interpretations, is the second stage in the six step gradient among the group we have termed senile. Here again we find 100%F, low F+%, and the content categories limited to A and anatomy. There is more spread in area here, and the subject escapes the childlike characteristic of generalizing from a detail, but the concept is often quite poor. There are many presenile characteristics here also in such remarks as "I'm lost there," or "Oh, this is a hard one," and in the questions put to the examiner. These indicate the feelings of insecurity and uncertainty which are often characteristic of the older age groups. But the animal responses are never specific, only "some kind of an animal," and many of the anatomy and Ad responses appear to be given because of position. There is only one popular response.

One would conjecture that this subject is able to follow most of the everyday routines adequately, but that his actions and responses, especially in a social situation may sometimes be vague, inadequate, and often imprecise though not incoherent.

Sample Record of Mrs. K.: Age 76 Yrs.: Senile Group
(3) Variety of Anatomy

D	F−	anat.	I. Well, here is the vital vertebrae. (*Inquiry:* Two top center rounded humps. This was one case in which inquiry was of little value other than perhaps in again pointing out the area. She went so rapidly, and was so intent upon her own ideas, that inquiry was of little avail.)
D	F−	anat.	I'm interested in this nerve. It begins in the vital vertebrae and cerebrum here. (*Inquiry:* Points to midline.)
		Refusal	II. ∨ It was upside down, I guess. I don't understand the red splash. There isn't the vertebrae, nor none of the organs of the chest or cranium. (She gives the card back to the Ex.)

D	F−	anat.	III. Abdominal section from waist down. (*Inquiry:* Light gray shading at center bottom. *Reminded you?* The inside.)
D	F−	abstr.	A nervous condition. (*Inquiry:* Center red. *Reminded you?* Rheumatism or sciatic nerve. It controls so much of the lower limbs. Here she proceeds to tell in great detail what parts control sections of the body.)
Do	F+	anat.	IV. You have the lower limbs, have you? (She shakes her head.) (*Inquiry:* Usual boots. She evidently sees these as legs though she continues with "limbs.")
D	F−	anat.	Course this just seems to be the same right from the vital down to the coccyx. (*Inquiry:* Indicates top as "vital" and traces midline.)
D	F−	anat.	Shoulder blades and scapula. (*Inquiry:* Points to right and left of upper center.)
Dd	F−	anat.	Lumbar region here is perfectly plain. (*Inquiry:* Lower part of lower center head.)
D	F±	anat.	V. A contraction of the vertebrae. (*Inquiry:* At first designates the bottom center projections, then includes whole center of blot.)
D	F−	anat.	VI. This is the complex and the vital vertebrae here where it's attached and it goes right into the cerebrum, and that's a wonderful part of the anatomy because it controls a great deal of the troubles and everything else. (*Inquiry:* Midline of whole blot is vertebrae and top D is cerebrum.)
Dd	F−	anat.	Two white spots between the scapula and the upper regions. I seen the opening there. Would you name them? That controls the organs of the chest, the upper diaphragm. (*Inquiry:* Two light center spots in lower D.)

W	F−	anat.	Stomach, upper tubes of stomach, pancreas, upper intestine, female abdominal organs above and male abdominal organs below. The vagina, a wonderful organ for the female body. (*Inquiry:* She begins to name the male and female organs in detail, becoming more and more confused. She changes the location of parts several times. She includes the whole blot, however, before she is finished, and apparently feels that it is all to be accepted as one.)
Dd	F+	anat.	VII. The rectum. (*Inquiry:* Center of third tier, bottom.)
Dd	F+	anat.	The vagina. (*Inquiry:* Midline of third tier.)
Dd	F−	anat.	VIII. (Examiner suggests these might look like something else, but she ignores this.) What's this they call this little tube that's so often cancerous? (*Inquiry:* Dark part of top midline. *Idea?* She only continues with further enumeration.)
D	F−	anat.	Stomach. (*Inquiry:* Left center blue.)
Dd	F−	anat.	Pancreas. (*Inquiry:* Dark dot on L center blue.)
D	F−	anat.	Upper vertebrae. (*Inquiry:* Usual center ribs.)
S	F−	anat.	Abdominal cavity. (*Inquiry:* White space between center blue and pink.)
D	F−	anat.	Uterus. (*Inquiry:* Small triangular white space in midline between blue and pink.)
D	F±	anat.	Scrotum. (*Inquiry:* Center pinks.)

	↗?C		
D	F−	anat.	Terminus for red blood organs. (*Inquiry:* Bottom pink and orange.)
S	F−	anat.	IX. Lower jaw. (*Inquiry:* Top of center space detail.)
D	F−	anat.	Vital region. (*Inquiry:* Midline.)
Dd	F−	anat.	Scapula. (*Inquiry:* rounded part of green toward center.)
S	F−	anat.	Chest cavity. (*Inquiry:* Lower part of center space detail, including slits.)
Dd	F−	anat.	Lumbar region. (*Inquiry:* Bottom of green, toward center.)
D	F−	anat.	Hips. (*Inquiry:* Outer parts of lower pink.)
Dd	F+	anat.	Rectum. (*Inquiry:* Bottom midline.)
Dd	F−	anat.	Outlet of both male and female. (*Inquiry:* Again bottom midline.)
D	F±	anat.	X. Well, here we have different colors. Well, this ought to be the kidneys. (*Inquiry:* Side browns.)
D	F−	anat.	Is this the ovaries in the female? (*Inquiry:* Center yellow.)
D	F−	anat.	Bladder in both sexes. (*Inquiry:* Top green.)
D	F+	anat.	This little dingus here is in the chest. There's nothing in the chest but the heart and lungs. Is that the lungs because there are two? (*Inquiry:* Top gray.)
D	F±	anat.	Nerve plexus. (*Inquiry:* Side blue.)
D	F−	anat.	That ought to be the diaphragm. (*Inquiry:* Center blue.)

Best: IV. A good showing from the posterior.

Least: IV. Cause it shows nothing but just the dark shadow of the interior.

R=36 (1 refusal)   Time: 35 minutes

1W=3%W   36F=100%F   35 anat.=97% anat.

19D=53%D   4F+, 5F±, 27F−=18%F+   1 abstr. (anat.)

11Dd   Reactivity: 0M : 0ΣC   0P
4S=44%Dd
1Do

COMMENT This would appear to be an excellent example of the compulsive senile with the *idée fixe*. Many of our subjects felt that the blots should be anatomic in character, and although anatomy responses customarily increase with age, in this case the form is poor and the responses are probably based on the position on the card. It was impossible to change her idea of interpretation, and in some instances there seemed to be just an enumeration of parts. In attempting to clarify her response, often both area and interpretation became more confused.

This woman had been a nurse, but had done no nursing for forty years. She reported during the interview that "blood upsets me. I don't like operations." It would have been interesting to have had earlier protocols for her in order to see what other variants there may have been in the emotional and intellectual structure.

One would surmise that this woman is extremely compulsive and follows one idea without much regard for its coherence or relevance. It is difficult to stimulate a change in her behavior, though the manifestations of her reactions may have enough variety for her to appear more lucid than she actually is. There appears to be little effective contact with the environment.

Sample Record of Mr. R.: Age 76 Yrs.: Senile Group
(4) Perseveration of Anatomy

W	F±	anat.	I. (Continuously smiling. Very friendly.) V Skeleton. (*Inquiry:* Whole.)
W	F−	anat.	II. V Looks like a skeleton. (*Inquiry:* Whole. This continues throughout. He always indicates the whole blot when asked what reminded him.)
W	F+	anat.	III. Looks like a skeleton. I'm all right inside and out, as far as I know.
W	F−	anat.	IV. Skeleton.
W	F−	anat.	V. Looks like a skeleton.

W	F−	anat.		VI. That looks like a skeleton.
W	F−	anat.		VII. That's a skeleton.
W	F−	anat.		VIII. Skeleton.
D	F+	A	P	Rat.

(*Inquiry:* Usual animals.)

W	F−	anat.	IX. Skeleton.
W	F−	anat.	X. Skeleton.

R=11   Time: 5 minutes

10W=91%W   11F=100%F   1A=9%A

1D=9%D   2F+, 1F±, 8F−=22%F+   10 anat.=91% anat.

Reactivity: 0M : 0ΣC   1P

COMMENT This is the kind of magic repetition which we find in the very young child. Such a characteristic, so strong in the child of 2 and 3 years, has usually disappeared by the age of 4 years. However, with the child, the repetition is more likely to be "doggie," "kitty," or "tree," while with the aged person it is usually "skeleton" or some anatomic part. This suggests the difference between the initiation of widening concepts and coming to grips with the environment, and the dying back of the intellect and the emotions, so that the concern is more with the self and the grasp on life.

Sample Record of Mrs. McN.: Age 88 Yrs.: Senile Group
(5) Anatomy Limited to Spine, Womb, and Rectum

D	F±	anat.	I. (Trembles.) Well, I don't know as I could tell you. Well, would this be the spine? Are these the ends? (*Inquiry:* Indicates midline as "spine," and top and bottom center as "ends." Here again inquiry usually brought only a reiteration of response and indication of area.)
Dd	F±	anat.	Is this where you pass your urine? (*Inquiry:* Top center.)
Dd	F±	anat.	II. May I ask is this the rectum? (*Inquiry:* Bottom red, center.)
D	F−	anat.	I don't know if this would be—this–you'll have to tell me—would this be the womb? (*Inquiry:* Usual center hands.)

D	F−	anat.		III. I guess you got me stuck on this. Spine. (*Inquiry:* Center gray and black.)
D	F−	anat.		And of course if that's the spine this is the— oh, I don't know—entrance to the womb. Where you pass your water. (*Inquiry:* Center red.)
D	F+	anat.		IV. This entrance to the womb. (*Inquiry:* Top center.)
D	F+	anat.		And if that's so, this must be entrance to the spine. (*Inquiry:* Lower center head.)
D	F−	anat.		V. (Hands tremble.) That's a puzzle. I would say that this was the entrance to the womb. (*Inquiry:* Top projections.)
D	F−	anat.		Never studying these things you know. Rectum up through here? (*Inquiry:* Lower center projections.)
D	F−	anat.		VI. Mmmm! Well, I would say that this was the entrance to the womb, but goes further in. (*Inquiry:* Includes all of top D.)
D	F−	anat.		Entrance to spine, I should judge. I'm not very much posted on these things. Never had any children or anything. (*Inquiry:* Midline of bottom D.)
Dd	F−	anat.		VII. That must be the entrance here and here. (*Inquiry:* Indicates top and bottom center of third tier.)
Dd	F±	anat.		VIII. Well, I guess this is the rectum. (*Inquiry:* Center of bottom orange.)
Dd	F−	anat.		And this is the entrance to the womb. (*Inquiry*: Top of center gray.)
D	F+	A	P	What are those little fellers on the side? Little bears? Is that right? (*Inquiry:* Usual animals.)

D	CF	flower		This looks like a violet or pansy. (*Inquiry:* Pink and orange. *Reminded you?* Color.)
Dd	F±	anat.		IX. If I turn, V entrance to womb. Is that right? (*Inquiry:* Center of pink.)
D	F−	anat.		V This would be the rectum. (*Inquiry:* Center to white slits.)
D	F+	anat.		X. V This would be the spine. (*Inquiry:* Top gray.)
D	F−	anat.		V This would be entrance to womb. (*Inquiry:* lower green.)
D	F+	A	P	Crabs? (*Inquiry:* Usual side blue.)

Best: X.

Least: III.

R=22	Time: 13 minutes	
16D=73%D	21F=95%F	2A=8%A
6Dd=27%Dd	5F+, 5F±, 11F−=55%F+	19 anat.=87% anat.
	1CF	1 flower
	Reactivity: 0M : 1ΣC	2P

COMMENT   Here we see about the same configuration in the total scores as in the preceding cases in the senile group. There is still strong anatomic perseveration, but it is limited in this instance to three parts. At this stage in the senile process, we can again see the similarity of behavior to that of the very young child in the appearance of only two popular responses. The child of 2 or 3 years will have very few popular responses but occasionally there is a thrust which makes one feel he is beginning to participate and respond to cultural influences. The old person suddenly interjects a popular response, an affirmation perhaps of his identity with the group and his right to belong. With the old person this is not necessarily a thrust backward, but a sudden recollection of himself and the experiences he has in common with the group.

But, as in the preceding protocols, the emotional and intellectual impoverishment is marked. The sudden flash of color at VIII would indicate some emotional integrity, but the restriction of the rest of the protocol would make this appear minimal.

Sample Record of Mrs. S. B.: Age 82 Yrs.: Senile Group
(6) *Anatomy and Excretion*

W	F—	anat.	I. (Looks on back.) Why I don't know if it's a picture they took of me! (Ex. says no.) I thought not. Couldn't see any resemblance. (*What do you see?*) I don't know. It looks as if it might be the inside of somebody. (*Inquiry:* Whole. She cannot indicate why, or what reminded her.)
W	F±	A	II. Well, that looks to me like a bat. (*Inquiry:* Black only.) (*Else?*) No, I don't.
W	F—	anat.	III. Another one? Well, it looks like some parts of a body, but I couldn't tell you just
W	F—	elim.	what. Just the separate parts. You know, you had your bowels move or something like that—the flow out.
			(*Inquiry:* Whole. The parts of the body and the bowel movement are the same. She is unable to specify and seems to get the two mixed.)
W	F—	anat.	IV. Oh, oh, oh, oh! Well, I suppose that's some part of the body. (*Inquiry:* Whole.)
Do	F+	Hd	And that looks like the feet. (*Inquiry:* Human feet.)
W	F—	anat.	V. Another one? Well, it looks like some parts of the body. I couldn't tell you what. I don't know. These look like the lower part of the body. (*Inquiry:* Whole, with lower projections as "lower parts of the body.") (Looks on back of card.)
W	F—	anat.	VI. (Sighs.) Another one yet! You got me there. I suppose it's some part of the body, but couldn't tell you what it looked like. (*Inquiry:* Whole.)

W	F−	anat.		VII. Whew! Well, it looks like that might be the back, and then the other parts that come up from it but can't tell you what the parts are. (She smiles in a friendly way.) (*Inquiry:* Third tier is the "back," and the rest of the blot is "other parts that come up from it.") How do they make these? (Ex. explains.) Taken from X-rays?
W	F−	anat.		VIII. Now that looks like the back, and those come up around there. (*Inquiry:* Center orange and pink is "back," and includes whole as "those come up around there.")
W	F−	anat.		IX. Well, you've got me there! I can't tell. (Looks on back.) Could it be the picture of the front of anybody? (Ex. says it could.) Well I thought so. (*Inquiry:* Whole.)
D	F±	A		X. (Long careful regard.) Well, I give that up, I guess. It looks like two turtles on each side. (*Inquiry:* Usual side blue.)
D	F+	A	P	And then this—two animals of some kind. (*Inquiry:* Top gray animals.)
D	F+	A		But what these are? That looks like a mouse. (*Inquiry:* Side brown.)
				But I can't figure on those. (Indicates pink.)

Best: X.

Least: IV.

R=14	Time: 12 minutes	
10W=71%W	14F=100%F	4A=28%A
3D=21%D	3F+, 4F±, 9F−=37%F+	1Hd=8%H
1Do=8%Dd	Reactivity: 0M : 0ΣC	8 anat. =64% anat.
		1 elim.

1P

COMMENT   One of the nurses in an institution we visited during this study commented: "Our greatest problem (with the old people) is to get the food into them, and then to get it out again. And that's their greatest concern too."

As we have seen, the number of anatomic responses seems to increase as the emotional and intellectual capacity deteriorates. Concern with physical processes may be generalized, or it may even appear to be restricted to very specific parts of the body. And now elimination is added. It would almost seem that with this subject the physical processes are in command. Even the popular responses have all but disappeared here.

CHAPTER NINE

Other Dimensions of Classification

Out of the complex of genetic factors and life-history events that determine individuality, certain broad classes of variables have time and again appeared as important. Restricting a population on any one of these variables of classification reduces the differences that appear among individuals within that population. And so a certain portion of the variation among individuals can be considered "accounted for" by these variables.

Our findings in this study have convinced us that the single scheme most fruitful for classifying old age Rorschachs is a functional one—one that separates normal, presenile, and senile groups. Differences found within any one of these groups are markedly reduced over differences within our total old age group. But differences still do exist.

To attempt still further to account for these differences, and to determine the effectiveness of other classificatory schemes, we have re-sorted our sample along other dimensions. Three of these dimensions—age, sex, and socio-economic status—are traditional classifications in developmental research. Another classification, of more restricted pertinence, is that of residential status: institutional or noninstitutional.

Age and Socio-Economic Status

It appeared desirable to make a joint classification of subjects on both age and socio-economic status (SES). Such a two-way classification provides a means of assessing the consistency of over-all trends in score with either age or SES, since it portrays the SE trends for each age level, and the age trends for each SE level. That is, a trend in score from upper to middle to lower SE level at age 70 should appear also at ages 80 and 90, if it is to be considered consistent.

CLASSIFICATION OF SUBJECTS ON SOCIO-ECONOMIC STATUS Of the numerous items of information which allow classification of individuals

116

into socio-economic hierarchies, the items most consistently available for our sample were those of education and occupation during young adulthood. These have in previous studies provided the most satisfactory indices of SES, and they appeared to be the most likely to be reliably reported in the sometimes rambling accounts given by these old people.

Both sorts of information were not always provided by the subjects; sometimes only one was given, and, more rarely, neither. Consequently, we hoped to develop an index of SES which could be assigned on the basis of either occupation or education. This would provide a check on the probable accuracy of individuals who gave both sorts of information, and would allow classification of those who gave only one. Since we desired only a coarse grouping into broad SE classes, this task seemed feasible.

To construct this index, we assembled the histories of all subjects for whom both sorts of information were available, and classified them jointly on years of schooling and on occupational level on the Minnesota Scale (18). Of our subjects, 59.5 per cent could be jointly classified. By inspection, we determined the groupings that appeared to provide the highest degree of correspondence between the two classifications. The resulting scale made up of three levels—which we have termed A, B, and C—and the equated educational and occupational criteria are listed in Table 12.

TABLE 12. SCALE OF SOCIO-ECONOMIC STATUS
Equated Criteria of Classification by Educational or Occupational Level

Socio-economic class	Occupation			Education	
	Minn. scale level		Description	Years of school	Description
A	I–II		Professional, semiprofessional, managerial	12+	Graduated H.S. and beyond
B	III–V		Clerical, skilled or semi-skilled, retail business	8–11	Graduated grammar school or entered H.S.
C	VI–VII		Slightly skilled or unskilled	0–7	Did not graduate from grammar school

The joint classification of percentage of subjects in the educational and occupational groups is given in Table 13. This table shows that 85 per cent of the subjects on whom the information is available are identically classified by either education or occupation. Where classification of the same subject differs by the two methods, the ratings are in adjacent categories.

In classifying each subject on this SES scale, the occupational criterion was used wherever possible. Women were classified on the basis of husband's occupation, own occupation, or own education, in that order. In this way 91.5 per cent of our total sample could be assigned SES ratings.

TABLE 13. JOINT CLASSIFICATION BY OCCUPATION AND EDUCATION
Percentage of Subjects in Each Minnesota Scale Class at Each Educational Level
N = 119

Years of school	Occupational level		
	I–II	III–V	VI–VII
12+	39	4	0
8–11	7	39	0
0–7	0	4	7

It is evident that classification on such a system as we have used is not highly reliable. The source of information, in the first place, is not fully dependable, since some old people undoubtedly forgot or distorted information. The correspondence between the occupational and educational criteria is not absolute. The necessity of rating women on the basis of husband's occupation, and of combining women's and men's occupational levels in the same scale militates against reliability. With so many sources of error, the reliability of our classification is probably only moderate. Such lack of reliability tends to obscure true relationships between SES level and other scores. Thus the group differences we have found are conservative, and the relationships which do appear are the more significant.

The joint distribution of cases in our total sample by our socio-economic index and by age in decades is presented in Table 14.

TABLE 14. AGE AND SOCIO-ECONOMIC LEVEL
Number of Cases of Each Socio-Economic Level at Each Age

Age in years	Socio-economic level			Total
	A	B	C	
70	42	38	11	91
80	29	43	7	79
90	2	9	2	13
TOTALS	73	90	20	183

The joint distribution of means by age and SES for the major Rorschach scoring categories is presented in Table 15. Table 16 presents for each age and each SE level the percentage distribution of cases classified normal, presenile, and senile.

RESULTS *By Age.* An examination of Table 15, which presents mean Rorschach scores at each age level, shows that clear-cut trends in scores with age are disappointingly and surprisingly meager. For the most part even the marginal totals do not show over-all age trends. And usually when such a trend does appear, the age trends at the different SE levels for that score are contradictory (see Anat%, for example).*

We can discern apparent over-all age trends as follows: R, m, and Anat% tend to decrease with age; A% and H% tend to increase. Of these, however, only R and H% show any degree of intra-sample consistency.

The pattern of behavioral characteristics reflected in our classification of subjects into qualitative groups—normal, presenile, and senile—does not show any consistent trend with age. In fact, the proportions of cases in each qualitative group at ages 70 and 90 are nearly identical.

We conclude that for our particular sample, and for the population of old people it represents, sheer chronological aging has virtually no effect on Rorschach performance.† At most it serves only to decrease the total responsiveness (decreased R) of individuals, and apparently to increase interest in others (increased H%)—perhaps through increasing concern with and dependence on interpersonal relations.

By Socio-Economic Status. Despite its lower reliability of assessment, SES stands in sharp contrast to age as an important dimension of classification. Virtually every scoring category shows a direct trend in marginal totals with decreasing SES. These trends are largely supported by the intra-sample trends at each age level. The summary table, Table 17, presents the most important and consistent of these trends.

Besides these single-score relationships with SES, there is a trend in the qualitative patterns of Rorschach responses which we have grouped under the headings normal, presenile, and senile. A decreasing proportion of individuals are classified as normal, and an increasing proportion are classified as senile, as one moves from level A to B to C.

---

* The importance of a cell which reverses a trend in mean scores is proportional to the number of cases in that cell. Therefore the four cells for ages 70 and 80 at SE levels A and B, which form a square in the upper left corner of each distribution, are most important in establishing trends. Individual cells at 90 years cannot be given much weight in confirming or contradicting a trend.

† In no way, of course, does this invalidate the concept of patterned behavior changes through maturation. In infancy and childhood, when growth is extremely rapid and relatively uniform, these maturational stages are for most individuals so closely related to chronological age that we can speak of "age-changes," and even denote a particular pattern as "six-year-oldness," "seven-year-oldness," etc. With increasing maturity, individual differences in rate of growth cumulate, so that by old age, though individuals pass through the same patterned periods, chronological age is no longer a reliable predictor of the stage of the individual's development.

TABLE 15. MEAN SCORES BY AGE AND SOCIO-ECONOMIC LEVEL

Score	Age	Mean values				
		A	B	C	Total	SD
R	70	20.81	18.54	14.08	19.52	10.37
	80	15.84	15.16	15.14	15.27	9.11
	90	14.50	15.11	14.50	14.98	11.72
	TOTALS	18.25	16.59	14.47		
	SD	9.28	10.77	7.26		
D%	70	47.69%	45.97%	57.40%	48.04%	16.36
	80	44.31	46.19	48.14	45.67	17.26
	90	39.00	48.33	49.50	47.08	15.84
	TOTALS	46.11%	46.31%	53.16%		
	SD	14.48	17.27	16.03		
F%	70	55.64%	72.84%	73.64%	64.85%	27.37
	80	60.83	68.16	69.42	55.58	20.46
	90	42.00	58.11	69.00	57.31	10.01
	TOTALS	57.33%	69.13%	71.00%		
	SD	18.48	28.03	14.45		
M	70	2.19	1.37	1.27	1.96	1.30
	80	1.65	1.48	1.85	1.58	1.46
	90	3.00	3.00	1.50	2.77	2.45
	TOTALS	2.00	1.81	1.58		
	SD	1.67	1.24	1.85		
m	70	.50	.15	.36	.33	.58
	80	.45	.21	.00	.28	.64
	90	.00	.22	.00	.15	.58
	TOTALS	.47	.18	.20		
	SD	.72	.45	.41		

Score	Age	Mean values				
		A	B	C	Total	SD
W%	70	42.43%	41.82%	30.50%	40.84%	21.71
	80	48.28	42.14	40.29	44.22	23.95
	90	48.50	40.44	35.50	40.92	22.39
	TOTALS	44.29%	41.92%	34.63%		
	SD	19.72	24.30	25.25		
Dd%	70	11.29%	12.08%	11.80%	11.67%	12.42
	80	8.17	11.56	11.43	10.30	12.90
	90	13.50	11.11	15.50	12.00	16.81
	TOTALS	10.08%	11.73%	12.05%		
	SD	11.08	13.94	14.62		
F+%	70	87.36%	75.24%	71.09%	80.33%	19.37
	80	81.86	79.33	79.86	80.80	20.45
	90	74.00	82.00	79.50	80.38	8.31
	TOTALS	84.81%	77.87%	75.00%		
	SD	12.49	21.26	26.34		
FM	70	2.59	1.89	1.54	2.17	1.82
	80	2.21	1.62	1.57	1.84	1.85
	90	3.00	2.33	2.00	2.38	1.90
	TOTALS	2.45	1.81	1.60		
	SD	2.02	1.67	1.70		
F(C)	70	1.76	1.26	.81	1.44	1.72
	80	.38	.77	.43	.59	.89
	90	1.50	1.67	.00	1.38	1.80
	TOTALS	1.21	1.97	.60		
	SD	1.66	1.69	.75		

FC					
70	.59	.21	.18	.38	.69
80	.52	.26	.00	.37	.63
90	1.00	.56	.00	.54	.66
TOTALS	.58	.27	.10		
SD	.83	.51	.30		
ΣC					
70	1.69	.69	.54	1.13	1.54
80	1.07	.70	.36	.79	1.33
90	1.50	.83	.00	.81	1.17
TOTALS	1.44	.69	.43		
SD	2.22	.97	.69		
H%					
70	18.43%	15.16%	12.09%	16.30%	11.52
80	15.28	18.02	23.71	17.52	13.79
90	27.50	25.67	12.50	23.92	15.87
TOTALS	17.42%	17.58%	17.05%		
SD	12.12	13.70	12.59		
P					
70	6.58	5.13	4.36	5.77	2.33
80	4.93	4.80	4.84	4.96	1.88
90	4.50	6.00	5.00	5.62	3.63
TOTALS	5.86	5.06	4.50		
SD	2.13	1.87	3.06		

CF					
70	1.07	.34	.45	.69	1.05
80	.72	.44	.14	.52	.88
90	1.00	.56	.00	.54	.78
TOTALS	.93	.41	.30		
SD	1.19	.71	.57		
A%					
70	49.88%	54.29%	53.09%	51.73%	21.22
80	49.45	54.72	54.00	52.72	21.21
90	48.50	54.22	74.50	56.46	17.43
TOTALS	48.84%	54.44%	58.47%		
SD	15.12	23.63	22.81		
Anat.%					
70	6.38%	15.63%	20.64%	11.96%	23.25
80	11.31	8.86	9.00	9.77	20.85
90	0	0	0	0	
TOTALS	8.16%	10.83%	15.79%		
SD	14.85	24.08	29.34		

TABLE 16. PERCENTAGE DISTRIBUTION OF NORMAL, PRESENILE AND
SENILE CASES BY AGE AND SOCIO-ECONOMIC LEVEL
N = 183

| | Age | | | | | | Socio-economic group | | | | | |
| | 70 | | 80 | | 90 | | A | | B | | C | |
	No.	%	No.	%	No.	%	No.	%	No.	%	No.	%
Normal	23	27	9	12	3	23	21	29	13	14	1	5
Presenile	61	67	58	73	10	77	47	64	67	74	15	75
Senile	7	6	12	15	0	0	5	6	10	11	4	20
TOTALS	91	100	79	100	13	100	73	100	90	100	20	100

TABLE 17. CHANGES IN MEAN RORSCHACH SCORES WITH DECREASING
SOCIO-ECONOMIC STATUS

R: Mean score *decreases* consistently with decrease in SES, from an over-all mean of 18.3 for all cases in level A, to 14.5 for those in level C.

W%:   Mean score *decreases* consistently, from an over-all mean of 45% in level A, to 35% in level C.

D%:   Mean score *increases* fairly consistently, from 45% in level A to 53% in level C.

F%:   A sharp and consistent *increase* in mean score, from 57% in level A to 71% in level C.

F+%:   A fairly consistent *decrease* in mean score, from 85% in level A to 75% in level C.

M: A consistent *decrease* in mean score, from 2.0 for level A to 1.6 for level C.

FM: Mean score *decreases* consistently, from 2.5 in level A to 1.6 in level C.

F(C):   Mean score shows an over-all tendency to *decrease*, from 1.2 for level A to .6 for level C.

FC:
CF: Mean scores *decrease* consistently, from means of .6FC, .9CF, and
ΣC: 1.4 ΣC in level A to .1FC, .3CF, and .4ΣC in level C.

A%:   The over-all *increasing* trend in means, from 49% at level A to 58% at level C, is fairly consistently supported by intra-sample trends.

Anat.%:   The over-all *increasing* trend in means, from 8% at level A to 16% at level C, is not well supported by intra-sample trends.

P: A fairly consistent *decrease* in mean score, from 5.9 at level A to 4.5 at level C.

Taken together, these trends in Rorschach scores give a clearly patterned picture of psychological differences between groups at different socio-economic levels. Moving from upper to lower levels we see the following trends: productivity and responsiveness decrease; the abstract, generalizing intellectual approach declines in favor of more obvious, practical interests; and perceptual accuracy and sensitivity decrease. There is a decline in all types of emotional enlivenment, including both "inner" living and responsiveness to environmental stimulation. An increasing restriction and stereotypy of behavior appears with decreasing SE level, together with decreasing adaptiveness and participation in common thinking.

Furthermore, it appears that more individuals at lower social levels than at upper ones decline or deteriorate into behavior considered senile. Lacking longitudinal material, we cannot confirm this trend for individual subjects. Nevertheless, the responses of the senile group are so different from responses found in younger adult Rorschachs from any level of the population that an actual process of decline seems most likely. This conclusion would be in keeping with recent findings (Owens, 26) that the curve of intelligence in old age does not fall off sharply for individuals of higher educational levels, as it does for those of lower levels, but remains more level.

Sex Differences

Mean scores for female and male subjects in each qualitative group are presented in our master table, Table 9. The likelihood of a true sex difference between means for men and women can be estimated not only by the *t* test of significance, but also by the consistency of direction of the difference at the normal, presenile, and senile levels. Further data on sex differences are presented in Table 18, which shows the proportion of men and women in each age, socio-economic, and qualitative classification.

TABLE 18. PROPORTION OF MEN AND WOMEN IN EACH AGE, SES, and QUALITATIVE GROUPING

	Age			SES			Group		
	70	80	90	A	B	C	Normal	Presenile	Senile
	No. %	No. %	No. %	No. %	No. %	No. %	No. %	No. %	No. %
Female	73 52	58 41	9 6	52 41	64 50	11 9	30 22	100 71	10 7
Male	28 47	28 47	4 7	22 39	25 45	9 16	11 18	40 67	9 15
Homogeneity χ^2	P>.10			P>.10			P>.10		

The differences most consistently found between the sexes in Rorschach scores are presented in a summary table, Table 19.

This differential patterning of scores gives a picture of differences in the psychological structure of male and female which in some ways resembles the roles traditionally assigned to them. The female is portrayed as more responsive and garrulous, more practical and detailed, more generally responsive to environmental stimulation and more sensitive in her emotional susceptibility. She appears as more creative and imaginative,

TABLE 19. DIFFERENCES BETWEEN THE SEXES IN
MEAN RORSCHACH SCORES

R:	*Females* have consistently and significantly higher means at all levels.
W%:	*Males* have a higher mean W% at all levels.
D%:	*Females* have consistently and significantly higher mean D%.
F+%:	*Males* show higher means at all levels, significantly higher in senility.
M:	*Females* have consistently higher mean scores.
m:	*Males* have higher mean scores in the normal and presenile groups (no m given by senile subjects).
F(C):	*Females* show higher mean F(C) scores at all levels.
FC:	*Females* have significantly higher mean scores in the presenile group, though the trend is not consistent in other groups.
CF: ⎫ ΣC: ⎭	*Females* have consistently higher mean scores.
H%:	*Males* are consistently higher in mean H%.
Anat%:	*Females* are significantly higher in mean Anat% at the senile level; the trend is not clear at less deteriorated levels.
P%:	*Males* have consistently higher mean P%, significantly so in senility.

and more concerned with her self and her own bodily processes. Men, on the other hand, have more concern for the intellectual aspects of life. They take a more abstract, generalizing approach, are more accurate in their perception, and show greater intellectual adaptation to the life around them. Surprisingly, they show a greater interest in other persons than do women.

There is a suggestion that for men the decline of old age is sharper than for women. Though equal proportions of men and women in our sample reach 90 years, a greater proportion of men are considered senile than women (the difference is not statistically significant). The suggestion is further supported by the superiority of women over men in the movement sectors of the Rorschach—an area in which men appear to have had slightly higher mean scores in earlier life than women.

Perhaps the most provocative finding in this area is the apparent tendency for sex differences to *increase* with increasing deterioration of the subjects. In 13 out of the 26 Rorschach variables presented in the master table the largest absolute sex difference between means falls in the senile group—this despite the fact that the seniles have zero, or near-zero scores on many of the determinants, which restricts the possibility of differences appearing. Also, despite the lower power of the *t* test with the smaller number of cases in the senile group, the greatest number of significant sex differences appear in this group. In the normal group only 1 of the 26 scores shows a significant sex difference; 4 of the presenile sex differences are significant, and 7 of the senile differences.

This increase in sex differences stands in contradistinction to the decrease in individual differences. With increasing senility individuals within either sex group resemble each other more and more, and less and less is revealed of individual characteristics. On the other hand, the sexes move further and further apart in their response processes. This is highly suggestive of some sort of innate difference between the sexes in psychological structure which becomes more apparent with the waning of the individual differences that earlier had partially masked it.

Institutional Status

Differences between the Rorschachs of institutionalized subjects and those living at home did not impress themselves upon us in preliminary inspections of the protocols. (It was this similarity between institutional and noninstitutional subjects, in fact, that we felt justified our combining of subjects from both sources.) A finding of complete identity between the groups would have been surprising, but the functional developmental differences in the normal–presenile–senile sequence, and the sex and SES differences apparently obscured the residential differences.

Because of this, it appeared necessary to control the factors of age, sex, and SES in assessing differences between institutionalized and noninstitutionalized subjects. Therefore, we dealt with pairs of cases, one member of each pair residing in an institution, the other at home. Both members of each pair were of the same sex, in the same broad SES group, and within five years of each other in chronological age. Ninety-six of our total 200 cases could be so paired. The distributions of the pairs by sex, age, occupational and educational levels, and type of institution are presented in Table 20.

Distribution of institutional and noninstitutional subjects on our

TABLE 20.   DISTRIBUTION OF MATCHED INSTITUTIONALIZED AND
NONINSTITUTIONALIZED SUBJECTS

Sex:
  35 female pairs, 13 male pairs

Age:
  Noninstitutional mean = 78.7; range = 70–97
  Institutional mean   = 79.3; range = 70–93

Occupational level:	
Upper (Minn. Scale I–II)	32 pairs
Middle (Minn. Scale III–V)	14 pairs
Lower (Minn. Scale VI–VII)	2 pairs

Years of schooling:	
Below 8 years	2 pairs
8–11 years	17 pairs
Above 11 years	29 pairs

Type of institution:	
Benevolent institution	31 cases
Private institution	11 cases
County old peoples' home	6 cases

qualitative classifications is given in Table 21. The mean Rorschach scores for the institutional and noninstitutional groups, and the mean differences between pairs are presented in Table 22.

The χ^2 homogeneity test shows a significant difference in distribution of the two groups into our qualitative classifications. A much larger proportion of the noninstitutionalized members of the pairs is classed as normal; many more of the institutionalized cases as senile.

By the t test of significance of differences between paired groups, the noninstitutionalized members of the pairs are shown to have significantly higher scores on F + %, M, FM, FC, and P. Institutionalized cases are higher in F% and Anat%. The groups are quite similar in area scores.

Thus, compared with the institutionalized group, the noninstitution-

TABLE 21.   QUALITATIVE GROUPINGS OF INSTITUTIONAL AND
NONINSTITUTIONAL SUBJECTS

Percentage in Each Category

	Noninst.	*Inst.*
Normal	31	8
Presenile	65	71
Senile	4	21

Homogeneity $\chi^2 = 11.84$;
P < .01

TABLE 22. DIFFERENCES BETWEEN RORSCHACH SCORES OF
INSTITUTIONAL AND NONINSTITUTIONAL SUBJECTS
Mean Scores, Mean Differences, and Significance of Differences
between Matched Groups

Score	Noninst. mean	Inst. mean	Mean diff. $\overline{SE_{diff.}}$	Significance level
R	20.44	17.44	3.00/2.24	0
W%	43.69%	45.77%	1.08/2.43	0
D%	45.73%	44.98%	.74/1.98	0
Dd%	10.21%	8.69%	1.52/2.39	0
F%	56.10%	66.25%	10.15/3.95	*
F+%	86.50%	74.42%	12.08/3.99	**
M	2.13	1.52	.60/.31	*
FM	2.85	1.62	1.23/.38	**
m	.38	.31	.05/.12	0
F(C)	1.33	1.13	.21/.30	0
FC	.66	.35	.31/.16	*
CF	.77	.65	.13/.23	0
C	.15	.08	.06/.07	0
ΣC	1.31	.95	.36/.31	0
A%	48.15%	46.73%	1.42/4.57	0
H%	17.27%	16.08%	1.19/2.78	0
Anat%	6.38%	17.63%	11.25/4.07	**
P	6.48	5.42	1.06/.46	*
P%	33.88%	35.32%	1.45/3.27	0

Key: o = non-significant
  * = significant at 5% level
 ** = significant at 1% level

alized subjects are represented as being more "intact." They show greater productivity, greater perceptual clarity, more creativity, and better modulation of emotion. They are less constricted, and show far less concern with their selves and their bodily processes.

It is not possible to say, from our data, whether the greater deterioration of the institutionalized group is the result or the cause of institutionalization. Either is conceivable. It appears likely that those individuals who have "failed" more are the more likely to be institutionalized. On the other hand, there is the strong possibility that the relatively more restricted, less challenging life of the institution may itself have contributed to the decline. Despite efforts of the excellent institutional staffs to provide activities and stimulation, time hung heavy for many of these older people. "Taking my time? That's one thing I got plenty of. This [the Rorschach] is all I got to do today," commented one old gentleman. "You don't stay very alert, sitting around here," was the opinion voiced by one old lady, and para-phrased by several others.

It seems most likely that factors both of preliminary screening and subsequent hastening of deterioration operate to determine the resulting differences between the groups.

CHAPTER TEN

Old Age and Childhood

Normal, presenile, and senile—each of these three classifications appears to stand out as a clear-cut entity so far as the Rorschach response of the elderly human is concerned. Not only is there an appreciable difference in the quantitatively measurable determinants given by subjects in each classification, but also a qualitative difference in the character of the response.

While *normal* subjects give responses which in nearly every respect closely resemble those of the normal young adult, this is not true of the response of *presenile* subjects. These responses not only differ quantitatively from those of the normal young adult or normal older person, but in other ways as well. Chiefly the presenile response can be identified by the presence of so-called qualitative signs which do not customarily (though they may occasionally) occur in the normal record. These signs have been identified as A-list signs—responses which had occurred earlier, in childhood, but had largely dropped out in adulthood, and B-list signs—kinds of response not commonly seen in either childhood or normal adulthood.

Senile records were easily identified by the fact that in most, animal per cent or anatomy per cent, or both, was close to 100%, and that at the same time there was a very high F% and a very low F+%. Complete or virtually complete static perseveration was also common. Some of the qualitative signs of presenility, but not as a rule many, were occasionally present.

All of these changes can be identified by the clinician by referring to Chapters 6, 7, and 8 of this text; to Tables 9 and 10; and to the lists of A- and B-group qualitative signs, Tables 6, 7, and 8.

However, the change which commonly takes place as any subject approaches senility (though not in *all* subjects as they grow older) can be summarized more concisely and perhaps more graphically than has been done thus far in this volume.

We can do this by saying that as the normal individual matures into adulthood from childhood, his emotional and intellectual responsiveness and potential becomes increasingly "mature," complex and well structured. As measured by the Rorschach test, the number of responses given increases, and fewer cards are refused, form becomes increasingly good, content becomes more varied, responses to both emotional and environmentally structured stimuli become fuller, human movement responses come to exceed animal movement, color responses become more modulated, shading responses increase in number, there is less perseveration, and animal per cent decreases.

All of these ways of responding occur increasingly as the individual matures, and to a large extent continue, at about the same as the normal adult level, in many persons whose chronological age is over 70. Such persons in our group have been designated as "normal," on the basis of their Rorschach response at least.

However, as the individual progresses into presenility and eventually to senility, *the direction of development seems to reverse itself*, and as the subject deteriorates the response increasingly resembles that of a younger and younger person.

As Table 23 will demonstrate, the Rorschach response of the "normal" old person resembles in nearly every respect that of the normal young adult. The chief exception is the color responses, which in proportion and type are like those of the 7-year-old. However, the Rorschach of the presenile individual, in addition to containing many qualitative kinds of responses (A-list signs) which are like the responses of childhood, resembles quantitatively that of the 2- to 10-year-old child. In most respects it is like that of the 5- to 10-year-old child, with color responses "below" the other responses, at about a 3-year-old level.

In senility, the response has gone even farther back into childhood, being similar in most respects to that of the 2- to 3-year-old child, with color responses "lowest," about at a 2-year-old level.

The graphically minded reader may thus think of most of the customary Rorschach determinants as occurring along a bellshaped curve—increasing up through normal adulthood and normal old age, and then falling away in presenility, and decreasing even further in senility. (Or as a horizontal diamond which reaches its widest point at adulthood, with its narrow ends representing early childhood, and presenility and senility.)

TABLE 23. EXTENT TO WHICH ADULT RESPONSES GO BACK TO CHILDHOOD

Score	Normals		Preseniles		Seniles	
	Mean value	Location	Mean value	Location	Mean value	Location
R	25.9	Normal adult	16	5–10 yrs.	12	3 yrs. and under
F%	50%	Normal adult	62%	5½–10 yrs.	92%	2 yrs.
F+%	93%	Normal adult	81%	5½–10 yrs.	50%	2–2½ yrs.
M	3.3	Normal adult	1.6	7–10 yrs.	.2	3 yrs.
FM	2.7		2.0		.3	3 yrs.
m	.7		.3		.0	2 yrs.
FC	1.0	About 7 yrs.	.3	3 yrs.	.0	2 yrs.
CF	1.3		.5		.2	
C	.2		.1		.1	
ΣC	2.1		.7		.2	
F(C)	2.1	Normal adult	.9	8–9 yrs.	.4	2½ yrs.
A%	46%	Normal adult	55%	4 yrs. and under	40%	2½ yrs.
H%	24%	—	17%	8–10 yrs.	5%	2½ yrs.
Content	A, H, 4 other categories	Normal adult	A, H, 3 other categories	2–6 yrs.	3 categories	2–2½ yrs.
			Dynamic perseveration	8 yrs.		
			Confabulation	3½–7 yrs.		
			Perseveration	4 yrs.		

Specifically,

1. The average number of responses given increases to adulthood, and then in presenility and senility decreases.
2. Content becomes more and then again less, varied.
3. Perseveration disappears—rendering the response more varied in maturity—and then comes in again.
4. F% decreases, then again increases.
5. F+% increases, then decreases.
6. Number of shading responses increases, then decreases.
7. Global responses decrease in proportion to detail responses, then increase.
8. Dd% increases, then decreases.
9. Number of both M and FM increases, then decreases.
10. Gradually M exceeds FM, but in presenility and senility, FM responses once again exceed M.
11. Color responses in presenility and senility once again resemble those of childhood both in number and kind.
12. The number of cards responded to without refusal increases then again decreases.
13. A% is high in childhood, low in normal adulthood, then high again in presenility and senility.

Table 23 summarizes the extent to which the response of normal, presenile, and senile subjects goes back into childhood.

CHAPTER ELEVEN

Area

As is the general custom, we have defined the areas of the blot chosen for interpretation as follows: W, DW, and WS all indicate that the entire blot is used for the response, or that the concept is a total concept even though minor parts of the blot are not used. D indicates that a detail of the blot frequently interpreted is used; and Dd, S, and Do indicate that a detail rarely interpreted, a space detail, or a fragmentary detail, taken from an ordinarily interpreted entire concept, is chosen. The W scorings are self-evident, while the D and Dd responses have been determined in accordance with Hertz's frequency tables.

Findings reported in the literature as to area of blot chosen by older subjects are limited and somewhat conflicting. Rorschach (40) himself noted an overemphasis on whole responses. Klopfer, too (28), with 50 cases averaging 73.5 years of age, found "high" W, "low" D.

On the other hand, Dörken and Kral (16) with 60 cases of senile dementia, averaging in age 76.3, found that their subjects on the average, in spite of considerable individual variation, appeared to give a nearly normal distribution of responses insofar as location was concerned.

Their interpretation, unlike our own, is that older individuals no longer show a predilection for a particular type of response based on personal idiosyncrasies, as such personality characteristics tend to become lost through deterioration, thereby leaving the patients free to respond on the basis of the blots' Gestalt qualities.

Kuhlen and Keil (29), also, reporting on responses of 100 men aged 65 to 80, found that the responses for their group were distributed among W, D, and Dd in about the same proportions as in younger adult groups.

Prados and Fried (39) with 35 cases, divided their subjects by decades —50 to 60, 61 to 70, 71 to 80. They found a decreasing W% with age as follows in the three groups: 61%, 52% and 43% respectively. D% increased with age: 37%, 46%, and 55%. Dd% remained consistent at 2%. For each of these groups, therefore, W% was considerably higher than that expected in the normal population. However they point out that with increasing age the pattern of location comes to be more in line with the expected adult norms.

Other investigators, Chesrow *et al*, Grossman *et al*, and Wenar, do not discuss area.

Our own findings are that in normal older subjects, distribution of area is not too different from that in the normal young adult, but with increasing deterioration W tends to increase considerably beyond that usually found in the normal adult.

However, our three main groups of subjects, i.e. normals, preseniles, and seniles, show probably less distinctive difference from one group to another with regard to area than with regard to any other category of response. The amount of D remains almost constant for the three groups, being 47% for the normals, 47% for the preseniles, and 45% for the seniles. Percentages for W and Dd vary slightly more (see Table 24).

TABLE 24.   AREA

	Mean number of responses		
Score	Normal	Presenile	Senile
W	6.4	5.3	4.6
DW	1.0	.7	.4
WS	.1	.1	0
W%	36%	43%	46%
D	12.8	8.0	6.8
D%	47%	47%	45%
Dd	4.5	1.2	1.2
S	.9	.2	.3
Do	.3	.4	.3
Dd%	15%	9%	8%

In the normals, the percentages are 36%W, 47%D, and 15%Dd. No one of these falls quite within the expected range for normal adults, both W and Dd being a little higher than is expected. But they are not far off.

The change in area perceived as the subject moves toward senescence is that the W increases at the expense of Dd—D remaining nearly constant. Thus in the presenile group the distribution is 43%W, 47%D, and 9%Dd. This manner of perceiving the blots is almost identical with that seen in the senile group which sees 46% wholes, 45% large details, 8% small details.

The fact that all of these changes are relatively so slight suggests perhaps that once the normal adult manner of seeing the blots has been attained, the individual's way of perceiving does not change appreciably as he declines into senility. Intellectual and emotional changes which accompany old age do not appear to influence the area of a stimulus to which the individual responds.

It is interesting to note that at only one age in the first ten years of life, does the area perceived resemble that of the very old person. Nine year old subjects see 42%W, 48%D, and 9%Dd which is almost identical with the presenile figures and close to those for the seniles.

However, older subjects seem to be going back toward, though they do not reach, the child's manner of perceiving in that with increasing deterioration, use of W area increases until it slightly predominates over the D area. We might expect, though this is only a hypothesis, that with even more deterioration our subjects might reach a time when they would give over 50% whole responses as do children ten years of age and under.

Different levels of W: In our revisions of both Child (6) and Adolescent (7) Rorschach responses, we have introduced a scheme for scoring W responses which subscripts any W according to its level of differentiation. Though this scheme fails to cover completely certain subtle differences among Ws, it appears to sort out some important varieties of W and to point out responses where further qualitative evaluation is called for.

W_0 A gross, undefined, global response to the whole card, where the content is inherently vague, formless, or diffuse, and where sub-parts are not distinguished, or only incidentally so. Examples: mud, pile of feathers, clouds, paint, insides, design, painting, shattered piece of glass, map (if not further elaborated).

W_1 *One*-piece figures which are definite objects. These are single, global forms, with sub-parts distinguishable (spontaneously or on request), but the whole thing is essentially *a* thing: a man, a bat, a face, etc. "A man: he has arms, legs, hat," etc., would still be a W_1: all the details are considered as "accessories" to the single basic figure.

W_2 The blot is differentiated into *two* major portions, then recombined. Nearly always it is split laterally into two sides: 2 elephants, 2 people shaking hands, lady seeing her reflection, etc. "Accessory" items may be included: "Two bears fighting—they have blood on their paws." Horizontal rather than vertical cleavage is also included here, for consistency, but the former is more likely to have more the strength of a W_3. (E.g., VI. "Bee coming out of a flower," "Lighthouse on an island.")

W_3 The blot is differentiated into *three or more* distinct portions and recombined. The pieces are definite in form; often two of them are duplicated. For example: "Two bears climbing up a mountain"; "Two women bending over pots"; "Two men quarreling about a woman."

W_x "The above scale cannot handle this W." This wastebasket category was included for the relatively few W that do not fit into the W_0-W_3 scale and that should not be forced into it. For example, it is used for "collection" Ws—multiple details grouped only loosely into a W ("Undersea scene with lots of fishes"). Also includes responses in which a large area is at one level, often W_0, but another area is more defined (VII: "A tiny church steeple down here and all clouds around it"). Inherently vague forms described in detail, such as map responses elaborated with bays, peninsulas, etc., are included here.

(Note:—WS and W̸ responses are also rated for W level: for example, WS_1 (most faces on Card I); WS_3 ("Rocket ship shooting through clouds toward two red planets"); W̸$_1$ ("Bearskin, not counting this part.")

When our original old age data were reviewed, and W responses classified according to this scheme, it appeared that for both men and women the largest number of W_3 responses occurred in the normal subjects, fewer in presenile subjects and none in the seniles. For women, the smallest number of W_2 responses occurred in senile subjects, and senile men gave neither W_2 nor W_3 responses. Thus as in other respects, as subjects moved on toward senility, they moved back toward a more childish way of responding.

Table 24A reports the percentage of normal, presenile and senile subjects who give each type of W response.

TABLE 24A. DIFFERENT LEVELS OF W RESPONSE

	W_0	W_1	W_2	W_3	W_x
		Women			
Normal	6%	45%	28%	13%	8%
Presenile	4	54	28	9	5
Senile	2	76	11	0	11
		Men			
Normal	7	41	26	19	7
Presenile	5	60	26	6	3
Senile	0	95	0	0	5

Of the Dd responses, rare details clearly predominate at all ages. The oligophrenic or fragmentary detail response, Do, is virtually nonexistent. The simple space response, S, has a mean occurrence of .9 in the normal group but virtually disappears thereafter.

These findings suggest that the older person, whether in normal, presenile, or senile category, tends to generalize his response. He is slightly less practical and concrete than he may have been earlier. But it is interesting that the ability to refine judgment and to observe the less obvious, holds up as well as it appears to do.

It is the quality of the responses in each of these areas which differs with each of our groups. Even though the average distribution of the areas chosen for interpretation does not appear to be greatly disparate from one group to another, we find less good form as the subjects progress from a normal to a presenile level and into senility.

Our findings with regard to area do not agree with those of Prados and Fried on normal old subjects under 70, but are approached by their figures for their ten subjects over 70 in whom they find a W of 43%, D of 55%, and Dd of 1%. Prados and Fried interpret their high W as a result of a vagueness and a certain inability to cope with the test. Our findings approximate the figures of Dörken and Kral on their 31 senile psychotic subjects aged 65 to 88, in that D exceeds W and Dd is small. Dörken and Kral give the mean percentages of 31%W, 51%D, 9%Dd, and 8%DdS.

Our interpretation of our findings on area, and particularly of the fact that area chosen changes so slightly from normal to presenile to senile subjects, is that area chosen remains—more than any other determinant— a function of the individual's own personal manner of response, rather than a function of the age or state of intellectual and emotional adequacy of the subject. These latter factors do of course have their influence but it is less than for other Rorschach determinants.

Area by other Classifications

BY AGE   Though, as we have previously noted, the division of cases into normal, presenile, and senile categories appeared to yield the most conclusive material, we also worked out findings for all cases as divided into the more conventional age gradations: 70–80, 80–90, and 90–100. Area differences for these three groups were inconsistent as the following tabulation shows:

70 years	80 years	90 years
41%W	44%W	41%W
48%D	46%D	47%D
11%Dd	10%Dd	12%Dd

BY SOCIO-ECONOMIC STATUS   There is a decrease of W with decreasing socio-economic level; a tendency toward an increase of D with decreasing socio-economic level; but no consistent trend in Dd.

A level	B level	C level
44%W	42%W	35%W
46%D	46%D	53%D
10%Dd	12%Dd	12%Dd

INSTITUTION VS. NONINSTITUTION   The differences remaining when the groups are matched on age and SES are not significant.

Noninstitution	Institution
44%W	46%W
46%D	45%D
10%Dd	9%Dd

SEX DIFFERENCES   Considering our total population divided into normal, presenile, and senile groups, the males in each group give more whole responses (see Master Table 9), fewer D responses, and fewer Dd. This sex difference remains consistent for all three groups.

CHAPTER TWELVE

Determinants

FORM

Form responses, that is responses which involve neither movement, color, nor shading but which are determined only by the form or shape of the blot, are generally considered to reflect the degree of a subject's intellectual control. They give an indication of the intellectual ability of the subject, of his reasoning powers, of his critical ability.

Klopfer (27) comments that "The control of any subject of more than average intelligence, whose record contains more than 50%F can be called constrictive. Among presumably normal adult subjects, any F% between 50 and 80% invariably corresponds to signs of inflexibility, or in clinical terms, constriction with compulsive elements."

Klopfer believed that more than 50%F, in children as well as in adults, indicated rigidity and inflexibility. However, our own earlier findings (6) did not bear out this belief. In a population of normal Connecticut child subjects aged 2 to 10 years, the mean F% remained above 50% at every age. F% was at its highest at 2 years of age (90%), from which point it declined to 52% at 7 years, its lowest point. Thereafter it rose again to a mean of 63% at 10 years.

We have not as yet determined the mean F% for our adolescent subjects; in the normal adult, most investigators agree, it is ideally 50% or under.

In our group of "normal" old people, the mean F% is, interestingly enough, exactly 50%, just at the top limit of the normal range.

Its rise thereafter is sharp and marked. Our presenile group of old people has a mean F% of 64%, and the senile group an F% of 92%. The presenile group therefore approximates, in the extent to which form determines its response, child subjects aged 5½ to 10 years of age, whereas the senile subjects are more restricted in this respect than any child group except the 2-year-olds.

The only mention which we find in the literature of F% to be expected in old people is that of Dörken & Kral, whose subjects ranged in age from 66 to 86, and who found a mean F% of 55%.

Form responses obviously vary in the accuracy and sharpness with which the concept given matches the actual blot. The F+% is, according to Rorschach (40), "an indication of the clarity of the associative processes and, at the same time, of the length of the span of attention and the capacity for concentration."

In analyzing the responses of child subjects, form accuracy was scored not solely according to adult norms, but with reference to group frequency (Ames *et al.*, 6, pp. 32–39). A gradual direct increase of good form was found as the child grew older, the mean rising in almost straightline progression from 54%F+ at 2 years to 89% at 10. As early as 4½ years of age, F+% had reached 75%—the lower limit for a normal adult.

Chesrow *et al.* (15), with 20 subjects aged 64 to 83, found an F+% above 70% in all but 7 cases, and only 3 of these scored below 60%F+.

In our present subjects, both normal and presenile subjects maintained an F+% which fell within presumably normal limits. Mean F+% for normals was 93%, for preseniles 81%. Only in the seniles did the average fall below normal limits—down to 50%F+.

Thus clarity of associative processes, attention span and capacity for concentration all remain creditably high in not only our normal but also in our presenile elderly subjects. This means that the mean F+% for both these groups, who constituted all but 10 per cent of our 200 subjects aged 70 to 97 years of age, was well within normal limits.

By Different Classifications

BY AGE   Apparently there is a slight drop in F% with age. F+% remains virtually constant.

70 years	80 years	90 years
65%F	56%F	57%F
80.3%F+	80.8%F+	80.3%F+

BY SOCIO-ECONOMIC STATUS   There is at all age levels a consistent increase in F% with decreasing socio-economic level and a decrease in F+%.

A level	B level	C level
57%F	69%F	71%F
85%F+	78%F+	75%F+

INSTITUTION VS. NONINSTITUTION   There is a significant increase in F% and a significant decrease in F + % in the institution as compared with the matched non-institution group.

Noninstitution	*Institution*
56%F	66%F
87%F+	74%F+

SEX DIFFERENCES   Considering our three main groups—normal, presenile, and senile: the males have a lower F% in normals and seniles but higher in preseniles. F + % is higher in males in all three groups—especially in seniles (see Table 9).

MOVEMENT

Human Movement

Human movement responses, indicated by the scoring symbol M, are considered to give an indication of the richness of the inner life of the individual and to be an indication of inner creativity. The individual in whom M responses outweigh the sum of the color responses (ΣC) is considered to be introversive, one who is directed more by his own inner promptings and reflections than by immediate responsiveness to environmental stimuli.

Though the number of human movement responses can in the normal individual vary from 0 to 15, a person of average intelligence is generally expected to give 2 or 3 such responses, a subject of superior intelligence, 5 or more.

In our child subjects we found the number of M to increase in an almost steady progression from 2 to 10 years. During this period the increase was from an average of .07 per child at 2 years to an average of 1.70 at 10.

As to the literature on older people, Klopfer with his subjects found a mean M of 1.4; Dörken and Kral, a mean M of 1.1; Chesrow *et al.* a mean of 1.6. The mean age for all these groups of subjects was in the seventies. Prados and Fried obtained a mean M of 2.6 with 50-year-olds; of 1.9 with 60-year-olds; of 1.9 with 70-year-olds. Thus all their subjects over 70 have a mean M of 1+, which is similar to that found in our presenile group.

In our present cases the occurrence of human movement responses is as follows:

Normal older subjects (aged 70 to 97) give a mean M of 3.3, as many as would be expected in normal adults of any age. This suggests that so far as our subjects may be representative of a normal old population, a large number of individuals over 70 years of age (about one fifth in our group) show a remarkable intactness of those intellectual or psychic functions expressed in the M response.

This mean number of M responses falls sharply in presenility to 1.6 and practically disappears thereafter. The mean M of the senile group is only .2.

As in our study of children's Rorschach responses, we have classified M responses given by our subjects as static, extensor (moderate, and strong-to-violent), and flexor (passive, and lifting or holding.) In children, static responses predominate at 2 and 2½ years, at 3½, and at 4½ through 5½ years; extensor movements at other ages, especially from 6 through 10 years. Of the extensor movements, moderate extension prevails at the earlier ages, strong to violent extension from 8 years on. Flexor movements increase after 5 years, reaching their high points at 7 and 10 years but never predominating.

TABLE 25. CLASSIFIED TABLE OF M RESPONSES
Total Number and Percentage

		Normal (N = 41)		Presenile (N = 140)		Senile (N = 19)	
		No.	%	No.	%	No.	%
I.	Static	53	40	120	49	2	50
II.	Total extensor	57	43	96	40	2	50
	Moderate	39		53		1	
	Strong to violent	18		43		1	
III.	Total flexor	14	11	24	10	0	
	Flexor passive	6		5		0	
	Lifting, holding	8		19		0	
	Unclassified	9	7	3	1	0	
	TOTALS	133	100	243	100	4	100

In normal subjects over 70 years of age, at least so far as our population is concerned, extensor movements just barely predominate over static. But in our presenile subjects, once again as in earliest childhood, static movement definitely predominates over extensor and flexor. In the senile subjects, movement responses are so limited in number as to make their classification valueless.

As Table 25 indicates, human movement responses become more passive with increasing deterioration of subjects.

If, as Piotrowski believes (37, p. 53), the type of movement indicates the subject's conception of his role in life, self-assertiveness being indicated by extensor movements, compliance by flexor movements, and indecisiveness by blocked movement—then it is not too surprising that static movements increasingly predominate in older subjects.

An unclassified table of human movement responses in normal, presenile, and senile subjects (Table 26), indicates more specifically just

TABLE 26.   UNCLASSIFIED TABLE OF MOVEMENT RESPONSES
Total Number of Responses

	Normal (N = 41)	Presenile (N = 140)	Senile (N = 19)
Just two people (on Card III)	8	62	2
Sitting	3	6	0
Lying	1	3	0
Standing	6	6	0
Admiring own reflection	1	0	0
Looking, grinning, making faces	3	12	0
Talking, whispering	4	10	0
Controversy, spat, arguing	12	9	0
Oral activity (mouth wide open, smoking, biting, drinking, etc.)	15	7	0
Meeting or facing	0	5	0
Kneeling, praying	4	0	0
Holding, carrying, lifting, pulling	8	19	0
Hanging, suspended	2	0	0
Bowing	0	3	0
Dying	0	2	0
Walking	1	2	0
Posturing hands or reaching	7	17	1
Posturing with whole body, acting	12	12	0
Playing "Pease Porridge Hot"	3	3	0
Serving	5	5	0
Shaking, touching hands	6	11	0
Cooking	2	0	0
Kissing, making love to	3	3	0
Running	2	1	0
Climbing	1	4	0
Dancing	13	18	0
Fighting	2	10	1
Jumping	0	3	0
Swimming	0	1	0
Playing, or contest	0	6	0
Other	9	3	0

what kind of human movement is to be found in records of subjects over 70 years of age.

In normal older subjects, the seven leading kinds of behavior are in order of decreasing frequency: oral activity, dancing, controversy, posturing with whole body, holding-carrying-lifting, just two people, and posturing hands or reaching.

In presenile subjects the seven leading kinds of human movement are: just two people, holding-lifting-carrying, dancing, posturing hands or reaching, posturing with whole body, looking, shaking or touching hands.

In senile subjects there are in all only four human movement responses: just two humans (twice), people with hands up, "two fellers fighting."

TABLE 27. MOST COMMON TYPES OF HUMAN MOVEMENT
FOUND IN CHILDREN AND OLD PEOPLE

Children	*Normals*	*Preseniles*
Just two people (2–3½, 5, 6–10 years)	Just two people	Just two people
Shaking, touching or posturing hands (3, 10 years)	Posturing hands	Shaking, touching or posturing hands
Sitting (4, 9 years)		
Standing (4½, 8 years)		
Holding, lifting, carrying (7–10 years)	Holding, lifting, carrying	Holding, lifting, carrying
Dancing (8–10 years)	Dancing	Dancing
Looking (10 years)		Looking
	Posturing with body	Posturing with body
	Disputing	
	Oral activity	

Table 27 compares these seven most common types of human movement found in normal and presenile older subjects with the seven most common types of movement noted by us in child subjects aged 2 to 10 years of age. It will be seen that four of the most common movement responses found in normal old people coincide with those most prevalent in children. In presenile subjects, five of the seven most common types of movement coincide with those most prevalent in children.

All but one of the senile movement responses coincides with most common childhood movement responses.

This seems at first glance like a rather startling coincidence and suggests a marked return in presenility to behavior characteristic of the early years of life. However, so far as we know, no similar breakdown of human movement responses has been made for a group of young adults. Since the possible number of different types of human movement is not unlimited, and since our classifications are broad, a similar likeness might exist between normal young adults and our older subjects.

However, we can at least conjecture that here as in other respects, the Rorschach response of the old partially resembles that of the child.

A few sample characteristic human movement responses of our presenile group are reported here verbatim:

Card III. "They did come to life! They're not saying good morning to you, but making a real curtsy. Man and woman. This one almost has whiskers. This other has a long neck like me. Is this the punch after the wedding day that they're scooping up?"

Card VII. "Ha ha! What is it? Secrets of a master mason! Telling secrets. Giving you the words."

Card IV. "Oh! Now what has happened to them? Certainly down and out and I don't know why. Arms hanging down and toes turning up—sign of dying. You've not turned yours up, have you, dear?"

Card II. "Ha ha! Well if you could fill in there (top white) you should have a couple of fellers having a highball. I can't concentrate today—offside last two weeks."

Card I. "Man and woman dancing around these two children—twins perhaps. You know what they are of course. Just the same, they look, so you call them twins. (Looks on back.) Am I better than the others?"

Card III. "Well, now these two fellows are going away on a journey and they're each picking up their bags. They seem to be a little antagonistic to each other, don't they? (Yes). I thought so! Maybe that fellow has picked up that fellow's bag. Otherwise they're coming apart; they're parting."

Card II. "A couple of clowns playing bean porridge hot, bean porridge cold. How are you? (She says, addressing the figures in the card.) Well, I'll say two boys facing each other around a bowl of something."

Card VII. "Ho ho! That's kinda cute. Top could be two profiles. Of course, this part (bottom) looks like a heavy winged bat. These two, two women's faces saying, 'I know better and I know better.'"

Card IX. "That's a gay old pair; I think they're monks having a grand drink. I bet they're talking about people who have confessed to them and laughing about it."

Card IV. "I think that's Santa Claus. If I had my old girl down here (her doctor) she could tell. Walking off that way. I suppose that's no more Santa Claus than I am, if the truth were known."

Animal Movement

Animal movement (other than bears and apes in humanlike movement) is scored FM. Piotrowski considers that animal movement represents the individual's past conceptions of his role in life, conceptions which have shaped the individual's adjustment in the past, usually in early childhood, and that they are an approximate measure of vitality (37, p. 61). Klopfer suggests that they represent the influence of the most instinctive layers within the personality (27, p. 278).

Since FM responses are generally considered to reflect more primitive, instinctual drives than do M, it is to be expected, and actually turns out to be the case, that they occur more in childhood than do M responses.

In our own earlier study of the Rorschach in the first ten years of life (Ames *et al.*, 6) FM exceeds M at every age but 2 and 10 years when they are about equal.

In the normal young adult record, 1 to 2 FM are customarily expected.

Klopfer, with old subjects whose mean age was 73.5, found a mean FM of 3.2. Dörken and Kral with subjects of a mean age 76.3 found a mean FM of 2.8. Prados and Fried obtained mean FM's of 4.8, 5.0, and 5.1 with subjects in their 50's, 60's, and 70's respectively. All of these figures are somewhat higher than our own findings.

In our old people we find that FM responses occur to the following extent:

In normal older subjects, the mean FM is 2.7. It drops only slightly in our preseniles to 2.0. But in seniles it is virtually nonexistent—a mean of .3.

Comparing the number of M and FM responses we find that, as indicated, in children under 10, FM definitely exceeds M. In the normal young adult and in our normal older subjects, M generally exceeds FM. However, in presenility again as in early childhood, FM exceeds M—2.0 FM to 1.6 M. In senility the figures are .2 M, .3 FM.

TABLE 28. CLASSIFIED TABLE OF FM RESPONSES
Total Number and Percentage

		Normal (N=41)		Presenile (N=140)		Senile (N=19)	
		No.	%	No.	%	No.	%
I.	Static	33	29	67	24	0	
II.	Total extensor	67	59	181	65	6	100
	Moderate	29		54		1	
	Strong-to-violent	38		127		5	
III.	Flexor	13	12	32	11	0	
	TOTALS	113	100	280	100	6	100

Classifying FM responses as static, extensor (moderate, and strong-to-violent), and flexor we find that in every one of our three groups, strong to violent extension definitely predominates (see Table 28). This is exactly the same situation which we found in the first ten years of life when strong to violent extensor movements predominated at every age through ten years.

Comparing FM and M responses of older people from this point of view—as to what kind of movement predominates—we find FM responses considerably more active than M.

TABLE 29. UNCLASSIFIED TABLE OF ANIMAL MOVEMENT RESPONSES
Total Number of Responses

	Normal (N = 41)	Presenile (N = 140)	Senile (N = 19)
Sitting, perched	9	10	0
Standing	4	18	0
Vocalizing	5	5	0
Noses or paws together	8	11	0
Looking at, facing	1	23	0
Waiting	2	0	0
Lying down	4	0	0
Pulling something	1	2	0
Carrying, holding	5	9	0
Hanging from (or onto) something	7	14	0
Frightened	0	1	0
Bending	0	1	0
Clinging	0	1	0
Hunched up	0	3	0
Burrowing	0	1	0
Walking, stalking	5	6	0
Biting, eating, smelling	11	24	0
Going someplace	0	3	0
Sprawled, stretched out	6	7	0
Blowing bubbles	0	1	0
Being hatched or born	0	4	0
In motion	3	2	0
Floating	0	2	0
Playing	0	0	1
Motion of head	0	1	0
Social activity	0	1	0
Imitating	1	0	0
Meeting	2	0	0
Performing	1	0	0
Running	4	3	0
Jumping, springing	0	9	0
Climbing, crawling	15	53	3
Fighting	6	21	1
Flying	10	33	0
Dancing	3	2	1
Swimming	0	3	0
Waving	0	1	0
Other	4	5	0

We also, as with human movement, present a detailed unclassified table of all types of animal movement found in our three groups of subjects (Table 29). This table indicates that in our normal older subjects the six leading kinds of animal movement are, in order of decreasing frequency:

climbing, biting or eating, flying, sitting, noses or paws together, and hanging from something.

In preseniles, the six leading behaviors are, in order of decreasing frequency: climbing, flying, biting or eating, looking at, fighting, and standing. Thus though there is great similarity between the two groups, the movement responses given by the presenile subjects are slightly more active than those of the normals.

The very few animal movement responses of the seniles are climbing (three times), and fighting, dancing, and playing, once each. Thus climbing definitely predominates in every group.

Comparing the specific type of animal movement found in older people with that of young children, we find that the picture is strikingly similar. The presenile responses resemble those of slightly younger children more than do the normals as might be expected, though this distinction is not clear-cut. In children under 10, as well as in older people, climbing is definitely the outstanding kind of animal movement. Looking at or regarding is conspicuous at 4 years of age, flying from 4½ through 7, standing at 4½, 5, 6, 7, and 10 years; sitting at 8; fighting at 9; and noses or paws together at 7 years and following.

By Different Classifications

BY AGE Age trends for M are inconsistent, as are age trends for FM. There is an apparent decrease in mean m with age.

70 years	80 years	90 years
1.96 M	1.58 M	2.77 M
2.17 FM	1.84 FM	2.38 FM
.33 m	.28 m	.15 m

BY SOCIO-ECONOMIC STATUS At each level there is a consistent drop in both M and FM with decrease in socio-economic level. The trend in m is inconsistent.

A level	B level	C level
2.00 M	1.81 M	1.58 M
2.45 FM	1.81 FM	1.60 FM
.47 m	.18 m	.20 m

INSTITUTION VS. NONINSTITUTION There is a marked decrease in all three determinants from noninstitutional subjects to matched institutional subjects, though the difference in m is not significant.

Noninstitution	Institution
2.13 M	1.52 M
2.85 FM	1.62 FM
.38 m	.31 m

SEX DIFFERENCES   Sex differences in number of movement responses in the normal, presenile, and senile groups are as follows:

The men have fewer M in every group. Sex differences in FM are inconsistent. Men give more m than women in normal and presenile groups. No m responses are given by the seniles.

Inanimate Objects

The scoring symbol used to indicate inanimate objects in motion is m. This movement may be brought about by an outside force. It may take a fairly active form, as wind blowing or a top spinning, or it may be more passive, as objects crushed or broken.

As noted in our earlier Rorschach publication (6), we do not score m as strictly as does Piotrowski (37), who reserves this scoring for "inanimate movements caused by external or impersonal forces." With him, the "actual sensation of motion" is a prerequisite. Hanging objects, for instance, would not be included unless the individual reporting them experiences a sensation of pulling. However, we do not score it as loosely as does Klopfer for whom m means minor movement and includes such responses as "terrifying expressions and certain involuntary functions of human or animal bodies." We use m, as indicated, for inanimate objects in action, or being or having been acted upon.

Interpretations of the meaning of m given by different Rorschach workers vary somewhat, though none of the customary interpretations is directly contradictory to any of the others. Presence of m is generally considered to be a sign of aggressivity, repressed or overt; a sign of an inner tension, anxiety or struggle between conflicting emotions; or an indication that the subject feels his inner promptings to be hostile.

Piotrowski considers it an indicator of repression, and Loosli feels it to be a symptom of unemployed energy affording an area of inner conflict. Bochner and Halpern consider that m reflects tensions within the individual which have not been resolved or sublimated. These tensions, being unrelieved, are a constant irritant and source of frustration. All forms of m suggest the "expression of a desired attitude or way of life with the knowledge that this is unlikely ever to be attained." The nature of m, like the nature of M, can be revealing—an exploding bomb for instance having a quite different connotation from a flowing stream.

In children's records we have found very little m in the first ten years of life. Mean m scores for the different age groups ranged from a low of .05 at 2 years to a high of .82 at 7 years.

Many investigators consider that a normal adult record should contain no m responses. The only m mentioned in the literature on old people is a mean of .1 found by Klopfer in a group of subjects whose mean age was 73.5; and also a mean of .1 found by Dörken and Kral with subjects whose mean age was 76.3. This figure is lower than that obtained by us with normals and preseniles.

In our normal older population, the mean m for the group is .7. Thereafter m virtually disappears. The mean for the presenile group is only .2, and there are no m responses in our senile records.

TABLE 30. TABULATION OF m RESPONSES, INCLUDING →m
Number of Occurrences

	Normal	Presenile	Senile
Cracked, broken	1	1	1
Downward activity	6	6	0
Water, etc.	1	3	0
Other	5	3	0
Spinning, etc. in place	0	0	0
Shooting, etc.	0	0	0
Hanging	6	7	0
Explosions, tearing apart	2	2	0
Upward activity	6	6	0
Flames, smoke, etc.	3	2	0
Water, oil	1	1	0
Clouds, wind, etc.	1	3	0
Volcano erupting	1	0	0
Flying	3	0	0
Holding up	4	0	0
Animal skin stretched out, etc.	7	21	0
Miscellaneous	4	7	0

As to the quality of m responses in older people, we have tabulated all m responses and all tendencies toward m found in normal and presenile subjects (see Table 30). The categories in this table are similar to those used in our tabulation of inanimate movement responses in children, thus making possible a comparison of children's and older people's responses.

A rather clear-cut trend was found in the nature of m responses in the first ten years of life. At the earliest ages, 2 and 3 years, "cracked and broken" responses led in number. From then on, downward and upward activity predominated alternately: downward at 3½ and 4½ years; upward at 4, 5, and 5½ years; downward at 6 years; and finally upward at 7, 8, 9, and 10 years.

Quite different responses are found in old age. This is one of the several areas in which the behavior of the older people does not appear to return to that found in the child, but rather goes on to manifest its own special characteristics.

By far the outstanding m response in old people is one not found at all in our group of child subjects—an animal skin stretched out. This response occurs 7 times (17 per cent of the cases) in our normal group; 21 times (15 per cent of the cases) in preseniles. Next in frequency is an object hanging (5 times in normals, 7 times in preseniles).

Downward and upward movement occur next and about equally: downward activity 6 times in normals, 6 in preseniles; upward activity, 6 in normals, 6 in preseniles.

Many other types of inanimate motion do occur, as Table 30 shows, but too infrequently to be noteworthy. No primary inanimate movement response occurs in our senile subjects, and actually its occurrence is very infrequent in the other two groups.

COLOR

Color responses are classified in three categories: FC (form-color) interpretations, which are those inspired primarily by the form of the blot, but which include color as a consideration of the interpretation; CF (color-form) interpretations in which the determining factor is the color, but where form also contributes to the response; and C (pure color) in which the subject is influenced by the color alone.

In calculating the sum of color responses, the weighting of ½ point is assigned to FC, 1 point to CF, 1½ points to each C response.

FC interpretations are generally considered to be an index of adaptive affectivity, or at least a wish for affective adaptation. CF interpretations indicate more egocentric, suggestible, impulsive affects. C responses are considered indicative of nonadaptive, poorly integrated emotional reactions.

The stronger the color reactions, the more pronounced the emotional activity. The more these reactions fall in the CF and C categories, the less adaptive the subject is considered to be. The greater the color balance is on the FC side, the more controlled and adaptable he is or desires to be.

Color shock, considered by Rorschach as a sign of affective disturbance and as a positive sign of neurosis, does not seem to occur with any frequency in our older subjects, and therefore will not be discussed in this section.

In the subjects of the present study, except in the normal group, color responses are rather surprisingly limited. Though present in our normal group of old people to about the same extent—though not in the same proportion—as in the normal younger adult population, they fall off markedly in the preseniles, and virtually disappear in senility. The average ΣC in the normal group is 2.1; in presenility .7; in senility only .2.

In children under 10 years of age, we have found the average ΣC to range from .7 at 2 years of age to 2.9 at 7 years. It declines slightly between 7 and 10 years.

Thus at 7 years of age ΣC is equal to that found in our normal old people. At 3 years it is equal to that found in presenility. Senile adults give even fewer color responses than do 2-year-old children.

In the normal young adult population the optimal ratio of color responses has been considered about 3 FC, about 1 CF, no pure C. In young children, at every age but 2 years—when C predominates, CF responses are the leading kind of color response. FC responses become increasingly prominent as the child matures but have not by 10 years become the leading type.

Except for Prados and Fried's relatively young subjects (those in the fifties and sixties who had, respectively, FC means of 1.8 and 1.7; CF of 1.5 and 1.6; and C of .2 and .2) very little color is reported in older subjects. Klopfer, whose subjects had a mean age of 73.5, noted that color is found in only 36 per cent of his group, with means of .3FC, .7CF, and 0C. Prados and Fried's oldest subjects, aged 71 to 80, gave the following means: .2FC, .2CF, .3C. Dörken and Kral, whose subjects had a mean age of 76.3, gave color responses to the following extent: .7FC, .4CF, and .2C.

Except for Prados and Fried's younger subjects, findings of these investigators approximate our findings with our presenile group—especially in the case of Klopfer.

In our older subjects, in each of our three groups, CF responses predominate. This is as in the young child. However in normals and preseniles, FC responses come second and only in the seniles is the order of frequency CF, C, then FC—as at most of the children's ages.

A more specific analysis reveals the following comparison between children's and old people's color responses:

FC responses in children vary from a mean of .05 at 2 years to .5 at 10 years, reaching their high point of .7 at 7 years. In normal old people the mean FC is 1.0; in preseniles .3; in seniles 0. Thus normal old people show themselves more adaptable emotionally than are children at any time in the first ten years of life. The presenile mean is close to that of the

3-year-old. At no age in childhood is the mean FC as low as in senile subjects.

CF responses, the leading color responses in childhood, vary from mean .1 at 2 years to .8 at 10 years, reaching their peak of 1.5 at 6 years. The mean CF of normal old people is 1.3, approaching this 6-year-old high point. The presenile mean of .5 CF is close to that found in children in the first four years of life.

Mean C in children varies from .4 at 2 years to .3 at 10, its high point being a mean .8 at 7 years and its low point a mean of .1 at 3 years. In our older subjects, C is virtually nonexistent. Mean C in our normal old subjects is .2, in preseniles .1, in seniles also .1.

As indicated (see Table 9), in older people CF is the leading type of color response in every group. In normal and presenile subjects, FC responses come second, C responses least of any. In senile subjects, CF leads, C comes next, and FC occurs least, in fact not at all.

However, only in normal subjects do any type of color responses occur appreciably.

The number of older subjects giving any color responses in each group is as follows (see Table 10):

FC responses are given by 59 per cent of normal old subjects, 26 per cent of preseniles, no seniles. CF responses are given by 68 per cent of normals, 34 per cent of preseniles, 16 per cent of seniles. C responses are given by only 20 per cent of normals, 11 per cent of preseniles, 5 per cent of seniles.

Thus all three kinds of color responses are given by a decreasing number of subjects as senility approaches.

Color shock, as already noted, does not appear in this group of cases, unless the extreme lack of color response could be so considered.

Color naming, so prevalent in very young subjects, scarcely occurs in our older subjects. There are two instances of it in the normal old people, six in the entire presenile group, none in the seniles.

Qualitative Analysis of Color Responses

Color responses of old people were analyzed qualitatively as well as quantitatively. As in children, FC responses were so varied that no tabular summary is presented. In normal subjects, the six leading kinds of FC responses were, in order of frequency: clothing, flower, worms, butterfly or bird, leaf or tree, and food. In presenile subjects they were: flower, clothing, butterfly or bird, leaf or tree, fish or other sea-life objects. No FC responses were given by senile subjects.

Table 31 presents a qualitative analysis of the CF and C responses in normal, presenile, and senile subjects.

TABLE 31.   DISTRIBUTION OF CF AND C RESPONSES

	Normal (N = 41)	Presenile (N = 140)	Senile (N = 19)
CF RESPONSES			
Flower	21	20	1
Tree or leaf	13	15	0
Other nature responses	4	6	0
Food, fruit	3	4	0
Butterfly	3	3	0
Animals	3	1	0
Fire, explosion	3	1	0
Miscellaneous	3	0	0
Design, painting	2	3	0
Clothing, etc.	2	2	0
Anatomy and blood	2	4	2
C RESPONSES			
Blood	3	8	2
Nature (sun, sunset, sky, grass, etc.)	1	3	0
Food	1	3	0
Fire	1	2	0
Colorful language	1	0	0

The data indicate great similarity in the kinds of CF responses in normal and presenile subjects and the almost complete absence of CF of any kind in senility.

In both normal and presenile subjects, flower responses definitely lead, followed closely by tree or leaf. Nature responses in general come next, followed by food responses. Anatomy responses are relatively more frequent in seniles than in preseniles. Butterfly shares fourth place in the normal subjects and fifth place in preseniles with several other categories. Fire also shares fourth place in normal subjects but almost disappears in preseniles.

This is not too different from the situation in the first ten years of life when flower is the leading category, with butterfly, anatomy, fire, or tree assuming second place.

As to C responses, as the table shows, blood responses definitely lead with all three groups of older subjects. Other types of C responses are virtually absent in normals and seniles. In preseniles, nature and food responses tie for second place, followed by fire.

(Though the table shows more C responses occurring in presenile subjects than in normals, actually the proportions are about the same since our population contained about three times as many presenile as normal subjects.)

Pure C responses in old people are not too different from those in children, in whom we have found that paint responses predominate in the earliest years, then as the child grows older, nature, then blood, then fire. Old people do not give the paint response characteristic of the 2- and 2½-year-old, but do in their C responses closely resemble the 3- to 10-year-old.

By Different Classifications

BY AGE   Age trends are inconsistent though there is an apparent tendency for ΣC to decrease with age.

	Mean scores	
70 years	80 years	90 years
.38 FC	.37 FC	.54 FC
.69 CF	.52 CF	.54 CF
1.13 ΣC	.79 ΣC	.81 ΣC

BY SOCIO-ECONOMIC STATUS   There is a consistent drop in FC, CF, and ΣC with decrease in socio-economic level.

A level	B level	C level
.58 FC	.27 FC	.10 FC
.93 CF	.41 CF	.30 CF
1.44 ΣC	.69 ΣC	.43 ΣC

INSTITUTION VS. NONINSTITUTION   There is a decrease in all color scores in the institutional population.

Noninstitution	Institution
.65 FC	.34 FC
.77 CF	.65 CF
.15 C	.08 C
1.31 ΣC	.95 ΣC

SEX DIFFERENCES   In our three groups—normal, presenile, and senile—color trends seem quite inconsistent though ΣC is larger in females in every group. In normal subjects, males have more FC, but less CF and less C. In preseniles, males have less FC and CF but more C. In seniles, there are no FC responses in either sex, but women have more CF and more C.

SHADING

It is with regard to shading responses that our system of scoring differs most from the usual American scoring. And even here it need cause no great difficulty for the American student since the difference is in the direction of simplification.

We have followed Loosli's system (30) of scoring nearly all forms of true shading as F(C). Shading used for discernment of detail within the blot, for the play of light and shadow, for texture, for reflection, and for vista all fall in this one F(C) category. (All the foregoing are Binder's F(Fb).) In practice, Loosli also scores as F(C) the use of shading as non-dysphoric diffusion—that is when darkness or unpleasantness is not mentioned or directly implied as a feature of the diffusion: for example "clouds" or "smoke" on VII would be F(C). Responses based on a diffuse impression of the blot stemming from its darkness are scored Clob (FClob, ClobF).

Most investigators would agree that "the shading category in general appears to represent a careful, cautious, highly sensitive approach to the environment" (Hertz, 24). It is Loosli's belief that in every sort of shading response, the gray-black provokes uneasiness in the subject. His method of dealing with the anxiety-arousing situations is shown by the type of shading response that he gives. Loosli states:

All F(C), it seems to me, whether given with pleasure or not, is to be considered as a vigorous (and successful) reaction against the painful impression provoked by the gray. If the gray were not perceived as such, F(C) would be impossible. But the elaboration of that perception is quite different from the Clob; instead of abandoning himself passively to the diffuse impression, the subject takes a more active attitude. Rising above the initial reaction of displeasure, he studies the blot more closely, distinguishes shadings, and usually has success in making very fine interpretations (30, p. 48).

The F(C) responses indicate that the subject is concerned with adapting to the environment. Binder believes that shading responses given with pleasure, and given to the lighter parts of the blot indicate a "gently accommodating and delicately submissive adaptation to the environment, which is accompanied by positively toned emotions," while responses given anxiously and to darker portions show "an anxious, cautious, painfully conscientious form of adaptation to the environment" (Binder, 11). The F(C) seems to be less connected with the deeper emotional life of the subject than the Clob, representing a more "peripheral" emotional adjustment, and appears to be related to the FC, denoting an affective disposition still more sensitive than does FC.

In children's records, the mean $F(C)$ is low for the most part through the first ten years of life, though at most of these ages relatively many children do give this type of response, usually giving a single $F(C)$ response in an entire record. In fact, at 2 years of age more children use $F(C)$ than use any other single determinant except form. Gradually children use other determinants, but at every age in the first ten years, more children use $F(C)$ than use m, FC, or pure C. At every age from 4 years on, between a third and half of the children give shading responses. The mean number increases from .2 $F(C)$ per child at 2 years to 1.1 at 7, then drops to .6 at 10. The increase is not a straight-line progression; there are spurts and then slackenings in the frequency.

Analysis of all shading responses (including tendencies toward shading) found in our records of older people is presented in Table 32.

TABLE 32. DISTRIBUTION OF SHADING RESPONSES
(INCLUDING TENDENCIES TO SHADING)
(Total Numbers of Responses)

	Normal	Presenile	Senile
Diffusion: clouds, smoke	10	17	1
Light-shade: lights, shadow, reflections	7	8	0
Differentiation within blot:			
eyes, path, etc.	35	43	4
dogs within blot on IV	3	13	2
Texture:			
hard surface	5	7	0
soft surface (esp. fur)	32	45	0
fine differentiation	6	17	0
Vista	9	7	0

There are virtually no shading responses in the senile subjects, but in both normal and presenile subjects texture responses lead, soft texture, especially fur, being outstanding. Nearly as many subjects, in both groups, respond to differentiation within the blot as respond to texture.

Diffusion, as clouds and smoke, comes next; then vista, then differentiation within the blot. But all these occur very infrequently. Clob responses are almost completely absent in old age.

In analyzing shading responses in children we found a clear-cut trend with increasing age. Shading used as diffusion predominated up to 5½ years. Shading as differentiation of details within the blot predominated from 5½ to 7 and as texture from 7 to 10. Vista responses did not appear.

Thus responses of older people resemble most those of 5½- to 10-year-old children in quality. They do not characteristically resemble those of the child under 5 even though some diffusion responses do appear.

There are relatively fewer shading responses in preseniles than in normals but the qualitative distribution is very similar.

Shading responses are not mentioned in the available literature on Rorschachs in old age. The normal adult record generally contains from 2 to 3 F(C) responses. Our normal group of old people is within this range—the mean F(C) for our normal older subjects being 2.1.

This number drops sharply in presenility to .9, approximately the figure for 8-year-olds.

It again drops sharply to .4 in senility. This is close to the figure found in the first five years of life.

By Different Classifications

BY AGES   Age trends are inconsistent. Mean F(C) for the 70-year-olds is 1.44; for the 80-year-olds is .59; for the 90-year-olds, 1.38.

BY SOCIO-ECONOMIC STATUS   There is a tendency toward a decline in F(C) with decreasing socio-economic level, as follows. Mean F(C) for the A group is 1.21; for the B group 1.07; for the C group, .60.

INSTITUTION VS. NONINSTITUTION   The institutionalized group give fewer shading responses than do the matched noninstitutionalized population. Mean F(C) for the noninstitutionalized subjects is 1.33; for the institutionalized, 1.13.

SEX DIFFERENCES   In all three qualitative groups, women have more shading responses than men.

CHAPTER THIRTEEN

Content

The various systems for scoring the Rorschach—European and American—are all relatively uniform as to content categories used to classify responses.

The following categories appear in responses of the elderly subjects used in this study:

Animals (A); Animal detail (Ad); Humans (H); Human detail (Hd); Plant (Pl); Flowers; Object (obj.); Nature (Nat.); Architecture (Arch.); Food; Abstract (Abstr.); Scene; Fire; Explosion; Blood; Anatomy (Anat.); Geology (Geol.); Geography (Geog.); Mask.

In the normal adult subject, the expectation as to content is 35–50% animal responses, 10–15% human responses, and the occurrence of three to four other content categories.

In child subjects in the first ten years of life, our own findings were that as a rule approximately four different content categories were represented at each age. These changed with age as follows:

At 2 and 2½ years they were: animals, plants, objects, and humans. From 3 to 4½ years they were: animals, plants, objects, humans—humans replacing nature. From 5 through 7 years: animals, objects, nature, and humans—plants dropping out. At 8, 9, and 10 years they were: animals, objects, anatomy, and humans.

Thus the outstanding age changes were that humans became a prominent response at 3 years and following; plants dropped out as a main category after 5–6 years; anatomy came in conspicuously at 8–10 years. Animals and objects were among the leading categories at every age. Nature responses occurred conspicuously at every age even when they were not one of the four leading categories.

Content is not discussed to any extent in the literature on old people, except that nearly all investigators do give the mean A%, as follows:

159

Klopfer found a "high" A%; Dörken and Kral a mean A% of 57%; Chesrow *et al.*, an A% of 49%. Prados and Fried, with subjects in their fifties, sixties, and seventies, found increasingly high A percentages of 43%, 45%, and 49%.

Table 33 shows the mean number of times that each type of content occurs per subject in each of our three groups of subjects. As the table shows, though the number of different content categories represented narrows down considerably with increasing deterioration of the subject, there is more or less consistency in the leading categories. Animals, humans, and objects are among the four leading categories in all groups.

TABLE 33. DISTRIBUTION OF CONTENT CATEGORIES
Mean Number of Responses per Subject

	Normal	*Presenile*	*Senile*
A+Ad	11.4	8.6	4.0
H+Hd	6.0	3.0	.5
Object	3.3	1.8	.4
Plant, flower	1.8	.6	.1
Nature	.7	.3	.1
Anatomy	.5	1.4	8.4
Geol., geog.	.4	.1	—
Scene	.3	.1	—
Food	.3	.1	—
Architecture	.2	.1	—
Blood	.1	—	.1
Abstract	.1	.1	—
Fire, explosion	.1	—	—
Mask	.1	—	—
A%	46%	55%	40%
H%	24%	17%	5%
Anat%	2%	7%	47%

The behavior trends, as subjects progress toward senility, appear to be as follows:

In normal subjects the four leading categories are, in order: animals, humans, objects, and plants and flowers. In presenile subjects the four leading categories are: animals, humans, objects, and anatomy—plants and flowers falling to fifth place. In seniles the order changes in that anatomy responses lead, followed by animals, humans, and objects.

Thus animals, humans, objects are three leading categories in each group in that order. But in normal old people they are followed by plants and flowers. In preseniles, anatomy takes fourth place, instead of plants and flowers. And in seniles, anatomy rises to first place.

Table 34 indicates the four leading content categories through childhood and in our three groups of old people. As will be seen, humans are among the four leading content categories at all ages but 2 and 2½. Older people never lose the human category and therefore in this respect do not even in senility get back to the 2-year-old level.

TABLE 34. LEADING CONTENT CATEGORIES FOR
CHILDREN AND OLD PEOPLE

2–2½ years	*3–4½ years*	*5–7 years*	*8–10 years*
Animals	Animals	Animals	Animals
Plants	Plants	Objects	Objects
Objects	Objects	Nature	Anatomy
Nature	Humans	Humans	Humans

Normal	*Presenile*	*Senile*
Animals	Animals	Anatomy
Humans	Humans	Animals
Objects	Objects	Humans
Plant, flower	Anatomy	Objects

In some respects, as has been pointed out, the Rorschach response of the old person as he approaches senility tends to revert to or toward that of the very young child. That is, the response of the most deteriorated adult and the very young child are most alike.

We do not find this pattern, however, with regard to content of response. The category 'plant' for example occurs conspicuously in the youngest children and in the most intact older people. Anatomy occurs in the oldest children and in the most deteriorated older people.

At all ages, animals and objects are consistently among the leading content categories. Kinds of objects are so varied as to make analysis impractical. Animals, however, can be classified.

Table 35 presents this classification for our three groups of old people. There is, obviously, quite a shift in type of animal which occurs most con-

TABLE 35. TOTAL NUMBER OF ANIMAL RESPONSES GIVEN
BY EACH QUALITATIVE GROUP

	Normal (N = 41)	*Presenile* (N = 140)	*Senile* (N = 19)
Wild animals	90	229	12
Domestic animals	77	155	13
Butterfly, bat	76	222	15
Insects	75	113	6
Sea life and amphibians	71	122	16
Birds	48	86	1
Worms, snakes	10	7	1
Miscellaneous	74	392	12

spicuously. In normals, the four leading animal categories are, in order: wild animals, domestic animals, butterfly-bat, and insects. In preseniles: wild animals, butterfly-bat, domestic animals, and sea life. In seniles: sea life, butterfly-bat, domestic animals, and wild animals.

Thus the progression from normal to senile seems to be roughly— wild animals, domestic animals, butterfly-bat, sea life—with sea life coming in more strongly the more deteriorated the subject.

In children, the progression as the child matured was from domestic animals, to wild, to butterflies and bats, to birds. Thus no clear-cut comparison seems possible between these two trends.

By Different Classifications of Subjects

BY AGE   There is an increase in both A% and H% with age, and an apparent decrease in anatomy per cent with age, as follows:

70 years	80 years	90 years
52%A	53%A	56%A
16%H	18%H	24%H
12%anat.	10%anat.	0%anat.

BY SOCIO-ECONOMIC STATUS   There is an increase in A%, an inconsistent trend in H%, and a tendency toward increase in anatomy % with decrease in socio-economic status:

A level	B level	C level
48.84%A	54.44%A	58.47%A
17.42%H	17.58%H	17.05%H
8.16%anat.	10.83%anat.	15.79%anat.

INSTITUTION VS. NONINSTITUTION   There is a very slight decrease in A% and H% and a significant increase in anatomy, in the institutionalized group, compared with the matched noninstitutional group.

Noninstitution	Institution
48.15%A	46.73%A
17.27%H	16.08H
6.38%anat.	17.63%anat.

SEX DIFFERENCES   In our three groups, sex differences are as follows:

For A%: women have a slightly larger A% in normals and preseniles, but men definitely exceed in seniles.

For H%: men have a slightly larger H% in all three groups.

For anatomy %: slightly higher in normal women; slightly higher in presenile men; much higher in senile women.

CHAPTER FOURTEEN

Related Concepts

Best- and Least-Liked Cards

Each subject was asked routinely at the end of the test to indicate which card he liked best, and which he liked least. It was not always possible to get our senile subjects to make these judgments, but almost without exception they were obtained from the other subjects.

Table 36 indicates choices for best and worst, for male and female sub-

TABLE 36. BEST- AND LEAST-LIKED CARDS

	Card best liked			Card least liked		
	F	M	All	F	M	All
Normal	IX, X	X	X	IV	VII	IV
Presenile	X	IX, X	X	IV	VII	IV
Senile	X, IX	IX	IX, X	III, IV	—	III, IV

jects separately, for each of the three groups. As this table shows, in normal subjects, Cards IX and X are best liked by women, Card X by men. In preseniles, Cards IX and X are best liked by men and women both. In seniles, also, cards IX and X are best liked by women. Most men do not choose.

When we look back to the performance of children, we find that in the first ten years of life, Card X is definitely the outstanding card except at 2 years when Card II is preferred by both sexes.

As to least liked: In normal subjects, women dislike Card IV the most, men dislike VII. In preseniles, again, women dislike IV the most. Men dislike VII. In senile subjects, women dislike III and IV. Men do not express a preference.

Comparing the dislikes of older subjects with those of children, we note that in the first ten years of life there is considerable variety in preference, but that girls tend to dislike VI, IV, and II; boys to dislike I, VI, and

163

IV. The marked dislike of VII observed in older men is not seen in young boys.

It is interesting to conjecture as to why older women show such marked dislike for Card IV which some Rorschach workers consider to have strong connotations of sex and to suggest the male figure, while older men show such marked dislike of Card VII which some consider to have implications as to a subject's feelings for a mother or mother figure.*

Not only are these particular cards disliked, but also they are most frequently refused, as the following section on Refusals indicates.

Refusals

Though refusals are generally considered suspect when they occur in an adult record, among child subjects aged 2 to 10 years more than a fourth of the children refused at least one card at all but three age levels. The mean number of refusals per child, for this age range, gradually declines from 2.42 at 2 years to .58 at 10. The percentage of children refusing at least one card ranged from 14 at 3½ years, its low point, to 46 at 2 years, and 42 at 10.

In older people the mean number of refusals increases with increased deterioration of subjects. In our normal group, the mean number of refusals was .19; in preseniles .62; in seniles 1.42. In both normal and presenile groups, women refused slightly more cards than did men, but in the senile group there were only 2 refusals by women and 25 by men.

As to cards refused, normal women most often rejected Card VI. Normal men were varied as to card refused. Both presenile men and women refused VI and VII most. Senile women gave almost no refusals. Senile men refused Card VII the most.

Thus we arrive at the interesting discovery that Card VII is not only chosen as the most disliked card by older men, but that it is also refused the most frequently.

Timing

Though timing for individual responses was not recorded, total time of response in minutes was indicated for nearly all subjects.

Table 37 presents average time of total response in minutes for males and females separately in normal, presenile, and senile subjects, and also

---

* Some investigators believe that assigning certain special meanings to special cards is not only too stereotyped but unsubstantiated. We ourselves tend to find it helpful if not applied in too stereotyped a manner.

for the total normal, presenile, and senile populations. It also gives the range for each sex in each grouping.

As this table indicates, females in all three categories take much longer for their total response than do males. Not only is the mean time for females greater than for males, but also the range is wider for females.

TABLE 37. TIME IN MINUTES FOR TOTAL RESPONSE
Mean and Range for Each Group

	Normal		Presenile		Senile	
	Mean	Range	Mean	Range	Mean	Range
Female	23.3	11–65	15.8	6–40	16.7	3–35
Male	17.7	7–27	15.1	6–34	6.7	3–12
TOTAL	21.8	7–65	15.6	6–40	11.7	3–35

As might be expected, total time decreases steadily from normality through presenility to senility. For males and for the total group, the total timing decreases by about 50% from normality to senility. Females do not fall off quite as much in timing as do the males.

Only in senile males did the timing approximate, in brevity, that of the young subjects of our earlier study (6).

Number of Responses

There is a steady decrease in number of responses with increased deterioration of the subject. Normal subjects give a mean of 26 responses; preseniles, a mean of 16; and seniles a mean of only 13. Sex differences in every instance favor the females. In normal subjects, women give a mean of 27.33 responses, men, 22.64; in preseniles, women give a mean of 16.66 responses, men, 13.23; in seniles, women give a mean of 17.80 responses, men, 8.76.

There is, also, a consistent drop with age. Subjects in their seventies give a mean of 19.52 responses; those in their eighties, a mean of 15.27; those in their nineties, a mean of 14.98.

Furthermore, there is a consistent drop with socio-economic status. In our A group of subjects, the mean number of responses is 18.25; in the B group, 16.59; in the C group, 14.47.

Institutionalized subjects give fewer responses (mean of 17.44) than noninstitutionalized subjects (mean of 20.44).

Popular Responses

SELECTION OF POPULARS It has been found (Ames *et al.*, 6) that the responses given most commonly by groups of subjects at different ages in childhood differ to some extent from those of normal adults. Because of this, it seemed likely that old-age populars might not completely coincide with those of younger adults, and we decided to determine our scoring on the basis of frequency of occurrence of responses given by our sample.

To derive differing lists of populars for each of our three qualitative groups seemed clumsy and, because of the reduced N in the separate groups, inaccurate. A single list for the entire old age sample appeared more satisfactory. On the other hand, to derive a single list on the basis of all cases pooled would give undue importance to responses of the presenile cases, who are in the vast majority. For this reason, we tabulated frequency of each type of response for each group separately, and then weighted the three groups equally in arriving at an over-all figure.

We have followed the usual criterion that a particular response must be given by one person in six to be scored popular. In order not to overly restrict our list of populars, and unduly penalize the normal cases, we have considered popular any response given either by more than 16 per cent of the weighted total group or by more than 16 per cent of the normal group alone.

A listing of all responses which meet this criterion, with tabulation of their frequency for each of our groups, is presented in Table 38. It is of interest to compare this list with the populars for a normal young adult population, as determined by Hertz (24). In Table 38, all those forms in our list which are not found in Hertz's compilation have been italicized. Table 39 lists forms which are popular for Hertz's young adult group, but are infrequently given by our older group.

There is a quite striking consistency of patterning of frequencies for these forms. In nearly every case, our normal group has the highest intra-group agreement in naming these forms, but is rather closely followed by the presenile group. There is very little intra-group consistency of specific responses among the seniles. Although there may often be considerable similarity among the seniles in giving an anatomical interpretation to a particular blot, these interpretations are highly disparate with respect to the location and to the particular anatomic forms given. On just two forms do the seniles show greater frequency of accord than the other groups, and neither of these forms is popular for our group. One, the 'ribs' on Card VIII, is the only anatomical response achieving near-popular status; the other, 'boots' or 'shoes' on Card IV, appears to be a narrowing down of the entire human figure usually seen by our normal group.

DISTRIBUTION OF POPULAR SCORES   As follows from the above, the popular score drops as one progresses from normal to presenile to senile,

TABLE 38. POPULAR FORMS
Percentage of Each Group Giving Each
Response and Weighted Total Percentage

| Card | Location | Form | Percentages | | | |
			Normals	Preseniles	Seniles	Total
I.	W	Bird, bat, butterfly	45	50	21	39
	Center	*Human figure*[a]	22	10	16	16
II.	W	Two persons	56	30	5	30
	All black parts	Bears, dogs, animals	29	51	11	30
III.	W or W	2 persons	92	66	16	58
	Center red	*Bow*	34	19	11	21
IV.	W	Skin, fur rug	24	16	0	13
	W	*Animal, head at top*	20	23	16	20
	W	*Person*	24	6	0	10
V.	W	Bird, bat, butterfly	83	57	26	55
VI.	W or lower ⅔	Skin, fur rug	39	29	5	24
	Top projection	*Bird, butterfly*	24	8	0	11
VII.	W or top 2 tiers	Persons	44	18	0	21
	Top tier	Person's head	12	24	0	12
VIII.	Side figures	Animals	73	79	57	70
X.	Side blue	Crab, spider	59	44	16	40
	Lower green	Worm, caterpillar, snake	24	15	5	15
	Top gray	*Mice, bugs, animals*	34	31	11	25

[a] Italicized forms are those not popular for Hertz's young adult group.

TABLE 39. YOUNG ADULT POPULARS NOT POPULAR FOR OLD PEOPLE
Percentage of Each Group Giving Each
Response and Weighted Total Percentage

| Card | Location | Form | Percentages | | | |
			Normals	Preseniles	Seniles	Total
I.	W	Face	0	1	0	0
III.	Center red	Butterfly, moth	15	6	0	7
IV.	Lower sides	Boot, shoe	10	9	21	13
VIII.	Blue+gray	Tree	7	12	0	6
	Center white	Ribs	5	7	21	11
IX.	Pink	Face, head	14	8	0	7
	Pink+center	Tree (blot reversed)	0	0	0	0
	Green-brown	Animal face	5	5	0	3
X.	Lower green	Rabbit face	5	6	0	4

from a mean of 7.1P to 5.4P to 2.1P. Though all of the normals and pre-seniles, and 89 per cent of the seniles give at least a single P response, only 21 per cent of the seniles give as many as 4P, compared with 92 per cent of the normals and 83 per cent of the preseniles.

Those senile cases who do achieve as many as 4P belong entirely to that sub-group in which animal responses predominate over anatomy. The mean P% of this subgroup is 41%, in contrast to the 9%P given by the senile subgroup emphasizing anatomy.

When our subjects are considered with respect to age alone, the trends are inconsistent, and differences between the groups are very slight. Subjects in their seventies give a mean of 5.8P (34%P). Those in their eighties give a mean of 5.0 (36%P), and those in their nineties a mean of 5.6 (34%P).

Number of popular responses shows little difference among the socio-economic groups. For our upper, middle, and lower groups respectively the mean P is 5.9, 5.1, and 4.5; mean P% is 34%, 35%, and 34%.

There is, however, a difference in number of populars between our matched institutionalized and noninstitutionalized groups, the latter giving significantly more P.

CHAPTER FIFTEEN

Longitudinal Studies

Studies of human development must be considered limited in value when longitudinal data are completely lacking. Any study of the Rorschach responses of 70- or 80- or 90-year olds tells us how these subjects are responding *at this particular time in their lives.* But no single isolated Rorschach test tells us what aging as such has done to the individual subject.

If, for example, an 80-year-old gives an extremely restricted response —high F%, high A, narrow content, few responses—we cannot know for certain whether the response is restricted because the subject is 80, or because this particular subject has always given a restricted response.

Ideally we should have available for analysis yearly or bi-yearly Rorschach records on a large group of subjects. Then we would be in a position to evaluate properly the effect of aging on the Rorschach response.

Though Rorschach research on elderly subjects is relatively new, two studies of our own (1, 2) conducted since the first edition of this book was published, provide some longitudinal data. One of these studies reports findings on a group of sixty-one individuals over 70 years of age who were given a second Rorschach test after an interval of, on the average, four to five years. Age changes in scores and in type of response over the interval were reported. Also comparisons were made of the responses of the three different groups of subjects tested—two institutional groups and one group of individuals still living independently in their own homes. Subjects for this longitudinal study ranged in age from 70 to over 100. Individuals of all levels of social status and ability were included in our sample, but those of the higher levels were overly represented as compared with a total U.S. population.

Clearcut age trends were apparent for most major variables, as shown in Table 40 which gives mean scores for major variables for all groups.

TABLE 40. MEAN SCORES FOR MAJOR VARIABLES FOR ALL GROUPS
OF LONGITUDINAL SUBJECTS

		Victoria* Mean	*Masonic** Mean	*New Haven* Mean	*All* Mean	S.D.
N	1st test	26.3	17.5	27.2	21.2	(11.5)
	2nd test	24.3	13.9	18.9	17.4	(10.3)
Refusals	1st test	.1	.6	.2	.4	(.8)
	2nd test	0	1.2	.3	.7	(1.6)
W%	1st test	31.8	40.9	34.8	37.6	(23.3)
	2nd test	34.1	49.3	45.6	44.6	(24.4)
D%	1st test	52.1	48.1	49.0	49.3	(17.8)
	2nd test	51.3	41.8	48.4	45.3	(18.5)
Dd%	1st test	13.6	11.2	15.7	12.5	(14.2)
	2nd test	13.7	8.8	5.9	9.7	(13.8)
F%	1st test	57.6	65.1	65.8	63.3	(18.7)
	2nd test	61.3	67.8	63.2	65.4	(19.9)
F+%	1st test	82.9	75.8	89.4	79.7	(18.6)
	2nd test	75.5	75.4	85.1	76.8	(19.6)
M	1st test	2.4	1.7	2.0	1.9	(1.9)
	2nd test	3.4	1.6	1.6	2.1	(2.4)
FM	1st test	3.3	1.3	2.8	2.1	(1.6)
	2nd test	2.4	1.5	3.6	2.0	(2.3)
m	1st test	.4	.3	.9	.4	(.7)
	2nd test	.5	.5	.9	.5	(.8)
ΣC	1st test	2.1	1.0	1.4	1.3	(1.1)
	2nd test	1.4	.4	.2	.6	(1.1)
F(C)	1st test	2.1	.9	1.7	1.3	(1.6)
	2nd test	1.4	.6	.7	.8	(1.5)
No. content categories	1st test	6.1	3.9	5.8	4.8	(2.0)
	2nd test	5.5	3.4	4.6	4.4	(2.2)
H%	1st test	17.6	18.3	13.4	17.4	(14.0)
	2nd test	17.6	23.2	15.8	20.7	(18.6)
A%	1st test	50.6	52.9	47.3	51.4	(18.2)
	2nd test	54.6	55.9	54.7	55.4	(21.1)
No. anatomy responses	1st test	2.1	3.3	2.2	2.9	(6.6)
	2nd test	.6	1.0	.8	.9	(1.9)

*Note that the institutional group rated higher in occupational and educational level (the Victoria group) gave the clearly superior response of the two institutional groups tested.

Number: Means for all groups decreased on the second test. And 69% of subjects had a smaller N, plus 7% who had the same number.

Correct form: F+% was slightly less for all groups on Test 2, though only 42% of subjects had a smaller F+%, plus 5% who remained the same on both tests. Decrease in correct form appeared to be the most customary trend with increasing age. However, relatively intact individuals used various devices for maintaining a high F+. These included refusing difficult cards, giving a lowered N—that is perhaps giving "easy" responses but not trying for difficult ones;

hiding F— in increased movement responses; and by giving an increase of "easy" animal responses.

Color: Here we found the most clearcut and consistent age changes. For every group, mean ΣC was lower on the second than on the first test. 26% of subjects gave no color response even on the first test, 56% more had less color on Test 2 than on Test 1. This left only 13% of all subjects in whom ΣC increased, plus 5% in whom ΣC was present but equal on both tests.

Shading: Every group gave a lower mean for shading responses on the second than on the first test; and the majority of individual subjects gave either no shading on either test, or if shading was present, less on the second test.

Content: For every group there was at least a slight decrease in number of content categories on Test 2, and 56% of individual subjects gave fewer different content categories on Test 2. Mean A% was higher for every group on the second test. As to mean H%, except for the Victoria Home subjects whose H% was identical on the two tests, other groups gave a higher H% on the second test and 50% of individual subjects gave a higher H% on Test 2.

A perhaps surprising number of responses (a mean of between 3 and 4 per subject) was found to remain constant—that is the same response was given after the interval of from 4 to 5 years.

Slightly more variability was found for such variables as area, F%, and movement.

Area: All groups gave a higher W% and a lower D% on the second than on the first test, and all but the Victoria Home group also gave a lower Dd% on the second test. D% predominated over W% in all groups on both tests except for the Masonic group in whom W% predominated on Test 2.

F%: In the population as a whole and in both institutional groups, F% increased with age. However in the New Haven group it was lower on the second than on the first test.

Human movement increased on Test 2 in the Victoria Home group, fell off slightly, on the average, in the other two groups. Animal movement fell off slightly in the Victoria group and increased slightly in the other two groups. Noteworthy among human responses was the increased number of interpersonal M which came in with increased age.

Test responses for both Tests 1 and 2 for each individual were identified as "normal", "presenile", and "senile". Of our total population, 24 subjects did not change their status between Tests 1 and 2; 5 improved with age; 32 gave a somewhat less intact response on the second than on the first test.

The presence of certain kinds of response which have been identified as especially characteristic of presenility (A-list signs which are those ways of responding found earlier, in childhood, which largely disappear in maturity and then re-appear in old age; and B-list signs which to a large extent appear for the first time conspicuously in old age) was noted, and age changes in these signs were described (1).

The most common trend in old age appeared to be toward an increasing restriction of Rorschach response as subjects grow older. *Individual subjects as they grow older actually do proceed in the direction of change predicted from group averages.* Thus the majority of present subjects, with increasing age, showed decreased N, fewer content categories, fewer color responses. They showed also an increased F% and a lower F+%, and a higher A%. All of this adds up to a picture of the psyche of the aging individual as being extremely static, stereotyped and restricted. (Though the better preserved, even while following this path, may not go far toward restriction.)

A few of our better endowed old people appeared to stabilize their response, and showed with increasing age a lower F%, higher F+%, and increased M, especially interpersonal M.

Comparison of the two different institution populations showed that the group rated higher in occupational and education level, that is the "Victoria" group, gave the clearly "superior" Rorschach response when compared on the basis of actual scores, of the incidence of interpersonal M, on the incidence of A and B list items, and on the basis of stabilization or restriction of response with increased age, with the less well educated group.

As to sex differences—on Test 1, men's records were considerably more restricted than those of women in that men gave fewer N, more refusals, a higher F%. Differences remained about the same on the second test except that here men had a lower F% and more M than did women.

This first of our two longitudinal studies of age changes in the Rorschach response of elderly subjects included only two test responses each for each subject. A second study included fewer subjects but more responses for each subject. Thus a series of from three to six Rorschach tests were given at approximately two year intervals to six elderly subjects aged between 70 and 102 years of age. All subjects were among those who made up the original group whose responses were reported in the original edition of the present volume.

All subjects showed a common trend toward restriction of response.

Thus all showed a decrease of N, decrease in variety of content categories, and a decrease or eventual dropping out of color with increasing age.

Like subjects reported in earlier studies, several of the present subjects, as they grew older, showed the further restriction of an increasingly high F%, increasingly low F+%, lower M and FM, and high A%.

However, several of the subjects though inevitably showing some of the restriction characteristic of increasing age, tended to stabilize in their response and then to develop in a manner which may be specially characteristic of well preserved old age. For these individuals, F% decreased, F+% increased, and both human and animal movement, especially interpersonal movement, came in strongly. Nearly half of these interpersonal movement responses fell into one of two categories: two people either arguing, disputing, competing, not liking what the other is doing. Or engaged in friendly activity or discussion. FM to some extent reflected the same kinds of involvement.

Or, the response might expand in the direction of abstract or idealized response. Increase in F+ was brought about by decreased N, increased refusal, increased A%, or by hiding poor form in M scores.

Special kinds of responses characteristic of presenility (A-list items or ways of responding common in childhood, absent in maturity, reappearing in old age; and B-list items or ways of responding absent or infrequent in childhood and normal adulthood but appearing in old age) were conspicuous in present subjects. B-list items predominated in the better-preserved subjects.

Slight sex differences were observed in that females gave more responses, higher D%, more M, more F(C), more color. Males had a higher mean W% higher F+%, more m, higher mean H%, higher P.

Though the majority of responses were neutral in emotional tone, unpleasant concepts became relatively conspicuous in relation to pleasant concepts as subjects grew older.

The predominant trend with increasing age was toward restriction, but on occasion a later test was a little "better" than an earlier test. Though the customary trend was toward presenility and eventual senility, many long-lived individuals did not appear to proceed far along this path.

As with subjects in our longitudinal study of a larger number of elderly individuals for whom only two tests apiece were available, results of this particular study showed that repeated tests on aging individuals confirm the behavior changes implied by findings in the original edition of

TABLE 41. MRS. A.E., 77-88 YEARS.

Variable	77 years	79 years	82 years	84 years	86 years*	88 years
Number	38	14	16	11	13	14
Area	18%W 55%D 27%Dd	57%W 35%D 8%Dd	50%W 44%D 6%Dd	72%W 27%D	46%W 54%D	57%W 43%D
F% F+%	52%F 92%F+	29%F 100%F+	37%F 100%F+	27%F 100%F+	15%F 100%F+	7%F 100%F+
Movement	7M 4FM 1m	6M 3FM 1 tend m	6M 3FM 1 tend m	3M 3FM	5M 2FM	5M 6FM 1 tend m
F(C)	1 F(C)	0 F(C)	1 tend F(C)	1 F(C)	1 tend F(C)	0 F(C)
Color	2FC 1CF 2C	–	–	–	0FC 1CF 1C	–
A% H%	34%A 37%H	29%A 50%H	44%A 44%H	45%A 45%H	30%A 46%H	57%A 43%H
No. content categories	7	5	3	3	4	2
No. A-list signs	4	4	3	3	3	3
No. B-list signs	8	11	8	8	5	8
Classification	Normal to intact presenile	Intact presenile	Intact presenile	Intact presenile	Intact presenile	Intact presenile
P%	21%	28%	31%	36%	38%	36%

* At 86 years, Mrs. E., about three months before Test 5, suffered a severe cerebral hemorrhage and was not expected to recover. However, she did recover and fully resumed her normal life and activities.

this book. That is, the individual aging subject, as he matures, does actually change in ways predicted by our original findings established in non-longitudinal research.

To give the full flavor of the kinds of change in response which we may expect in well preserved old age we give here some detail information on one of our best documented cases, that of Mrs. A.E. for whom Rorschach protocols are available at 77, 79, 83, 84, 86 and 88 years of age, covering an 11 year period. Like other subjects in her group, Mrs. E. lived independently in her own home. She was both physically and mentally active—doing her own shopping and gardening, looking after her own financial affairs, and for recreation reading widely and enjoying double acrostic puzzles. She was also considerably interested in politics and until she was 84 worked at the polls as an election clerk.

Her health was excellent except for a severe cerebral hemorrhage when she was 86, just before her fifth examination. She was hospitalized and not expected to live, but after two months in a hospital and nursing home, returned home. Her 86-year-old Rorschach was given while she was still convalescing, and *her Rorschach response anticipated her return to virtually her full earlier degree of activity.*

This full series, covering more than 10 years of this well-endowed and resilient subject's later life, gives us the clearest view which we have yet obtained of the changes which take place in the human psyche with increasing age. As will be seen, a marked change, in the direction of simplification, took place between 77 and 79 years of age. Thus N was reduced from 38 to 14; area shifted from primarily detailed to primarily global; F% was sharply reduced; F+% was increased; and relative amount of M was sharply increased. Color dropped out. A% was reduced.

The Rorschach picture then remained remarkably stable from 79 through 86 years (see Table 41), with N ranging only from 11 to 16, area remaining predominantly global, M and FM numerous, no color, low F (range from 15 per cent to 37 per cent), 100%F+ at every age, and content categories ranging from 3 to 5. Then, following her illness at 86 years of age, the response became slightly more vigorous and in many ways more like that seen at 77 years than at any other time thereafter. N increased; response became again predominantly detailed; A% was lowered and color came in.

And then again at 88 years, as earlier at 79 years and following, a slight deterioration set in with W% increasing and again predominating, color dropping out, A% again increasing, and number of content categories reduced. However it should be noted that even at 88 years of age this subject gave 14 responses, 100%F+, 5M, 6 FM, and 53%H.

Mrs. E., like even the best-preserved elderly subjects, showed some inevitable signs of increased restriction as she grew older. Thus over a ten year period from 77 to 88 years her N decreased from 38 to 14, color dropped out, A% increased from 36% to 57%, number of content categories decreased from 7 to 2. However, there was much in her series of responses which showed stabilization and expansion. Thus F% decreased from 52 per cent to 7 per cent; F+% increased from 92 per cent to 100 per cent. Relative number of both human and animal movements increased ... H% increased from 37 per cent to 53 per cent. Classification changed between 77 and 79 years from normal-intact presenile to intact presenile, and remained at intact presenile for the next nine years. At every age, B-list signs far exceeded A-list signs, though both were strongly present at every age.

Most characteristic of her response at all ages was the consistently high H% (37 per cent to 53 per cent), and the predominance of strongly interpersonal human movement responses (57, 85, 66, 100, 80 and 100 per cent of M at successive ages were interpersonal). The nature of this engagement varied from extremely pleasureable: (III) "Two very self-satisfied gentlemen going for a walk and having a grand time," to extremely hostile: (II) "Oh I see real animosity in the faces of these two people."

An example of the changing interpersonal interest is shown in her responses, at successive age levels, to *Card IX:*

77 years

	CR			
	→			Another bright one. Certainly looks like witches
W₃	M	(H)		having a grand old time. Throwing things back and forth and catching, though I don't see what it would be. Up in the tops of trees. Pink is a bright flowerbed down there underneath the trees. (*Inquiry:* The witches in the trees and the color below made me think of flowers.)
	m			Ropes on a vessel. (*Inquiry:* Green claws into
	→			pink? The number of different ropes which
Dd	F±	obj.	O	hang on a vessel.)
Dd	F(C)	Hd	O	< Profile, face, eye, nose, beard and head-

dress. What I thought was an eye is a button on the side of the hat. (? Unusual small detail, dependent on shading, where green and orange mix.)

D F+ Hd   Pink man with moustache or side whiskers, his eye is quite plain and his collar. Looks like Taft. The elder Taft. Kind of stout.

79 years

D M H   That's a gay old pair. I think they're monks having a grand drink. I bet they're talking about people who have confessed to them and laughing about it. (? Orange as monks, holding up glasses and drinking.)

D F+ H   Can you see two things, disconnected, in one picture? Two men, moustaches, heads too big and eyes, good-natured. Too bad their bodies are so small. (*Inquiry:* usual figures in pink.)

82 years

D K H   Well I should think by the fingernails they must be Chinese; isn't it the Chinese who have such long fingernails? They're pointing with their thumbs (top proj.) each to his own fingernails, each thinks that he has the longest. (Else?)

Dbl F+ obj.   Two little statues there (white in gray) but I don't seem to see why they're there. (Don't have to.) Oh I thought it had to be all together.

84 years

W₂ M H O   Well I think they're wise men having a discussion. With many gestures. I suppose wise men would be amiable but they don't look too amiable. I have an idea they're having a contest.

They climbed up there to see how long they could stay in that precarious position.

86 years

D	CF	plant	Well that's undoubtedly two witches. *Couldn't be anything else!* Their tall pointed caps. And very angry. (?) Well by the way they're gesticulating . . . I can't tell what they're holding. They're evidently up in the trees, aren't they? (?) They're green and the way people are perched in them. Grass and flowers beneath—looks vertical but probably horizontal.
D	C	plant	

88 years

D	M	(H)	Well those are two witches aren't they? I can't tell anything except they're having a heated dispute. All I can see. (?) Oh yes. Oh! Some why some . . . animals . . . fierce with their mouths open. (Usual deer). Perhaps the people are just discussing their danger and trying to point out to each other something they may do to escape. (This whole card could be scored DW M H.)
D	FM	A	

More than any other subject, perhaps, Mrs. E.'s responses reflect what we may assume to be her own personal problems and attitudes. Thus consider the response to Card X, on Test 4:

Ha ha! Two small animals (top gray). I don't know what kind. They've climbed up those very steep places (pink). And now they're afraid. And they're hanging on for their very lives. Talking it over and each says, 'How long can we hold out, and *who* will come to our aid?'

Or, the response to Card V on the 5th test:

Bird with very heavy wings. He seems to be trying to rise from the ground but it's very difficult. He's getting one wing up a little higher than the other already. But he's a very patient bird and he'll keep on trying.

Or again, response to Card IV on the 6th test:

Well this is apparently a terrible ogre. He's in a tearing rage. He's lifting up his voice to heaven and complaining about the way people are treating him and each other. He's sure the whole world is coming to destruction and he's utterly helpless to prevent.

Mrs. E.'s chief interest and concern as reflected in her series of Rorschach protocols thus appears to be interpersonal relations—how individuals (rather than Mankind as in the case of one of our other subjects, Mrs. J.) get along. Extremes both of excellent rapport and of great enmity and competition were expressed—in the earliest years friendly relations predominated; but in the later years, hostility.

Thus, in summary, as the normal individual matures, ordinarily his emotional and intellectual responsiveness and potential become increasingly mature, complex, and well-structured. As measured by the Rorschach, the number of responses given increases, fewer cards are refused, form becomes increasingly accurate, content more varied, responses to both emotional and environmentally structured drives fuller. Human movement responses come to exceed animal movement, color responses become better modulated, shading responses increase in number, there is less perseveration, and animal percentage decreases. This normal adult response continues to be given in many individuals well past the seventieth year of life.

But as the individual goes on to presenility and eventual senility, the direction of development appears to reverse itself. As the subject deteriorates, his response to the Rorschach becomes increasingly like that of a younger and younger person, and the changes described above are reversed.

However, in spite of the increased restriction characteristic of old age, and the similarity of response in some respects from one subject to another, the Rorschach appears even in extreme old age to be a useful tool for revealing personality characteristics as well as developmental level.

CHAPTER SIXTEEN

Supplementary Tests

As we outlined the several classifications or behavior levels of Rorschach performance described in this volume, it was suggested to us by Dr. Kurt Pelz, Medical Director of the Masonic Home and Hospital in Wallingford, where much of the testing was carried out, that such classifications might be of substantial practical as well as theoretical value.

It became evident as our work progressed that many individuals who seem superficially to be relatively intact, might actually, on examination, prove to be functioning at a rather deteriorated level. In fact it is quite generally admitted by those in charge of the care of elderly patients that the manner and verbalization of such patients or even their performance on some standard intelligence tests is often a misleading clue as to their actual level of competence.

Thus a careful evaluation of elderly patients could be of great value to hospital and other personnel in helping them care for and work with such individuals.

Though Dr. Pelz agreed with our own opinion that the Rorschach was a delicate and effective test to be used for such evaluation, it seemed to him that its use required a more specialized training than that to be found in most of those actually dealing with the elderly. At his suggestion we explored the possibility of using other psychological tests in order to determine the behavior or functional level of elderly individuals (34, 35).

We offered the hypothesis that in spite of seeming intactness of function (good vocabulary, reasonably good memory, apparent social adequacy) many elderly individuals are functioning, at least in some respects, at what amounts to a preschool level. For this reason, preschool and early school-age tests may yield a better indication of level of performance and possible function than will the type of adult intelligence and performance test customarily given.

We also suggested that in order to measure effectively decreasing levels of effective performance in elderly subjects, the clinician needs to understand the successive steps in the breakdown of any given function, which may well turn out to be the reverse of the development of that function in childhood.

Subjects used to test this hypothesis were 100 guests of the Masonic Home and Hospital in Wallingford, Connecticut, who were each given a Rorschach test. From this initial group of 100 subjects, 60 were chosen for further testing, not on the basis of degree of psychological intactness or deterioration but merely on the grounds of willingness, cooperativeness and enough visual and auditory acuity to make further participation in the study practical. On the basis of the Rorschach, 7 subjects were classified as normal; 24 as intact presenile; 16 as medium presenile; 13 as deteriorated. Mean ages for these several groups were 76.3 years; 80.5 years; 83.3 years; and 84.2 years, though total range in age of individual subjects was from 69 to 92. In all, 35 female and 25 male subjects were tested. All levels of social status and ability were represented in comparison with the total U.S. population.

After subjects were classified as normal, intact presenile, medium presenile or deteriorated on the basis of Rorschach performance, they were given a battery of tests chosen from those customarily used at the Gesell Institute (24a). Mean scores for each group of subjects on each of these individual tests supported the classification made on the basis of the Rorschach alone and indicated clearcut differences between the different groups as follows:

a. Gesell Cubes: Subjects are presented with ten one inch cubes and are asked to build a tower of ten, and then to copy a 3 cube bridge, a 5 cube gate, and a set of 10 cube steps. Normal and intact subjects succeeded on all cube tests; medium preseniles failed only steps; deteriorated subjects failed all but the tower of ten.

b. Gesell Copy Forms: Subjects are asked to copy a circle, cross, square, triangle, divided rectangle and diamond. Only with deteriorated subjects were there any conspicuous failures. Deteriorated subjects failed on diamond and divided rectangle.

c. Gesell Incomplete Man: Subjects are asked to complete the incomplete figure of a man. This test appeared to give good clues as to level of intactness, but considerations were largely qualitative and required some

TABLE 42. DEVELOPMENTAL LEVEL OF RESPONSE TO SUPPLEMENTARY TESTS

	Normal N = 7 Mean age 76.3 years	*Intact presenile* N = 24 Mean age 80.5 years	*Medium presenile* N = 16 Mean age 83.3 years	*Deteriorated presenile* N = 13 Mean age 84.2 years
Rorschach:	15N (6 years) 1.9 M:1.1sC (10 years) 64%F/85%F+ (8 years) 4.4 content categories (4½ yrs.)	13N (3½ years) 1.4M:6sC (7 years) 58%F/85%F+ (7 years) 3.6 content categories (3 yrs.)	11N (2½ years) .9M:7sC (6 years) 64%F/5½ years) 3.6 content categories (3 yrs.)	7N (2 years) .5M:.5sC(3½ years) 76%F/60%F+ (3 years) 1.9 content categories (2 yrs.)
Gesell Cubes:	Tower Bridge (5 yrs.+) Gate Steps	Tower Bridge (5 yrs.+) Gate Steps	Tower Bridge (4 yrs.) Gate	Tower (3 yrs.)
Gesell Forms:	Circle Cross Square (6 yrs.+) Triangle Rectangle Diamond	Circle Cross Square (6 yrs.+) Triangle Rectangle Diamond	Circle Cross Square (6 yrs.+) Triangle Rectangle Diamond	Circle Cross Square (5 yrs.) Triangle
Visual I:	All (5 yrs.+)	11 (5 yrs.)	10.2 (5 yrs.–)	4.7 (Unscoreable)
Visual III:	8.9 (8-9 yrs.)	2.8 (5 yrs.–)	.8 (Unscoreable)	.9 (Unscoreable)
Incomplete Man:	8.6 parts (6 yrs.) Arm, finger, leg, foot, ears, neck	7.8 parts (4½ years) Arm, finger, leg, hair, eyes, ear, neck	6.3 parts (4 years) Arm, finger, leg, hair, ear, neck	3.4 parts (3 years) leg, arm, and one other
Lowenfeld Mosaic:	Patterned designs Objects (6 yrs.+)	Patterned designs (5 yrs.)	Non-patterned designs, patterned designs (4 yrs.)	Non-patterned designs (3 yrs.)
Range of Behavior Ages:	4½-10 years	3-7 years	2½-6 years	2-5 years

skill in test interpretation. However, normal subjects did add all necessary parts; deteriorated subjects added usually on a very poor quality arm, leg and some one other part.

d. Monroe Visual I: Subjects are asked to match simple forms. Only deteriorated subjects showed any conspicuous inability to deal with this test effectively. Thus failure on Visual I supported failure on bridge, gate and steps, and on copy rectangle and diamond in classifying any given subject as deteriorated.

e. Monroe Visual III: This test requires the copy of forms from memory. Here the breakdown of response came much earlier, making this a more sensitive test for our purposes. Though normal subjects had a mean score of 8.9 (which equals the performance of the average 8-9 year old child), intact preseniles gave a mean score of only 2.8, and medium preseniles a score of only .8. Thus any failure to make a substantially successful response to this test appeared to indicate that the subject was presenile at best.

f. Lowenfeld Mosaic Test: Subject is presented with a box of multi-colored plastic pieces and is requested to "make something" with them on a sheet of white paper. Here any response which must be classified as non-representational without pattern indicates that subject was presenile or below. Successful construction of even the simplest object indicates intact personality or better.

g. WISC: This is the standard Wechsler Intelligence Test. Scores for tests in this battery could not be converted into either I.Q. scores or developmental ratings for elderly subjects, but there was a gradual and consistent falling off of scores with increasing deterioration of subjects. However, the WISC appeared to be less useful than other tests in the battery for determining level of functioning in elderly subjects. *Vocabulary and information tests appeared to be particularly deceptive in indicating a spuriously high level of performance.*

A tabular summary of these findings is given in Table 42.

These findings appeared to confirm the suggested hypothesis that preschool and school age tests do permit an adequate differential diagnosis between groups of normal, intact presenile, medium presenile and deteriorated subjects.

Range of behavior ages on individual tests in this battery was for our subjects: 4½ to 10 years for normal subjects; 3-7 years for intact preseniles; 2½-6 years for medium preseniles; and 2-5 years for deteriorated subjects.

Degree of intactness appeared to be largely independent of chronological age of subjects. Clearcut sex differences were not evident.

Of the tests used, some appeared to be more effective than others in actual practice.* Gesell Copy Forms had the disadvantage that all subjects except the most deteriorated were able to pass all subtests successfully. The Gesell Cubes were somewhat more discriminating—medium presenile subjects failed the steps, and deteriorated subjects failed all but the tower. However, there is a somewhat difficult test to give especially for subjects with poor manual control or for the bedridden. Visual I is responded to successfully by all but the most deteriorated. The Lowenfeld Mosaic appears to be nicely discriminating but even more so than with the cubes, it can be awkward to give to the elderly subject because of its many pieces.

This leaves, of the supplementary tests tried, only Visual III and the Gesell Incomplete Man test which are both relatively easy to give and nicely discriminating.

Research currently under way is still searching for tests to make up a battery which can supplement or take the place of the Rorschach. We are at present trying a battery which consists, besides the Rorschach, of: Gesell Incomplete Man, Visual III, the Bender Gestalt, and a test now being researched by Dr. Frances L. Ilg of the Gesell Institute called the Tree Test. In taking this test, the subject is given an 8 x 11 piece of white paper and a box of colored crayons and is asked to draw a tree.

This current research has a threefold approach. First, to see how well accepted each of these tests may be by elderly people; second to work out norms for these supplementary tests for subjects grouped on the basis of their Rorschach response as normal adult, various levels of presenile, or senile; third to determine the extent to which any given individual is consistent or inconsistent in his or her test performance.

That is, of any given group of subjects, does the one who gives the most intact or most effective Rorschach response also perform most effectively on the various other tests. Or is the response inconsistent? Preliminary results suggest that though in general there is fairly good consistency, in some instances performance on some one test (and this seems particularly true of Visual III) may be quite out of line with response on other tests in the battery.

---

* The Gerontological Apperception Test (Wolk, 51) was tried but did not seem useful for our purposes.

Our ultimate aim is to find a battery of tests for old people which will be easy to give, well accepted, and highly discriminative of different levels of intactness. It may also be possible to show that certain kinds of intactness (perhaps memory for forms as shown on Visual III) *may* be deceptive in suggesting an intactness of function not borne out on other tests.

There is much yet to be discovered about the functioning of the elderly individual.

CHAPTER SEVENTEEN

Summary

This study aims to determine whether or not patterned age changes take place in the human organism in old age as they do in childhood. The tool used in this investigation is the well-known Rorschach inkblot test.

Accepting the fact that an individual's physiological age is not necessarily the same as his chronological age, we inquire whether or not there may also be a discrepancy between psychological and chronological age, and if so, whether this discrepancy can be demonstrated by means of the Rorschach test.

If patterned changes as reflected in the Rorschach response do take place with increasing age, it should be possible to determine how well or how poorly any given individual is "holding up" psychically as he advances in age.

Literature on Rorschach responses of older subjects is limited. Rorschach himself found in old people a coarctated *erlebnistypus*, inaccurately seen forms, and a highly restricted thought content. Except for Klopfer's 1946 study, subsequent reports do not go too far beyond these initial suggestions of Rorschach. Gilbert in her 1952 survey summarizes Rorschach studies to date as revealing a reduced and shallow emotional responsiveness, efficiency, and productivity, little inner conflict, reduced control of emotional demands, constriction, impotence, and a recurrence of the primitive manifestations of childhood.

However, most investigators have found marked individual differences among older subjects—some elderly persons showing extremely well integrated and healthy personalities.

The present study discusses Rorschach responses of 200 subjects between the ages of 70 and 100. This group included 102 70-year-olds, 85 80-year-olds, and 13 90-year-olds. There were 140 women and 60 men. The basic criteria for selecting subjects were that they should be over 70, and reasonably healthy, active, and alert. Sixty-seven of our subjects were living in their own homes; 133 were in institutions for the aged.

Following the usual approach in developmental research, we divided our subjects into three groups: the 70-year-olds, 80-year-olds, and 90-year-olds. We expected to find marked differences between these three groups. But on analysis of our data, consistent differences between the three groups were not forthcoming. Some subjects in each age bracket responded virtually as would the normal adult. And some of the subjects in the very oldest age bracket responded more adequately than those in the younger.

Obviously, this classification by age was not, as at younger age levels, the most fruitful one. Thus we sought a different basis of grouping of cases. Our clinical impression of this material which we had gathered was that some real and measurable change was going on in the Rorschach response in old age. We wished to find an ordering of cases which would highlight these changes.

Though many of our subjects gave a response virtually indistinguishable from that of the normal adult, many others did not. Of these others, some gave a response which seemed patently indicative of senility. But there were many others—the majority of the cases, in fact—who were not yet senile but whose responses clearly differed from the normal. *And all differed more or less in the same way.* We identified this intermediate group of individuals whose responses—superficially normal—had nevertheless departed from strict normality, as *preseniles.* By no means yet senile, they nevertheless could no longer be considered normal; and we therefore decided on this intermediate category.

We thus arrived at the following classifications: normal, presenile, and senile. Subjects were classed as normal when the total patterning of their records was about as rich and varied as one would expect to find in any normal adult, when scoring approximated that of the normal, and when they showed few or none of what we had identified as the "qualitative" signs of presenility.

Subjects were considered senile when the animal percentage or the anatomy percentage, or both together, was close to 100% and when at the same time there was a very high F% and a very low F+%. Complete or virtually complete static perseveration was also a basis for classification in the senile group.

The presenile subjects, by no means yet senile, nevertheless differed significantly in their responses from the normal individual. Quantitative scoring changes were chiefly high A% and F%, low F+%, low number of responses, and little variety of content.

In addition, the presenile and senile subjects differed from the normals by showing very specific qualitative signs of aging. On the basis of clinical impressions gained in administering the test and "working through" the records, we proposed a large number of such signs. These we listed as two separate groups, as follows: Group A included those kinds of response which do occur in children's records but not in those of normal adults. Group B included those responses which to our knowledge do not occur commonly in children or in normal adults. Frequency of occurrence for each item was tabulated for each of our tentatively identified groups. Items originally proposed which did not allow discrimination between our three qualitative groups were discarded. A- and B-list signs which did turn out to be useful in discriminating presenile from normal and senile subjects are given below:

A-list signs, present also in childhood

A1.	Thinks own concept is right or wrong
A2.	F% over 50%
A3.	A% over 50%
A4.	Static perseveration
A5.	Dynamic perseveration
A6.	"Perfect" this or that
A7.	Low F+% (80% or under)
A8.	Tells own experiences
A9.	Gives qualifying remarks
A11.	M+FM=0
A14.	Interest in other people's responses
A16.	Qualifying verbs
A17.	Initial exclamations
A20.	Low R (15 or fewer)
A21.	Narrow content (4 or less)
A22.	Refusals
A25.	Looks on back of card
A29.	Would know what it was if it were a picture of something else
A31.	Suggests changes in the blot to make it fit his concept
A32.	Says "too hard" or that he doesn't know, and then responds adequately
A33.	Bird or animal response to men on III

B-list signs, not seen conspicuously in childhood or normal adulthood

B1.	One or more anatomy responses
B2.	Concept of "oughtness"
B3.	Abstraction or idealistic concept
B4.	Quarreling

B5.   H% of 15% or more
B6.   New shading response, inside upper side portions of IV
B7.   Complains that brains aren't good, is stupid or dumb, etc.
B8.   Describes people as "having a high old time"
B9. $\Sigma C = 0$
B10.   Thinks there is a trick
B11.   Soothing, reasonable tone of voice
B12.   Quotes a nursery rhyme
B13.   Mention of midline
B14.   Mention of symmetry
B15.   Laughter
B16.   Questions card, addressing it directly
B17.   Compliments card
B18.   "Yeah," confirming comment to own response
B19.   Discusses own response with self, pro and con
B20.   Questions Ex. as to what "answer" is
B23.   F− on populars
B24.   Physical excuses for poor performance (headache, pain in arm, etc.)
B26.   Implies without naming
B29.   Split up middle
B30.   Indefinite use of "something," "somebody"
B31.   Dogs on VIII watching other part of blot, or other new connections
        between parts of blot
B32.   Thinks Ex. knows the answer
B33.   Legs off on Card III
B36.   Perseveration of remarks
B37.   "Of course"
B40.   Subject says he is "stuck"
B42.   Stories about bats
B43.   One blot connected with another
B44.   General expressions of insecurity or inadequacy
B45.   Prefaces responses with "Well"

Having proposed this basis for classification of subjects, we divided our records into the three groups. The major task of the remainder of our study was essentially one of describing the resulting groups: detailing the central tendencies and variabilities of behavior in each, and assessing the degree to which they hang together as clinically valid clusters.

Responses of Normal Subjects

The response of the normal elderly person is virtually within normal limits except for area. The mean figures for area are 36%W, 47%D,

15%Dd. This is slightly more W and Dd and slightly less D than is expected in the normal adult. With respect to area perhaps more than any other determinant, our group of normal old people diverges from the younger normal population. Furthermore, it is in this respect that our own three groups (normal, presenile, senile) are least clearly distinguished one from the other.

Number of responses—mean of 25.9—falls well within the normal range. Mean F% is 50%, just at the top limit for any presumably normal distribution. Mean F+% is 93%, well within normal limits.

The mean experience balance is 3.3M : 2.1ΣC. Movement response scores are virtually identical to those expected in the normal adult—3:3M, 2.7FM, .7m. On the color side there is a slight but not excessive divergence from the expected normal adult scores: 1FC, 1.3CF, .2C. Thus CF slightly exceeds rather than amounting to only half FC as prescribed. Pure C is almost nonexistent.

Shading also is within normal limits, the average being 2.1. The average Clob response is only .1.

As to content, the mean A% of 46% is within normal limits. H% is 24%—higher than the normal expectation.

Three to four other content categories usually appear—objects, plant or flower, nature and anatomy being the leading content categories, in that order.

Of the so-called "qualitative signs" which identify presenility, only a few appear in one quarter or more of the normal older group.

The picture of the "normal" 70- to 100-year-old individual which we obtain from the Rorschach is thus not unlike that of the theoretical "average" normal adult. Furthermore, individual records vary in character from one to the other about as much as would occur in a group of normal young adults. The stereotypy of behavior which is so conspicuous in senility and even in presenility and which makes records often strikingly similar one to the other, does not appear in the "normal" subjects.

The general behavior of our normal older subjects during the test situation, i.e., his response to the examiner and to the test, does not differ consistently or conspicuously from that of any normal adult.

Responses of Presenile Subjects

Presenile responses are distinctive and clearly distinguishable from either normal or senile responses with respect to most determinants. For example—the presenile subject gives on the average 16 responses, far less than does the normal subject. As to area, the averages are 43%W, 47%D, 9%Dd. Thus there are more global and fewer small detail responses than in the normal.

As to accurate form, presenile subjects hold up very well, with an average F+% of 81%. The proportion of responses determined by form alone is only 64%. Both of these figures change markedly in senility.

Animal movement now exceeds human with averages of 1.6M, 2.0FM and .3m. CF exceeds FC with averages of .3FC, .5CF, 1C. All of these figures are considerably less than in the normal record. ΣC, for example, is only .7 in preseniles as against 2.1 in normals. The basic equation in presenility is 1.6 M : .7ΣC.

The number of shading responses falls off in presenility to an average of .9. Clob responses have virtually disappeared.

The number of different content categories is less here than in normality: anatomy, object, and plant or flower being the only conspicuous responses besides human and animal. Animal percentage reaches its high point in this group (average of 55%). H% has dropped to 17%.

However, the presenile response is set off even more distinctively by the qualitative items which characterize it. These signs may be listed as follows:

A-list signs, present also in childhood

1. Items which especially distinguish the presenile subjects and occur less in normal and senile old people:
   Think that there is a "right" and "wrong" answer (68 per cent)
   Interject long personal anecdotes (52 per cent)
   Much qualification of response (56 per cent)
   Animal movement equals or exceeds human (64 per cent)
   Seeing a bird or animal instead of human on III (25 per cent)
   Giving delaying initial responses (60 per cent)
   Saying "I don't know" and then making an adequate response (60 per cent)
   Dynamic perseveration (2 per cent)
   Interest in how "well" others have done (16 per cent)
   Describing thing seen as a "perfect" one of its kind (18 per cent)
   Comments that cards get "harder and harder" or "worse and worse" (30 per cent)

2. Items which do not reach their peak in presenility, but occur increasingly as the response deteriorates:
   Static perseveration (in 32 per cent of presenile subjects)
   One or more refusals (36 per cent)
   Looking on the back of the card (12 per cent)
   Could identify picture if it were of something else (3 per cent)

B-list signs, not seen conspicuously in childhood or normal adulthood

1. Items which especially distinguish the presenile response:
   General vagueness of expression (61 per cent of preseniles)
   Argue and discuss with selves about accuracy of response (59 per cent)
   Ask suspiciously what test is for, even though this has been explained fully
       (21 per cent)
   Express belief that Examiner knows the answer (24 per cent)
   Perseveration of remarks (61 per cent)
   Express sense of oughtness (16 per cent)
   Excessive laughter (25 per cent)
   Make excuse for not giving better response: brains not good (44 per cent);
       physical excuse (15 per cent)
   Give concept by implication only (16 per cent)
   Describe things as "split up the middle" (25 per cent)
   Speak in gentle, pleased, reasonable tone of voice (25 per cent)
2. Behavior strong in presenility but even stronger in senility:
   Compliment the cards or the artist (10 per cent)
   Confirm own response by saying "Eah!" (19 per cent)
   Express insecurity as to ability to give a good response (62 per cent)
   Comment that subject is stuck or stumped (17 per cent)
   Gives F− response on populars (20 per cent)
   ΣC of 0 (47 per cent)
   Emphasis of midline (30 per cent)
   Anatomy response (mean of 1.4)
   Tells stories about bats (7 per cent), compliments own performance (6 per
       cent), addresses questions directly to the cards (5 per cent)
   Thinks there is a "trick" to the whole thing (3 per cent)

The presenile individual, as revealed by his Rorschach response, may thus be described in the following terms. He is uncertain of self and suspicious of others. There is a vagueness of both perception and expression.

There are several paradoxes in behavior. Thus though suspicious and egocentric, the presenile individual shows considerable interest in other people. Though vague and uncertain much of the time, he is at other times extremely certain, definite, and rigid.

There is marked restriction of both intellectual and emotional processes, though most are more introversive than extratensive. Though given to easy laughter and ready tears, these individuals do not seem to be the victims of or even the possessors of strong emotions.

Subjects in this group are both garrulous and repetitive. They have high standards for themselves and also for others. But there is a general lack of attention to small detail—even though conversationally they may be extremely detailed.

The responses of some of our presenile women subjects reflect a positive and constructive idealism.

Among presenile subjects no clear-cut gradient of performance (such as found in senile subjects) has been identified. However, we may roughly identify three groups: 1) those who are only slightly removed from the normal performance; 2) those who show clearly many or all of the qualitative and quantitative signs of presenility; and 3) those who give evidence of rapidly approaching senility. It is the second group with which we have been chiefly concerned in our descriptions of presenility.

This group of individuals, during the Rorschach examination, behaves not too differently from the normal older person, except for a little more than "normal" suspiciousness, hesitancy, worry about adequacy of response. Most establish a good friendly rapport with the Examiner, understand the instructions, and seem interested in the test. Emotional attitude toward the cards varies, as in any group of normal adults.

Behavior diverges from that of the normal individual in the following ways:

The presenile individual tends to "take over" the situation more than does the normal. He responds as he wishes, not as the Examiner has suggested, and often diverges from the task at hand to stories of his own experiences. He expects full responsiveness from the Examiner to such anecdotes, and to anything else that he may say or do.

Even after the test is completed it is often extremely difficult for the Examiner to break away. The purpose of the Examiner's visit is quickly forgotten, and the presenile subject settles down for a good long chat—or actually, monologue. There is much reference to present or former illness, family and former friends, approaching demise, to the Deity and his plans, and the purpose of life.

There is little interest expressed in the Examiner's evaluation of the test response. This seems quickly forgotten once it is completed in spite of often considerable worry during the test as to how "well" the subject was doing.

Responses of Senile Subjects

The Rorschach response of the senile subject is restricted, stereotyped, and often very similar in many characteristics from one subject to another. It is quite easy to identify both quantatively and qualitatively. It differs clearly both from the normal and the presenile response.

The response of the senile individual is outstandingly characterized by the predominance of animal responses, anatomy responses, or both. The statistical averages of 40% animal and 47% anatomy which we have found in senile subjects do not present a true picture of the individual response. Though a few senile subjects give a fairly equal number of these two types of content, in the majority either animal or anatomy predominates, and sometimes reaches 100%.

We have, therefore, divided our senile subjects into two main groups: those in which animal responses markedly predominate (mean of 69%) and those in which anatomy markedly predominates (mean of 83%).

The subjects who give predominantly animal responses give only a few responses (mean of 8.7), nearly 50 per cent of which are whole responses. Accurate form is considerably higher in this group than in the other, even though below normal limits (71%F+). P% is high—41%.

Subjects who give chiefly anatomy responses give many more responses (mean 17.8), have a slightly lower percentage of whole responses, and a much lower F+% (32%F+). P% is lower—9%.

All senile records do not appear to reflect the same degree of intactness of individual personality. Within the category of "senility" we have identified a rather clear-cut gradient of performance, from what appear to us to be the most intact to the most deteriorated individuals.

In the best-preserved subjects, animal responses predominate, and there are few if any anatomy responses.

Slightly less intact individuals give a combination of animal and anatomy.

The most deteriorated, however, give exclusively or almost exclusively anatomy responses. And even here there are gradations. The most intact within this group give a good variety of parts of the body, and the form is fairly good. Subjects who are holding up less well do not have a good variety of anatomy responses and tend to perseverate on just one or two body parts, as "skeleton," "spine," or "heart."

Even more deteriorated subjects give almost exclusively sex parts.

Next come those who see the blots as pictures of themselves.

Last and most deteriorated among our nonpsychotic seniles, are those who name either the organs of excretion or excretory products.

The senile group as a whole is distinguished by its extremely poor form (50%F+), and its very high F% (92%). The *Erlebnistype* is extremely restricted—.2M : .1ΣC. Movement responses are on the average .2M, .3FM, 0m. Color responses are 0FC, .2CF, .1C.

Thus the response of the senile subject tends to be ambi-equal as well as coarctated. This suggests that there is little motivation from within and very limited adaptability. Though the amount of emotionality expressed is slight, such as it is it is primarily egocentric. The picture of the senile psyche which is thus revealed is one of marked restriction and intellectual underproductivity and impoverishment.

There are no Clob responses, and shading responses average only .4.

The mean number of responses is only 13. Other than animal and anatomy responses, the only type of content which occurs conspicuously is human. Animal, anatomy, and human responses together reach a mean of 92% and very few other types of content appear.

As to area, this group is not too different from our other groups of old people. W% is 46%, D% is 45%, Dd% is 9%. The D response is thus about the same as in normal and presenile subjects, but W% has, obviously, increased at the expense of Dd.

Qualitative characteristics of the senile response are identified among the so-called A- and B-list items. Though outstandingly characteristic of the presenile protocol, a number of these behaviors are also found in the senile record, as follows:

A-list signs, seen earlier in childhood

Static perseveration occurs in 47 per cent of subjects
Looking on back of card (36 per cent of subjects)
Refusal of at least one blot (42 per cent)
Belief that there is a right and wrong "answer" (47 per cent)
Interruption of response with personal anecdote (42 per cent)
Comment that it is "too hard" followed by good response (36 per cent)
Could identify picture if it were of something else (5 per cent)

B-list signs, not characteristically seen in childhood or normal adulthood

Anatomy responses occur in 63 per cent of records
ΣC of 0 (in 78 per cent of records)
Emphasize midline (63 per cent)
Give F− on usual populars (53 per cent)
Complain of being stuck or stumped (36 per cent)
Verbalize feelings of uncertainty or inadequacy (58 per cent)
Initial "stalling" comments (53 per cent)
Compliment blot (10 per cent)
Worry that "brains" are not good (31 per cent)
Excessive laughter (15 per cent)
Perseverative comments (53 per cent)

We thus see in the response to the Rorschach a picture of the senile subject as extremely restricted, underproductive, stereotyped, intellectually and emotionally impoverished, uncritical and insecure. Little interested in those about him, his interest gradually narrows down to a complete concern with self and bodily parts and functions, particularly a concern with the eliminative functions. Subjects seem to be much more influenced by their own inner drives than by environmental stimuli. There appears to be rather marked emotional lability but no deep emotion.

However, while the actual examination was taking place, subjects were for the most part friendly and cooperative, even though not always too coherent in what they said or in their understanding of the Examiner. Cooperation was often better than in presenility, due to less suspiciousness of the Examiner and her intentions. Conversation was often garrulous and repetitive. Frequently the Examiner found it difficult to break into their verbalization in order to give the test.

Old Age and Childhood

Normal, presenile, and senile—each of these three classifications appears to stand out as a patterned entity so far as the Rorschach response of the elderly human is concerned.

The changes which commonly take place as any subject proceeds from normal through presenile to senile responses may be characterized as in many respects exactly the reverse of the changes which take place from childhood to adulthood.

As the normal individual matures, ordinarily his emotional and intellectual responsiveness and potential become increasingly "mature," complex, and well structured. As measured by the Rorschach, the number of responses given increases, fewer cards are refused, form becomes increasingly accurate, content becomes more varied, responses to both emotional and environmentally structured drives become fuller, human movement responses come to exceed animal movement, color responses become more modulated, shading responses increase in number, there is less perseveration, and animal percentage decreases.

This normal adult response continues to be given in many individuals well past the seventieth year of life. Those of our older subjects who respond in this way have been classified as "normal."

But as the individual goes on into presenility and eventually senility, the direction of development appears to reverse itself. As the subject deteriorates, his response to the Rorschach becomes increasingly like that of a younger and younger person.

Thus, the "normal" older person gives responses which, except for color, are quantitatively like those of any normal adult. Color responses, both in proportion and type, are like those of the 7-year-old child.

The presenile response (in addition to containing many qualitative kinds of response—A-list signs—which are like the responses of childhood) resembles quantitatively those of 2- to 10-year-old children, with color responses being the most immature, at a 3-year level.

In senility, the response has gone even farther back into childhood, being similar in most respects to that of the 2- to 3-year-old child, with color responses at about a 2-year level.

The graphically minded reader may thus think of many of the customary Rorschach determinants as occurring along a bell-shaped curve—increasing up through normal adulthood and normal old age, and then falling away in presenility, and decreasing even further in senility. (Or as a horizontal diamond which reaches its widest point at adulthood, with its narrow ends representing early childhood, and presenility and senility.)

Specifically:

1. The average number of responses given increases to adulthood, and then in presenility and senility decreases.
2. Content becomes more and then again, less varied.
3. Perseveration disappears, rendering the response more varied in maturity, and then comes in again with presenility and senility.
4. F% decreases, then again increases.
5. F+% increases, then decreases.
6. Number of shading responses increases, then decreases.
7. Global responses decrease in proportion to detail responses, then increase.
8. Dd% increases, then decreases.
9. Number of both M and FM increases, then decreases.
10. Gradually M exceeds FM; but in presenility and senility, FM responses once again exceed M.
11. Color responses in presenility and senility once again resemble those of childhood both in number and kind.
12. The number of cards responded to without refusal increases, then again decreases.
13. A% is high in childhood, low in normal adulthood, then high again in presenility and senility.

Other Classifications

AGE AND SOCIO-ECONOMIC STATUS   Subjects on whom the necessary information was available were classified into one of three broad groupings of socio-economic level, based on education and occupation. These subjects constituted 91.5 per cent of our total sample. Jointly with socio-economic status (SES) the same subjects were classified on age level by decades: 70, 80, or 90 years. This two-way classification provided a means of checking the consistency of apparent general trends in score with either age or SES. That is, a trend in score from upper to middle to lower SE level at age 70 should appear also at ages 80 and 90, if it is to be considered consistent.

The resulting trends in scores by age are for the most part highly inconsistent. Apparent trends from one age to the next at one SE level are often reversed at another. Only in the case of two variables do any regular trends appear: R tends to decrease and H% to increase with increasing age.

Socio-economic status, unlike age, shows a consistent relationship to a number of scores. With decreasing SE level, there is a tendency for the following scores to decrease: R, W%, F+%, M, FM, F(C), FC, CF, and ΣC. Conversely, D% and F% tend to increase with decreasing SE level.

This gives a clearly patterned picture of decreasing responsiveness, productivity, intellectual power, and emotional enlivenment of behavior with decreasing SES, and of increasing restriction in all areas of the personality.

INSTITUTIONAL STATUS   It appeared important to hold constant the factors of age, sex, and SES, when assessing differences between individuals who reside in institutions and those who do not. Therefore, we dealt with pairs of cases, one member of each pair in, and one not in an institution, and both members of the same sex, in the same broad SE group, and within five years of each other in age. We could pair 96 cases, of our total 200, in this way.

Mean differences of the paired scores were tested by the *t* test. It was found that the noninstitutionalized cases, on the average, had significantly higher scores on F+%, M, FM, FC, and P, while the institutionalized cases were significantly higher in F% and Anat%. The groups were highly similar in area scores.

Thus it appears that even when they are equated on age, sex, and on the genetic and life-history variables reflected in SES, significant differences still appear between the institutional and noninstitutional groups. The noninstitutionalized group is represented, on the average, as being more "intact"; showing greater productivity, perceptual clarity, creativity and modulation of emotion, less restriction and self-concern. Whether the deterioration of the institutionalized group is the result or the cause of institutionalization it is not possible to say. Probably both factors operate to determine the resulting differences between the groups.

SEX DIFFERENCES   Significance of differences between the sexes on Rorschach scores could be evaluated not only by the *t* test, but by consistency of direction of the difference in scores in all three of our qualitative groups.

Females achieved consistently higher scores on the following variables: R, D%, Dd, F, M, F(C), CF, ΣC, and Anat%. Males were consistently higher in: W%, F+%, m, H%, and P%. This difference in scoring portrays a tendency for women to be more responsive (garrulous?), more practical and detailed, more creative and emotional, more sensitive in emotional life, and more concerned with their own selves and their own bodily processes. Men, on the other hand, take a more intellectual, generalizing approach, are more accurate and more conforming in perception, and, surprisingly, show greater interest in others.

Differences between men and women are most sharply marked in senility, where most men fall into the "predominantly animal" response group, while most women fall into the "predominantly anatomy" response group. Men at this level give a much briefer, simpler, more accurate, stereotyped, and banal type of response, while women give a longer, more detailed response, with predominantly inaccurate form perception, and tremendous concern about anatomical parts.

Area, Determinants, Content

The mean number of responses diminishes from an average of 26 in normal older subjects, to 16 in preseniles and 13 in seniles.

Area varies less with increasing deterioration of subject than does any other category of response. Detail responses exceed or at least equal global responses in all three groups of subjects. Dd responses diminish. Thus mean W% is in the three groups, respectively, 36%, 43% and 46%. D% is 47%, 47% and 45%. Dd is 15%, 9%, and 8%.

The number of responses determined by *form* alone nearly doubles, from a mean of 50% in normal older people, to 64% in preseniles, and 92% in seniles. F+% goes in exactly the opposite direction and at about the same rate, being 93% in normal subjects, 81% in preseniles, and 50% in seniles.

M exceeds *FM* in normals only and decreases steadily and sharply, from a mean of 3.3 in normals to 1.6 in preseniles and .2 in seniles. FM also decreases, from 2.7 in normals, 2.0 in preseniles, and .3 in seniles. Likewise, m decreases, in fact, disappears. It averages .7 in normals, .2 in preseniles, 0 in seniles.

Shading responses, like other determinants, decrease with increasing deterioration of subject, being 2.1 in normals, .9 in preseniles, .4 in seniles.

ΣC decreases from 2.1 in normals to .7 in preseniles, to .2 in seniles. In every group, CF exceeds FC and C. Thus normal subjects give on the average, 1.0FC, 1.3CF, and .2C responses. Preseniles give .3FC, .5CF, and .1C. Seniles give 0FC, .2CF and .1C.

A% goes from 46% in normals to 55% in preseniles. It decreases to 40% in seniles because of the high number of anatomy responses in that group even though many senile subjects give nothing but animal responses.

H% decreases—from 24% to 17% to 5%. Anatomy increases from 2% to 7% to 47%.

Percentage of Subjects Giving Each Kind of Response

As to the percentage of subjects giving each kind of response, findings are as follows:

Area: 100 per cent of normals, 96 per cent of preseniles, and 95 per cent of seniles give at least some global responses. Detail responses are given by 98 per cent of normals and preseniles, and by 89 per cent of seniles. Sixty-three per cent of normals, 45 per cent of preseniles, and 32 per cent of seniles give Dd.

Form responses are given by all subjects in all three groups.

Movement: human movement responses are given by 98 per cent of normal subjects, 84 per cent of preseniles, but only 16 per cent of seniles. Animal movement is given by 80 per cent of normals, 78 per cent of preseniles, but only 21 per cent of seniles. Inanimate movement is given by 49 per cent of normals, 19 per cent of preseniles, no seniles.

Shading responses are given by 78 per cent of normal subjects, 52 per cent of preseniles, but only 21 per cent of seniles.

FClob responses are given by 7 per cent of normals, 1 per cent of preseniles, no seniles.

Color: FC responses are given by 59 per cent of normal subjects, 26 per cent of preseniles, no seniles. CF are given by 68 per cent of normals, 34 per cent of preseniles, 16 per cent of seniles. C are given by 20 per cent of normals, 11 per cent of preseniles, 5 per cent of seniles.

Content: animal responses are given by 100 per cent of normals and preseniles, and 89 per cent of seniles. Human responses are given by 98 per cent of normals, 89 per cent of preseniles, 42 per cent of seniles.

Related Factors

As to *card preferences*, "normal" women subjects prefer Cards IX and X, "normal" men prefer X. Presenile men and women, and senile women prefer IX and X. Senile men subjects do not express a preference. In children, Card X was an outstanding favorite.

Normal and presenile women dislike Card IV most; normal and presenile men dislike VII. Senile women dislike Cards III and IV; men do not express a preference. Girls in the first ten years of life disliked most Cards VI, IV and II; boys disliked I, VI, and IV.

When we consider *refusals*, we find that the mean number of refusals increases with increased deterioration of subjects. In our normal group the mean number of refusals is .19; in the preseniles, .62; in seniles, 1.4. Women refuse slightly more cards than do men.

Normal older women refuse Card VI most often; men vary. Both men and women in the presenile group refuse VI and VII most often. Senile women give almost no refusals; men refuse Card VII most.

As to *duration of total response*, females in all three categories take much longer for their total response than do males. Both the mean times and the range are greater in females. Total time of response decreases steadily from normality through presenility to senility. For males and for the total group, total timing decreases by about 50 per cent from normality to senility.

There is a steady decrease in number of responses with increased deterioration of subject. Normal subjects give a mean of 26 responses; preseniles a mean of 16; seniles a mean of only 13. There is also a fairly consistent drop with age, and with decreasing socio-economic status. Institutionalized give fewer responses than do noninstitutionalized subjects.

All three groups give approximately one third popular responses.

Sixty-one individuals over 70 years of age were given a second Rorschach test after an interval of, on the average, four to five years; six other elderly subjects, a series of from three to six Rorschach tests apiece.

Analysis of longitudinal data indicated that individual subjects as they grow older actually do proceed in the direction of change predicted from group changes. Thus the majority of subjects, with increasing age, showed decreased N, fewer content categories, fewer color responses. They showed also an increased F% and lower F+%, and a high A%. All of this added up to a picture of the psyche of the aging individual as being extremely static, stereotyped and restricted. (Though the better preserved, even when following this path, may not go far toward restriction.) A few of the better endowed old people appeared to stabilize their response and showed, with increasing age, a lower F%, high F+%, and increased M, especially interpersonal M.

Subjects rated higher in occupational and educational level gave the clearly superior Rorschach response. Sex differences were somewhat irregular.

Slight variations from the customary deterioration with age may be expected in repeat Rorschachs, but when they constitute improvement, such changes are usually small. That is, a subject might in a year's time "fail" considerably, but any "improvement" tends to be slight. And regardless of quantitative changes which occur on retest, each subject tended to give a retest response which was unquestionably his own and not to be confused with that of any other subject. There was a slight suggestion that the rate of change may slow down in extreme old age, since our very oldest subjects changed the least on retesting.

Supplementary Tests

It becomes increasingly evident that many individuals who seem superficially to be relatively intact prove on examination to be functioning at a rather deteriorated level. An appreciation of the actual level of functioning can aid hospital and other personnel in their treatment of elderly persons. We see the Rorschach as an ideal test for evaluating the behavior level of the elderly individual. It is, however, possible to use other psychological or behavior tests to supplement or supplant the Rorschach.

Though the Gesell Cube test, Gesell Copy Forms, Gesell Incomplete Man, Monroe Visual I and Visual III, and Lowenfeld Mosaic Test can each in its own way evaluate behavior level, the Gesell Incomplete Man and Visual III seem easiest to give and most effective in making this evaluation. Current research is being carried out which uses these two tests plus the Bender Gestalt and the Tree Test. Our aim is to find a battery of tests for old people which will be easy to give, well accepted, and highly discriminative of different levels of intactness.

In brief summary, we have found the Rorschach test to be an apparently extremely sensitive instrument in determining the extent to which people over 70 resemble younger adults in their intellectual and emotional functioning, and the extent to which their responses show changes related to aging.

It appears that many individuals in their seventies, eighties, or even nineties give a Rorschach response very similar to that of the young, active adult. Other individuals even in their seventies show already the deteriorating effects of aging.

Age alone does not, therefore, appear to be a safe criterion for determining the intactness of psychological functioning of the older person. By means of the Rorschach we have been able to classify a research population of older people as follows: normal subjects who regardless of age are responding as would a vigorous, healthy younger person; presenile subjects who are beginning to show signs of psychological aging; senile subjects who show very marked signs of aging.

APPENDIX

Clinical Summary Tables

The following three summary tables, Tables 43, 44, and 45, are presented for the special use of the clinician. These tables assemble the formal Rorschach scoring data for the groups we have classified as normal, presenile, and senile. The material is taken from Tables 9 and 10, but is organized here for each qualitative group, rather than by scores for all three groups. Thus each table gives a composite picture of the "typical" normal, presenile, and senile scoring, together with an indication of the variability found among normals, preseniles, and seniles.

Together with Tables 6, 7, and 8, our A- and B-lists, they should prove useful in classification of individual old people's protocols.

TABLE 43. SUMMARY TABLE: NORMALS

Means, Percentiles, and Percentages of Cases Using One or More of Each Scoring Category

Score	Percentage using 1+	Mean score	1	25	50	75	99
R	100	25.9	9	17.5	21.5	32.0	61
W		7.4					
WS	12	.1					
ΣW	100	7.6	2	5.9	7.9	10.1	14
W%		36%	4%	25%	33%	45%	100%
D	98	12.8	0	8.5	11.3	16.5	33
D%		47%	0	41%	50%	56%	69%
Dd	63	4.5	0	0	1.5	5.0	29
S	41	.9	0	0	.8	1.7	5
Do	24	.3	0	0	.6	1.0	3
ΣDd	71	5.7	0	.9	2.1	7.0	31
Dd%		15%	0	1%	10%	26%	52%
F	100	14.4	2	8.0	10.0	15.0	46
F%		50%	22%	39%	51%	63%	78%
F+%		93%	74%	90%	94%	99%	100%
M	98	3.3	0	1.8	3.6	4.3	9
FM	80	2.7	0	.9	2.8	3.8	8
m	49	.7	0	0	.1	.8	3
F(C)	78	2.1	0	.7	1.7	3.0	8
FClob	7	.1					
ClobF	2	—					
FC'	7	.1					
C'F	0	0					
FC	59	1.0	0	.1	.8	1.4	5
CF	68	1.3	0	.4	1.1	1.9	6
C	20	.2	0	0	0	.4	2
ΣC	85	2.1	0	.4	1.9	2.9	8.5
A+(A)	98	8.7					
Ad+(Ad)	71	2.8					
A+Ad	100	11.4	1%	7.0	10.0	13.3	39
A%		46%	1%	36%	45%	55%	77%
H+(H)	98	3.5					
Hd+(Hd)	59	2.5					
H+Hd	98	6.0	0	3.1	4.6	7.0	29
H%		24%	0	15%	23%	30%	55%
Anat	44	.5					
Blood	10	.1					
Anat+Blood	49	.6					
Anat%		2%					
Object	85	3.3					
Plant, flower	68	1.8					
Nature	41	.7					
Geol., geog.	17	.4					
Scene	22	.3					
Arch	15	.2					
Map	2	—					
Mask	7	.1					
Design	5	—					
Abstract	10	.1					
Fire, explos.	10	.1					
Food	24	.3					
P	100	7.1	3	5.8	7.0	9.0	10
P%		33%	5%	17%	31%	46%	72%

Means, Percentiles, and Percentages of Cases Using One or More of Each Scoring Category

Score	Percentage using 1+	Mean score	Percentiles 1	25	50	75	99
R	96	15.7	4	11.9	14.7	19.0	42
W	96	6.0					
WS	9	.1	0				
ΣW	99	6.2	0	4.7	6.1	7.6	12
W%		43%	0	28%	39%	57%	100%
D	98	8.0	0	5.2	8.3	9.3	26
D%		47%	0	36%	47%	58%	85%
Dd	45	1.2	0	0	.2	1.5	17
S	17	.2	0	0	0	0	2
Do	22	.4	0	0	0	.4	6
ΣDd	50	1.8	0	0	.6	2.6	18
Dd%		9%	0	1%	6%	16%	45%
F	100	10.3	1	6.9	8.8	12.6	32
F%		64%	18%	54%	65%	75%	100%
F+%		81%	31%	73%	85%	93%	100%
M	84	1.6	0	.6	1.4	2.4	7
FM	78	2.0	0	.6	1.5	3.2	7
m	19	.3	0	0	0	.4	3
F(C)	52	.9	0	0	.6	1.4	9
FClob	1	—					
ClobF	1	—					

Score	Percentage using 1+	Mean score	Percentiles 1	25	50	75	99
FC'	1	—					
C'F	1	—					
FC	26	.3	0	0	0	.5	3
CF	34	.5	0	0	.3	.9	3
C	11	.1	0	0	0	0	2
ΣC	54	.7	0	0	.3	1.3	4
A+(A)	100	7.3					
Ad+(Ad)	65	1.4					
A+Ad	100	8.6	1	5.3	8.1	11.0	29
A%		55%	10%	42%	55%	68%	100%
H+(H)	80	2.0					
Hd+(Hd)	49	1.0					
H+Hd	89	3.0	0	.9	2.3	4.1	11
H%		17%	0	8%	17%	23%	65%
Anat	38	1.4					
Blood	4	—					
Anat+Blood	40	1.4	0	0	.8	1.9	28
Anat%		7%	0	0	2%	9%	74%
Object	72	1.8					
Plant, flower	39	.6					
Nature	20	.3					
Geol., geog.	6	.1					
Scene	10	.1					
Arch	7	.1					
Map	3	—					
Design, embl.	5	.1					
Abstr	3	.1					
Fire, explos.	4	—					
Food	8	.1					
Painting	1	—					
P	100	5.4	0	4.0	5.7	7.2	10
P%		37%	0	28%	34%	48%	71%

TABLE 45. Summary Table: Seniles

Means, Percentiles, and Percentages of Cases Using One or More of Each Scoring Category

Score	Percentage using 1+	Mean score	1	25	50	75	99
R	95	13.5	3	10.0	13.0	14.0	34
W	95	5.0					
WS	0	0					
ΣW	95	5.0	0	2.1	4.8	8.0	10
W%		46%	0	24%	46%	68%	100%
D	89	6.8	0	2.5	5.5	8.3	20
D%		45%	0	31%	54%	59%	85%
Dd	32	1.2	0	0	.4	1.0	11
S	16	.3	0	0	0	0	3
Do	26	.3	0	0	0	.5	1
ΣDd	63	1.8	0	0	.9	1.4	15
Dd%		8%			6%	14%	32%
F	100	12.5	2	10.0	13.0	14.0	31
F%		92%	50%	85%	95%	100%	100%
F+%		50%	0%	32%	50%	73%	100%
M	16	.2					
FM	21	.3					
m	0	0					
F(C)	21	.4					
FClob	0	0					
ClobF	0	0					

Score	Percentage using 1+	Mean score	1	25	50	75	99
FC'	0	0					
C'F	0	0					
FC	0	0					
CF	16	.2					
C	5	.1					
ΣC	16	.2					
A+(A)	84	3.5					
Ad+(Ad)	21	.5					
A+Ad	89	4.0	0	2.0	4.0	6.5	13
A%		40%	0	10%	45%	70%	100%
H+(H)	21	.3					
Hd+(Hd)	21	.2					
H+Hd	42	.5	0	0	0	.9	3
H%		5%	0	0	0	8.5	25
Anat	63	8.4					
Blood	5	.1					
Anat+Blood	63	8.4	0	0	9.0	12.0	33
Anat%		47%	0	0	55%	86%	100%
Object	31	.4					
Flower, plant	5	.1					
Nature	5	.1					
P	89	2.1	0	1.0	1.5	3.0	6
P%		20%	0	7%	10%	33%	100%

References

1. AMES, L. B. Age changes in the Rorschach responses of a group of elderly individuals. *J. Genet. Psychol.*, 1960, *97*, 257-285.
2. AMES, L. B. Age changes in the Rorschach responses of individual elderly subjects. *J. Genet. Psychol.*, 1960, *97*, 287-315.
3. AMES, L. B. Changes in the experience-balance score on the Rorschach at different ages in the life span. *J. Genet. Psychol.*, 1965, *106*, 279-286.
4. AMES, L. B. Changes in the Rorschach response throughout the human life span. *Genet. Psychol. Monog.*, 1966, *74*, 89-125.
5. AMES, L. B. Projecting the future of a projective technique. *J. Proj. Tech. and Person. Assess.*, 1970, *34*, 359-365.
6. AMES, L. B., LEARNED, J., MÉTRAUX, R. W., WALKER, R. N. *Child Rorschach Responses.* Rev. Ed., New York: Brunner/Mazel, 1973.
7. AMES, L. B., MÉTRAUX, R. W., WALKER, R. N. *Adolescent Rorschach Responses.* Rev. ed. New York: Brunner/Mazel, 1971.
8. ANDERSON, J. E. (Ed.) *Psychological Aspects of Aging.* Washington, D.C.: American Psychological Association, 1957.
9. BANHAM, K. M. Senescence and the emotions: A genetic study. *J. Genet. Psychol.*, 1951, *78*, 175-183.
10. BECK, S. J. *Rorschach's Test: Vol. I. Basic Processes.* New York: Grune & Stratton, 1944.
11. BINDER, H. *Die Helldunkeldeutungen im psychodiagnostischen Experiment von Rorschach.* Zurich: Art. Institut Orell Fussli, 1932 (English summary in *Rorschach Res. Exch.*, 1937, *2*, 37-42.
12. BOCHNER, R., and HALPERN, F. *The Clinical Application of the Rorschach Test.* New York: Grune & Stratton, 1945.
13. CARLSON, A. J., and STEIGLITZ, E. J. "Physiological changes in aging." Chapter in Tibbits, C. (Ed.) *Social Contributions by the Aging.* Ann. Am. Acad. Pol. Sci., 1952, *279*, 18-31.
14. CAVAN, R. S., BURGESS, E. W., HAVIGHURST, R. J., and GOLDHAMMER, H. *Personal Adjustment in Old Age.* Chicago: Science Research Associates, 1949.
15. CHESROW, E. J., WOSIKA, P. H., and REINITZ, A. H. A psychometric evaluation of aged white males. *Geriatrics*, 1949, *4*, 169-177.
16. DÖRKEN, H., and KRAL, V. A. Psychological investigation of senile dementia. *Geriatrics*, 1951, *6*, 151-163.
17. DUBLIN, L. I., LOTKA, A. J., and SPIEGELMAN, I. *Length of Life.* Rev. ed. New York: Ronald Press, 1949.
18. GESELL, A., and AMATRUDA, C. S. *Developmental Diagnosis.* New York: Hoeber, 1941.
19. GESELL, A., ILG, F. L., and AMES, L. B. (In collaboration with J. Learned). *Infant and Child in the Culture of Today.* (Rev. ed.) New York: Harper and Row, 1973.
20. GESELL, A., and ILG, F. L. (In collaboration with L. B. Ames and G. E. Bullis) *The Child from Five to Ten.* New York: Harper, 1946.

21. GESELL, A., ILG, F. L., and AMES, L. B. *Youth: The Years from Ten to Sixteen.* New York: Harper & Brothers, 1956.

22. GILBERT, J. G. *Understanding Old Age.* New York: Ronald Press, 1952.

23. GROSSMAN, C., WARSHAWSKY, F., and HERTZ, M. Rorschach studies of personality characteristics of a group of institutionalized old people. *J. Gerontol.,* vol. 6, Supplement to No. 3, Program of the Second International Gerontological Congress, Sept. 9-14, 1951, p. 97.

24. HERTZ, M. R. *Frequency Tables to Be Used in Scoring the Rorschach Ink-blot Test.* Ed. 3. Cleveland, Ohio: Western Reserve University, 1951.

24a. ILG, F. L., and AMES, L. B. *School Readiness: Behavior Tests Used at the Gesell Institute.* New York: Harper & Row, 1972 (Revised edition).

25. Institute of Child Welfare, University of Minnesota. *The Minnesota Scale for Paternal Occupations.* Minneapolis, Minnesota. Pamphlet (no date).

26. KAPLAN, O. J. "Psychological aspects of aging." Chapter in Tibbits, C. (Ed.) *Social Contribution by the Aging. Ann. Am. Acad. Pol. Sci.,* 1952, *279,* 32-42.

27. KLOPFER, B., and KELLEY, D. M. *The Rorschach Technique.* Yonkers: World Book Co., 1942.

28. KLOPFER, W. G. Personality patterns of old age. *Rorschach Res. Exch.,* 1946, *10,* 145-166.

29. KUHLEN, R. G., and KEIL, C. The Rorschach test performance of 100 elderly males. *J. Gerontol.,* vol. 6, Supplement to No. 3, Program of the Second International Gerontological Congress, Sept. 9-14, 1951, p. 115.

30. LOOSLI-USTERI, M. *Le Diagnostic Individual Chez L'Enfant au Moyen du Test de Rorschach.* Paris: Hermann & Cie, 1948.

31. MILES, C. C., and MILES, W. R. The correlation of intelligence scores and chronological age from early to late maturity. *Am. J. Psychol.,* 1932, *44,* 44-78.

32. MILES, W. R. Age in human society. Chapter 15 in Murchison, C. (Ed.) *A Handbook of Social Psychology.* Worcester, Mass.: Clark University Press, 1935, pp. 592-682.

33. OWENS, W. A. Unpublished study, reported in 1950 Newsletter, Division of Maturity and Old Age, American Psychological Association.

34. PELZ, K., PIKE, F., and AMES, L. B. Measurement of psychologic function in geriatric patients. *J. Amer. Geriatrics Soc.,* 1961, ix, *9,* 740-754.

35. PELZ, K., PIKE, F., and AMES, L. B. A proposed battery of childhood tests for discriminating between different levels of intactness of function in elderly subjects. *J. Genet. Psychol.,* 1962, *100,* 23-40.

36. PIOTROWSKI, Z. A. On the Rorschach method and its application in organic disturbances of the central nervous system. *Rorschach Res. Exch.,* 1936, *1,* 23-40.

37. PIOTROWSKI, Z. A. *A Rorschach Compendium,* Rev. ed. 3. State Hospital Press, Utica, New York, 1950.

38. POLLAK, O., with the assistance of Glen Heathers. *Social Adjustment in Old Age: A Research Planning Report.* New York: Social Science Research Council, Bull. *58,* 1948.

39. PRADOS, M., and FRIED, E. Personality structure of the older age groups. *J. Clin. Psychol.,* 1947, *3,* 113-120.

40. RORSCHACH, H. *Psychodiagnostik Methodik und Ergebnisse eines Wahrnemungsdiagnostischen Experiments,* ed. 4, Berne, Switzerland: Huber, 1941. English edition, Berne, Switzerland, 1942.

41. SCHAFER, R. Rorschach imagery in aging patients. (Announcement of a study). *J. Projec. Tech.,* 1952, *16,* 385, 386.

42. SHOCK, N. W. "Gerontology" (later maturity). Pages 353-370 of *Annual Review of Psychology,* vol. II, 1951. (Ed. Calvin P. Stone and Donald W. Taylor). Stanford, California, Annual Reviews Inc.

43. SHOCK, N. W. *Trends in Gerontology.* Stanford, California: Stanford University Press, 1951.

44. Social Science Research Council, Committee on Social Adjustment. *Social Adjustment in Old Age: A Research Planning Report.* New York: Social Science Research Council, 1945.

45. U.S. Bureau of the Census. Sixteenth Census of the United States: 1940 *Population,* vol. IV. Characteristics of Age, Part 1, U.S. Summary. Washington, D.C.: U.S. Government Printing Office, 1943.

46. U.S. Federal Security Agency. *Man and His Years: An Account of the First National Conference on Aging.* Raleigh, North Carolina: Health Publication Institute, Inc., 1951.

47. U.S. Federal Security Agency. *Fact Book on Aging.* Washington, D.C.: U.S. Government Printing Office, 1952.

48. VISCHER, A. L. *Dals Alter als Schicksal und Erfüllung.* Basel, Switzerland: Benno Schwabe Verlag, 1945.

49. VISCHER, A. L. *Seelische Wandlungen beim Alternden Menschen.* Basel, Switzerland: Benno Schwabe Verlag, 1949.

50. WENAR, C. Comparison of Rorschach findings on aging subjects with their psychiatric and social ratings. Reported in *Am. Psychologist, 7,* July, 1952 program of September meeting, p. 403.

51. WOLK, ROBERT L., and WOLK, ROCHELLE B. *The Gerontological Apperception Test.* New York: Behavioral Publications, Inc., 1970.

Index